# RICK STEVES' ITALY

## 1996

**John Muir Publications**
Santa Fe, New Mexico

**Other JMP travel guidebooks by Rick Steves:**
*Asia Through the Back Door*
*Europe Through the Back Door*
*Europe 101: History and Art for the Traveler*
    (with Gene Openshaw)
*Kidding Around Seattle*
*Mona Winks: Self-Guided Tours of Europe's Top Museums*
    (with Gene Openshaw)
*Rick Steves' Baltics & Russia* (with Ian Watson)
*Rick Steves' Europe*
*Rick Steves' France, Belgium & the Netherlands* (with Steve Smith)
*Rick Steves' Germany, Austria & Switzerland*
*Rick Steves' Great Britain*
*Rick Steves' Scandinavia*
*Rick Steves' Spain & Portugal*
Rick Steves' Phrase Books for French, German, Italian,
    Spanish/Portuguese, and French/Italian/German

John Muir Publications, P.O. Box 613, Santa Fe, NM 87504
© 1995, 1996 by Rick Steves
Cover © 1996 by John Muir Publications
All rights reserved.

Printed in the United States of America
First printing January 1996

Originally published as *2 to 22 Days in Italy* © 1993, 1994

Rick Steves can be reached at Europe Through the Back Door, Box 2009,
Edmonds, WA 98020, tel. 206/771-8303, fax 205/771-0833, online at
ricksteves@aol.com.

ISSN: 1084-4422
ISBN: 1-56261-265-4

Distributed to the book trade by
Publishers Group West
Emeryville, California

**Editor, Europe Through the Back Door:** Risa Laib
**Editors, John Muir Publications:** Peggy Schaefer,
Dianna Delling, Nancy Gillan
**Production:** Kathryn Lloyd-Strongin, Janine Lehmann
**Design:** Linda Braun
**Typesetting:** Cowgirls Design
**Maps:** David C. Hoerlein
**Research Assistance:** Steve Smith
**Printer:** Banta Company
**Cover Photo:** Rick Steves

# ITALY'S BEST DESTINATIONS

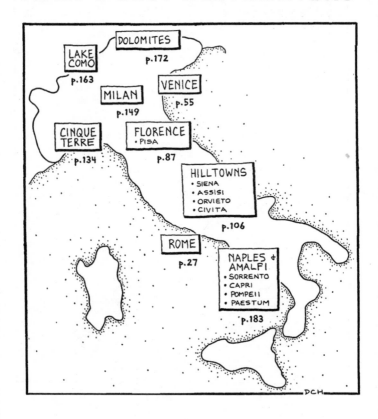

# CONTENTS

# HOW TO USE THIS BOOK

This book breaks Italy into its top big city, small town, and rural destinations. It then gives you all the information and opinions necessary to wring the maximum value out of your limited time and money in each of these destinations.

If you plan a month or less in Italy and have a normal appetite for information, this lean and mean little book is all you need. If you're a travel info fiend (like me), this book sorts through all the superlatives and provides a handy rack upon which to hang your supplemental information.

Italy is my favorite country. Experiencing its culture, people, and natural wonders economically and hassle-free has been my goal for over 20 years of traveling, researching, and tour guiding. With this book, I pass on to you the lessons I've learned, updated (in mid-1995) for 1996.

*Rick Steves' Italy* is a tour guide in your pocket. Places covered are balanced to include a comfortable mix of exciting big cities and cozy small towns, from brutal but *bello* Rome to *tranquillo* and traffic-free Riviera villages. It covers the predictable biggies and mixes in a healthy dose of "Back Door" intimacy. Along with the masterpieces of Michelangelo, you'll enjoy a *bruschetta* snack as a village boy pours oil and rubs fresh garlic on your toast. I've been selective, including only the most exciting sights. For example, of the many hill towns, I recommend the best four.

I don't recommend anything just to fill a hole. If you find no tips on eating in a town, I've yet to find a restaurant worth recommending above the others. For hassle-free efficiency, I favor hotels and restaurants handy to your sightseeing activities. Rather than list hotels scattered throughout a city, I describe my favorite two or three neighborhoods, and recommend the best accommodations values in each, from $8 bunks to fancy-in-my-book $120 doubles.

The best is, of course, only my opinion. But after two busy decades of travel writing, lecturing, and tour guiding, I've developed a sixth sense of what tickles the traveler's fancy.

## This Information Is Accurate and Up-to-Date

This book is updated every year. Most publishers of guide-books that cover a country from top to bottom can afford an update only every two or three years (and even then, it's often by letter). Since this book is selective, covering only the places I think make the top month or so in each country, I'm able to update it each summer. (For example, in 1995 I personally visited more than 90% of the hotels listed in this book.) Even with an annual update, things change. But if you're traveling with the current edition of this book, I guarantee you're using the most up-to-date information available. If you're packing an old book, you'll learn the seriousness of your mistake . . . in Italy. (I do send the new edition of this book to all my top listings each Christmas.) Your trip costs about $10 per waking hour. Your time is valuable. This guidebook saves lots of time.

## 2 to 22 Days Out . . . Modularity In!
## Italy's Top Destinations

This book used to be called *2 to 22 Days in Italy* and was organized as a proposed 22-day route. It's now restructured into a more flexible modular system. Each recommended module, or "destination" (as they're referred to in this book), is covered as a mini-vacation on its own, filled with exciting sights, homey, affordable places to stay, and hard opinions on how to best use your limited time. As before, my goal remains to help you get the greatest travel experience out of each day and each dollar. Each destination is broken into these sections:

**Planning Your Time**, a suggested schedule with thoughts on how to best use your time.

**Orientation**, including transportation within a destination, tourist information, and maps designed by Dave Hoerlein to make the text clear and your entry smooth.

**Sights** with ratings: ▲▲▲—Don't miss; ▲▲—Try hard to see; ▲—Worthwhile if you can make it; no rating—Worth knowing about.

**Sleeping** and **Eating**, with addresses and phone numbers of my favorite budget hotels and restaurants.

**Transportation Connections** to nearby destinations by train and tips for drivers with ideas on roadside attractions along the way.

The **Appendix** is a traveler's tool kit, with information on climate, telephone numbers, and public transportation.

Browse through this book, choose your favorite destinations, link them up, and have a great trip. You'll travel like a temporary local, getting the absolute most out of every mile, minute, and dollar. You won't waste time on mediocre sights because, unlike other guidebooks, I cover only my favorites. Since a major financial pitfall is lousy-though-expensive hotels, I've worked hard to assemble the best accommodations values for each stop. And as you travel the route I know and love best, I'm happy you'll be meeting some of my favorite Italian people.

## Costs

Six components make up your trip cost: airfare, surface transportation, room and board, sightseeing, shopping/entertainment/miscellany, and gelato.

**Airfare:** It's confusing and you can't save by going direct. Get and use a good travel agent. A basic round-trip U.S.A.-to-Milan (or Rome) flight should cost $600 to $1,000, depending on where you fly from and when. Consider "open-jaws" (into one city and out of another).

**Surface Transportation:** For a 3-week whirlwind trip of all my recommended destinations, allow $300 per person for public transportation (train and buses), or $500 per person (based on two people sharing car and gas) for a 3-week car rental, tolls, gas, and insurance.

**Room and Board:** While Italy is one of Europe's most expensive countries, you can still eat and sleep well there in 1996 for $60 a day plus transportation costs (that's $35 per person for a double with breakfast, $10 for lunch, and $15 for dinner). Students and tightwads do it on $40 a day ($15 to $20 per bed, $20 a day for meals and snacks). That's doable. But budget sleeping and eating require the skills and information covered later in this chapter.

**Sightseeing:** In big cities figure $5 to $10 per major sight, $2 for minor ones, $25 for splurge experiences (e.g., tours or gondola rides). An overall average of $15 a day works for most. Don't skimp here. After all, this category directly powers most of the experiences all the other expenses are designed to make possible.

## Italy's Best Three-Week Trip

| Days | Plan | Sleep in |
|------|------|----------|
| 1 | Arrive and see Milan | Milan |
| 2 | See Milan | Milan |
| 3 | Milan to the Riviera | Vernazza |
| 4 | Beach day in Cinque Terre | Vernazza |
| 5 | Riviera to Florence via Pisa | Florence |
| 6 | See Florence | Florence |
| 7 | To Siena via San Gimignano | Siena |
| 8 | Free day in Siena | Siena |
| 9 | Free day for hill towns or Assisi | Assisi or ? |
| 10 | To Città di Bagnoregio | Bagnoregio |
| 11 | To Rome, see Rome | Rome |
| 12 | See Rome | Rome |
| 13 | See Rome | Rome |
| 14 | Survive Naples | Sorrento |
| 15 | Pompeii, Amalfi Coast | Sorrento |
| 16 | Amalfi Coast, Paestum | night train |
| 17 | Venice | Venice |
| 18 | Venice | Venice |
| 19 | To Bolzano, into Dolomites | Castelrotto |
| 20 | Free day in mountains | Castelrotto |
| 21 | To Lake Como via Verona | Varenna |
| 22 | Relax on Lake Como | Varenna |

**Shopping/Entertainment/Miscellany:** This can vary from nearly nothing to a small fortune. Figure $1 per coffee, $2 per beer and ice cream cone, $1 per postcard, and $10 to $20 for evening entertainment.

## Prices and Discounts

I've priced things in lire (about L1,600 = $1). To figure lire quickly and easily, cover the last three digits and cut what's left by a third (e.g., a L24,000 dinner costs $16). Prices, hours, and telephone numbers are accurate as of mid-1995— but once you pin Italy down, it wiggles. While discounts are not listed in this book, seniors (60 and over), students (with International Student Identity Cards), and youths (under 18) may snare a deal—although many discounts are limited to European residents.

## Whirlwind Three-Week Tour of Italy

## Itinerary Priorities

       3 days: Florence, Venice
     5 days, add: Rome
   7 days, add: Cinque Terre, Siena
10 days, add: Città di Bagnoregio and slow down
14 days, add: Sorrento, Naples, Pompeii, Amalfi, Paestum
18 days, add: Milan, Lago di Como, Varenna, Assisi
21 days, add: Dolomites, Verona, Ravenna
(This includes everything on the route map above.)

Considering how you're likely to go both broke and crazy driving in big Italian cities, and how handy and affordable Italy's trains and buses are, I'd do most of Italy by public transportation. If you want to drive, consider doing the big intense stuff

(Rome, Naples area, Milan, Florence, and Venice) by train/bus and renting a car for the hill towns of Tuscany and Umbria and for the Dolomites. A car is a worthless headache on the Riviera and in the Lake Como area.

By train, consider seeing everything but Venice on the way south and sleeping through everything you've already seen by catching the night train from Rome (or Naples) to Venice. (This saves you a day, gives you a late night in Rome, and an early arrival in Venice.)

While you can fly easily into either Milan or Rome, I'd start in Milan (less crazy) and consider either starting or finishing the trip easy in Varenna on Lake Como (a quick hour by train from Milan).

General strategies (such as home-basing in Siena to do Florence, and drivers parking in Orvieto and catching the train into Rome) are covered in the text.

## Scheduling

Your day-by-day itinerary strategy is a fun challenge. Sundays have the same pros and cons as they do for travelers in the U.S.A. Sightseeing attractions are generally open but with shorter hours, shops and banks closed, and minor transportation connections more frustrating (e.g., no bus service to or from Cività). City traffic is light. Rowdy evenings are rare on Sundays. Saturdays are virtually weekdays with earlier closing hours. Hotels in tourist areas are often booked up at Easter, in August, and on Fridays and Saturdays.

Read through this book and note the days when most museums are closed. (Mondays are bad in Milan, Florence, and Rome.) Museums and sights, especially large ones, usually stop admitting people 30 to 60 minutes before closing time.

Plan ahead for banking, laundry, post office chores, and picnics. I've listed convenient laundromats throughout. Mix intense and relaxed periods. Every trip needs at least a few slack days. Pace yourself. Assume you will return. Drink your water *con gas*.

## When to Go

Italy's best travel months are May, June, September, and October. November through April usually has pleasant weather with generally none of the sweat and stress of the tourist season. Peak season (July and August) offers the longest hours and the most exciting slate of activities—but terrible crowds and, at times, suffocating heat. During peak times, many resort area hotels maximize business by requiring that guests buy dinner in their restaurants. August, the local holiday month, isn't as bad as many make it out to be, but big cities tend to be quiet, and beach and mountain resorts are jammed with higher hotel prices. If you anticipate crowds, arrive early in the day or call hotels in advance (call from one hotel to the next; your fluent-in-Italian receptionist can help you). Summer temperatures range from the 70s in Milan to the high 80s and 90s in Rome. In the winter it often drops to the 30s and 40s in Milan and the 40s and 50s in Rome.

Italy has more than its share of holidays. Each town has a local festival honoring its patron saint. February is Carnevale time in Venice. Italy (including most major sights) closes down on these national holidays: January 1, January 6 (Epiphany), Easter Sunday and Monday, April 25 (Liberation Day), May 1 (Labor Day), May 20 (Ascension Day), August 15 (Assumption of Mary), November 1 (All Saints Day), December 8 (Immaculate Conception of Mary), and December 25 and 26.

## Travel Smart

Many people travel through Italy thinking it's a chaotic mess. Any attempt at organization is seen as futile and is put off until they get to Switzerland. This is dead wrong—and expensive. Italy, a living organism that on the surface seems as orderly as spilled spaghetti, functions quite well. Only those who understand this and travel smart can enjoy Italy on a budget. Upon arrival in a new town, lay the groundwork for a smooth departure. Buy a phone card and use it for reservations, reconfirmations, and to double-check hours. Reread this book as you travel. Utilize local tourist information offices. Assume locals are friendly and would like to meet or help you. Ask questions. Seek and accept help. Wear your money belt, learn the local currency, and develop a simple formula to quickly estimate rough prices in dollars. Keep a sheet of paper in your pocket for organizing your thoughts, and practice the virtue of simplicity. Those who expect to travel smart, do.

## Tourist Information

Before your trip, send a letter to an Italian National Tourist Office (abbreviated "TI" in this book) telling them of your general plans and asking for information.

**Italian Government Tourist Offices:** 630 Fifth Avenue, #1565, New York, NY 10111, tel. (212) 245-4822; 12400 Wilshire Boulevard, #550, Los Angeles, CA 90025, tel. (310) 820-0098; or 401 N. Michigan Ave., #3030, Chicago, IL 60611, tel. (312) 644-0996. They'll send you the general packet, and if you ask for specifics (individual city maps, a publication called *General Information for Travelers to Italy*, the calendars of festivals, good hikes around Lake Como, wine-tasting in Umbria, or whatever), you'll get an impressive amount of help. If you have a specific problem, they are a good source of sympathy.

**Local Tourist Offices:** During your trip, your first stop in each town should be the tourist office (*turismo*, EPT, "i"). While Italian tourist offices are about half as helpful as those in other countries, their information is twice as important. Prepare. Have a list of questions and a proposed plan to double-check. If you're arriving late, telephone ahead. Use one TI as a map for your next stop. Be wary of the travel agencies or special information services that masquerade as tourist information offices, but serve fancy hotels and tour companies. They are crooks and liars, selling things you don't need.

While the TI is eager to book you a room, use their room-finding service only as a last resort. Across Europe, room-finding services are charging commissions from hotels, taking fees from travelers, and blacklisting establishments that buck their materialistic rules. They are unable to give hard opinions on the relative value of one place over another. The accommodations stakes are too high to go potluck through the TI. You'll do better going direct with the listings in this book.

## Recommended Guidebooks

Especially if you'll be traveling beyond my recommended destinations, you may want some supplemental information.

When you consider the improvements they'll make in your $3,000 vacation, $30 for extra maps and books is money well spent. Especially for several people traveling by car, the weight and expense are negligible.

*The Lonely Planet Guide to Italy* is thorough, well-researched, and packed with good maps and hotel recommendations for low-to-moderate-budget travelers. The hip *Rough Guide to Italy* (British researchers, more insightful), and the highly opinionated *Let's Go: Italy* (by Harvard students, better hotel listings) are great for students, vagabonds, and those planning to go beyond my recommended destinations. If you're a low-budget train traveler interested in the youth and night scene (which I have basically ignored), get *Let's Go: Italy*. The Italy section in *Let's Go: Europe* is sketchy.

**Cultural and sightseeing guides:** The tall green Michelin guides to Italy and Rome have nothing on room and board, but do have great maps for drivers and lots on sights, customs, and culture (sold in English in Italy). Among several good books specializing in Venice, Florence, and Rome, overachievers love the slick and user-friendly Eyewitness guides, which are packed with art and historical background. The Cadogan guides to various parts of Italy offer an insightful look at the rich and confusing local culture. Those heading for Florence or Rome should read Irving Stone's *The Agony and the Ecstasy* for a great—if romanticized—rundown on Michelangelo, the Medici family, and the turbulent times of the Renaissance.

**Rick Steves' books:** *Europe Through the Back Door, 14th Edition* (John Muir Publications, 1996) gives you budget travel skills and information on minimizing jet lag, packing light, driving or train travel, finding budget beds without reservations, changing money, avoiding rip-offs, hurdling the language barrier, staying healthy, travel photography, things to do in your bidet, Ugly Americanism, laundry, itinerary strategies, and more. The book also includes chapters on 40 of my favorite "Back Doors."

**Rick Steves' Country Guides** are a series of eight guidebooks (formerly the 2 to 22 Days Itinerary Planners) covering the Baltics and Russia; Great Britain; France; Spain and Portugal; Germany, Austria, and Switzerland;

Scandinavia; and Europe, as this one covers Italy. These are updated annually and come out each January.

*Europe 101: History and Art for the Traveler* (co-written with Gene Openshaw, John Muir Publications, 1996), which gives you the story of Europe's people, history, and art, is heavy on Italy's ancient, Renaissance, and modern history. A little "101" background knowledge resurrects the rubble.

*Mona Winks: Self-Guided Tours of Europe's Top Museums* (co-written with Gene Openshaw, John Muir Publications, 1996) gives you one- to three-hour self-guided tours through Europe's 20 most exhausting and important museums. Nearly half of the newly updated book is devoted to Italy, with tours covering Venice's St. Mark's, the Doge's Palace, and Accademia Gallery; Florence's Uffizi Gallery, Bargello, Michelangelo's *David*, and a Renaissance walk through the town center; and Rome's Colosseum, Forum, Pantheon, Vatican Museum, and St. Peter's Basilica. If you want to enjoy the great sights and museums of Italy, *Mona* will be a valued friend.

Italy is one country where a phrase book is as fun as it is necessary. My *Rick Steves' Italian Phrase Book* (John Muir Publications) is the only book of its kind, designed to help you meet the people and stretch your budget. It's written by a monoglot who, for 20 years, has fumbled happily through Italy, struggling with all the other phrase books. This is a fun and practical communication aid to help you make accurate hotel reservations over the telephone, tell your cabbie if he doesn't slow down you'll throw up, ask for a free taste of cantaloupe-flavored gelato, and have the man in the deli make you a sandwich.

## Maps

Don't skimp on maps. Excellent maps are available (cheaper than in the U.S.A.) throughout Italy at bookstores, newsstands, and gas stations. Train travelers can do fine with a simple rail map (such as the one that comes with your train pass) and free city maps picked up at TIs as you travel. However, drivers should invest in good 1/200,000 maps to really get the most out of their miles. Study the key to get the most sightseeing value out of your map.

The maps in this book, drawn by Dave Hoerlein, are concise and simple. Dave, who is well-traveled in Italy, designed the maps to help you locate recommended places and the tourist offices, where you'll pick up more in-depth maps (usually free).

## Transportation in Italy

### By Car or Train?

Each mode of transportation has pros and cons. Public transportation is one of the few bargains in Italy. Trains and buses are inexpensive and good. City-to-city travel is faster, easier, and cheaper by train than by car. Trains give you the convenience and economy of doing long stretches overnight. By train I arrive relaxed and well-rested—not so by car.

Parking, gas (about $4 per gallon), and tolls are expensive in Italy. But drivers enjoy more control, especially in the countryside. Cars carry your luggage for you, generally from door to door—especially important for heavy packers (such as chronic shoppers and families traveling with children). And groups know that the more people you pack into a car or minibus, the cheaper it gets per person.

### Train Travel in Italy

You can travel cheaply in Italy simply by buying tickets as you go and avoiding the more expensive express trains. A second-class Rome-to-Venice ticket costs about $45 (with express supplement). But Italy's train ticket system confounds even the locals, and for convenience alone, I'd go with the Italian State Railway's BTLC "Go Anywhere" pass (see train-pass box). Unlike the BTLC pass, Italy's Kilometric pass is a headache because it doesn't cover fast-train supplements. For travel exclusively in Italy, a Eurailpass is a bad value.

You'll encounter four types of trains in Italy. The *accelerato*, *regionale*, and *locale* are the miserable milk-run trains. The *diretto* is faster. The *espresso* zips along very fast, connecting only major cities. *Rapido* and Intercity trains are the sleek, air-conditioned top-of-the-line trains that charge a supplement (covered by the Eurail and BTLC train passes). While schedules say these require a reservation, those with train passes can hop on and grab unreserved seats. First-class tickets cost 50 percent more

## Cost of Public Transportation

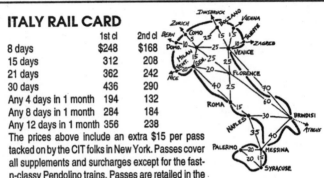

### ITALY RAIL CARD

|                        | 1st cl | 2nd cl |
|------------------------|--------|--------|
| 8 days                 | $248   | $168   |
| 15 days                | 312    | 208    |
| 21 days                | 362    | 242    |
| 30 days                | 436    | 290    |
| Any 4 days in 1 month  | 194    | 132    |
| Any 8 days in 1 month  | 284    | 184    |
| Any 12 days in 1 month | 356    | 238    |

The prices above include an extra $15 per pass tacked on by the CIT folks in New York. Passes cover all supplements and surcharges except for the fast-n-classy Pendolino trains. Passes are retailed in the USA through travel agents, direct from CIT in NYC (800/248-8687), or cheaper and easy in Italy at CIT travel agencies and major train stations. Note: Flexi versions of passes are sold only in the USA.

**Italy:** Point-to-point 2nd class rail fares in $US.

### ITALIAN KILOMETRIC TICKETS

Also known as the Biglietto Chilometrico, this features coupons for unlimited trips totalling up to 3,000 kilometers that can be split by up to 5 people for about $264 first class and $156 second class (e.g., a group of five could go the 570 km from Venice to Rome on a Kilometric Ticket for $34 each, a substantial savings over the normal $45 regular ticket price). Like the Italy Rail Card, this is sold in the USA through CIT (Italian Tourist Company). Call 800/248-8687 for a busy signal, or buy the same passes cheaper and easily in Italy at CIT travel agencies and major train stations.

than second-class tickets. While second-class cars go exactly as fast as their first-class neighbors, Italy is one country where I would consider the splurge of first class. The easiest way to upgrade a second-class ticket once on board an impossibly crowded train is to nurse a drink in the snack car. Newsstands sell up-to-date regional and all-Italy timetables (L6,000).

Italian trains are famous for their thieves. Never leave a bag unattended. There have been cases of bandits gassing an entire car before looting the snoozing gang. I've noticed recently that police are riding the trains and things seem more controlled. Still, for an overnight trip, I'd feel safe only in a *cuccetta* (a $15 bunk bed in a special sleeping car with an attendant who keeps track of who comes and goes while you sleep).

Avoid big-city train station lines whenever you can. For about a L4,000 fee, you can buy tickets and reserve a cuccetta at a travel agency. Plan your rail journey with the fun and clever new computer train schedule terminals. Watch the locals use one and then give it a try yourself. Because of the threat of bombs, you won't find storage lockers in train stations. But each station has a *deposito* (or *bagagli*) where you can safely leave your bag for L2,000 a day (payable when you pick up the bag).

### Car Rental

Research car rental before you go. It's cheaper to arrange for car rentals through your travel agent while still in the U.S. Rent by the week with unlimited mileage. If you'll be renting for three or more weeks, leasing—which is a scheme to save on insurance and taxes—is cheaper. Explore your drop-off options (south of Rome can be a problem).

Your car rental price includes minimal insurance with a very high deductible. A CDW (Collision Damage Waiver) insurance supplement covers you for this deductible. Since deductibles are horrendous, usually the entire value of the car, I generally splurge for the CDW. Ask your travel agent about money-saving alternatives to this car rental agency rip-off. The way I understand it, the car rental agency makes up for its highly competitive, unprofitably low, weekly rental rates with the approximately $12 a day you'll spend for CDW.

A rail 'n' drive train pass can be put to thoughtful use. Certain areas (like the Dolomites and the hill towns of Tuscany and Umbria) are great by car, while most of the rest of Italy is best by train.

### Driving in Italy

Driving in Italy is frightening—a video game for keeps and you only get one quarter. All you need is your valid U.S. driver's license and a car. (According to everybody but the Italian police, international drivers' licenses are not necessary. The police fine you if they can't understand the expiration date.)

**Filling up:** Most cars take unleaded (green pumps, available everywhere). *Autostrada* rest-stops are self-service (but most expensive) stations open daily without a siesta break. Small-town stations are usually full-serve with short hours. Many 24-hour-a-day stations are entirely automated with machines that trade gas for paper money.

**Autostradas:** Italy's freeway system is as good as our interstate system. But you'll pay about a dollar for every ten minutes of use. (I paid L37,000 for the 4-hour drive from Bolzano to Pisa.) While I favor the autostradas for the time and gas saved, and because I find them safer and less nerve-racking than the smaller roads, savvy local drivers know which toll-free "superstradas" are actually faster and more direct than the autoroute (e.g., Florence to Pisa).

**Parking:** White lines generally mean parking is free. Blue lines mean pay—usually L1,500 per hour. If there's no meter, there is probably a roving attendant who will take your money. Study the signs. Many free zones are cleared out (by car owners or tow trucks) one day a week for street cleaning. Many free zones have a 30- or 60-minute time limit. *Zona disco* has nothing to do with dancing. Cars have a time disc which you set at your arrival time and lay on the dashboard so the attendant knows how long you've been parked. This is a fine system which all drivers should take advantage of. Garages are safe, save time, and help you avoid the stress of parking tickets. Take the parking voucher with you to pay the cashier before you leave.

**Theft:** Cars are routinely vandalized and stolen. Try to make your car look locally owned: hide the "tourist-owned" rental company decals and put a local newspaper in your back window.

## Sleeping in Italy

It's expensive. Cheap big-city hotels can be sleazy, depressing, dangerous, and rented by the hour. Tourist information services cannot give opinions on quality. A major feature of this book is its extensive listing of good value hotels with doubles ranging from $30 to $120 a night. I like places that are clean, small, central, quiet at night, traditional, inexpensive, friendly, with firm beds—and those not listed in other guidebooks. (In Italy, I'm happy to score six out of these nine.) Budget travelers have a wide range of money-saving alternatives to choose from—convents, youth hostels, campgrounds, and private homes. Whenever applicable, I've listed these.

### The Accommodations Description Code

To save space while giving more specific information for people with special concerns, I've described my recommended hotels with a standard code. When there is a range of prices in one category, the price will fluctuate with the season, size of room, or length of stay. Prices listed are per room, not per person.

   **S**—Single room or price for one person using a double.

   **D**—Double or twin room. Double beds are usually big enough for non-romantic couples.

   **T**—Three-person room (often a double bed with a single bed moved in).

   **Q**—Four-adult room (an extra child's bed is usually cheaper).

   **B**—Private shower (most likely) or bath in the room. Most B rooms have a WC (toilet). All rooms have sinks with hot and cold water. B rooms are often bigger and renovated, while the cheaper rooms without B often will be on the top floor or yet to be refurbished. Any room without B has access to a B on the corridor (free unless otherwise noted).

   **WC**—I include this only to differentiate between rooms in the same hotel that have only a B and those with BWC. With no WC mentioned, B rooms generally have a WC.

   **CC**—Accepts credit cards: **V**=Visa, **M**=MasterCard, **A**=American Express. Many also accept Diners (which I ignored). If CC is not mentioned, assume they accept only cash.

   **SE**—When it seems predictable, the likely availability of an English-speaking staff person is graded A through F.

### Hotels

Double rooms listed in this book will range from about $30 (very simple, toilet and shower down the hall) to $120 (maximum plumbing and more), with most clustering around $60. It's higher in big cities and heavily touristed cities and lower off the beaten path. Three or four people can economize (and become more desirable in the eyes of the hotelier who knows he'll fill all his rooms) by requesting larger rooms. Solo travelers find that the cost of a *camera singola* is often only 25 percent less than a *camera doppia*. Most listed hotels have rooms for anywhere from one to five people. If there's room for an extra cot, they'll cram it in for you.

Prices are often soft—especially if you are arriving direct. If there's no middleman, you're in a stronger position to bargain. Consider the supply-and-demand situation. Breakfasts are legally supposed to be optional, but initial prices quoted are often with bath and breakfast.

Italy has a five-star rating system, but while the stars can give you a general idea of price range, the government no longer regulates hotel prices. Prices are pretty standard, and you normally get close to what you pay for. Shopping around earns you a better location and more character but rarely a cheaper price. You'll save $10–$20 if you ask for a room without a shower and just use the public shower down the hall (although in many cases the rooms with the extra plumbing are larger and more pleasant). Generally rooms with a bath or shower also have a toilet and a bidet (which Italians use for quick "sponge baths"). Tubs usually come with a frustrating "telephone shower." If a shower has no curtain, they expect the entire bathroom to shower with you. Double beds are called *matrimoniale*, even though hotels aren't interested in your marital status. Twins are *due letti singoli*. The cord that dangles over the tub or shower is not a clothesline. You pull it when you've fallen and can't get up. A few places have kept the old titles, *locanda* or *pension*, indicating they offer budget beds. The Italian word for "hotel" is *albergo*.

Ancient Romans ate no breakfast at all, and the breakfast scene has improved only marginally. Except for the smallest places, a very simple continental breakfast is normally available. If you like juice and protein for breakfast, supply it yourself. I enjoy a box of juice in my hotel room and often supplement the skimpy breakfasts with a piece of fruit and a separately wrapped small piece of cheese. (A zip-lock baggie is handy for petite eaters to grab an extra breakfast roll and slice of cheese, when provided, for a fast and free light lunch.) The hotel breakfast, while convenient, is usually a bad value—$5–$8 for a roll, jelly, and usually unlimited *cafe con latte*. You can always request cheese or salami (L5,000 extra). I enjoy taking breakfast at the corner café. It's OK to supplement what you order with a few picnic goodies.

Rooms are safe. Still, zip cameras and money out of sight. More pillows and blankets are usually in the closet or available on request. Remember, in Italy towels and linen aren't always replaced every day—drip dry and conserve.

To reserve a hotel room from the U.S.A, write or fax (simple English is usually fine) to the address listed and identify clearly the dates you intend to be there. (A two-night stay in August would be "one room, two people, two nights, 16/8/96 to 18/8/96"—European hotel jargon uses your day of departure and European date system.) You may receive a letter response requesting one night's deposit. Send a $50 signed traveler's check or a bank draft in the local currency. More and more, travelers can reserve a room with a phone call or fax, leaving a credit-card number and expiration date as a deposit. You can pay with your card or by cash when you arrive; if you don't show up, you'll be billed for one night anyway. Ideally, the hotel receptionist will hold a room for you without a deposit if you promise to arrive by mid-afternoon and you call to reconfirm two days before arrival. If you get no answer to your fax request, consider that a "no."

Except during the busiest summer times, long-distance hotel reservations are not usually necessary. But when you know where you'll be tomorrow night, life on the road is easier if you telephone ahead to reserve a bed. My most highly recommended hotels get lots of my likable and reliable readers, and will usually hold a room with a phone call until 17:00 (5:00 p.m.) with no deposit. They are usually accustomed to us English-speaking monoglots. Use the telephone! I've listed numbers with area codes. See the Appendix for long-distance dialing instructions.

Upon arrival, the receptionist will normally ask for your passport and keep it for a couple of hours. Hotels are legally required to register each guest with the local police. Relax. Americans are notorious for making this chore more difficult than it needs to be.

While bed and breakfasts (*affitta camere*) and youth hostels (*ostello della gioventu*) are not as common in Italy as elsewhere in Europe, I've listed quite a few in this book. While big-city hostels are normally overrun with the *Let's Go* crowd, small-town hostels can be a wonderfully enjoyable way to save money and make friends.

## Eating Italian

The Italians are masters of the art of fine living. That means eating . . . long and well. Lengthy, multi-course lunches and dinners and endless hours sitting in outdoor cafés are the norm. Americans eat on their way to an evening event and complain if the check is slow in coming. For Italians, the meal is an end in itself, and only rude waiters rush you. When you want the bill, mime-scribble on your raised palm or ask, *"Il conto?"*

Even those of us who liked dorm food will find that the local cafés, cuisine, and wines become a highlight of our Italian adventure. Trust me, this is sightseeing for your palate, and even if the rest of you is sleeping in cheap hotels, your taste buds will relish an occasional first-class splurge. You can eat well without going broke. But be careful; you're just as likely to blow a small fortune on a disappointing meal as you are to dine wonderfully for $20.

### Restaurants

When restaurant hunting, choose places filled with locals, not the place with the big neon signs boasting, "We speak English and accept credit cards." Look for menus posted outside. For unexciting but basic values, look for a *menu turistico*, a three- or four-course set-price menu. Galloping gourmets order à la carte with the help of a menu translator. (The *Marling Italian Menu Master* is excellent. *Rick Steves' Italian Phrase Book* has enough phrases for intermediate eaters.)

A full meal consists of an appetizer (antipasto, L5,000 and up), a first course (*primo piatto*, pasta or soup, L5,000–L12,000), and a second course (*secondo piatto*, expensive meat and fish dishes, L10,000–L20,000). Vegetables (*contorni*, *verdure*) may come with the *secondo* or be available for extra lire (L5,000) as a side dish. Restaurants normally pad the bill with a cover charge (*pane e coperto*, about L2,000) and a service charge (*servizio*, 15 percent). These days, service is usually automatically added to the bill. Tipping beyond that is unnecessary.

As you can see, the lire will add up in a hurry. Light

and budget eaters get by with a *primo piatto*. Hungry paupers can even go with two: a minestrone and a pasta. Self-service places and a few lower-class eateries feed you without the add-ons. Family-run places operate without hired help and can offer cheaper meals. The word *osteria* (normally a simple local-style restaurant) gets me salivating.

Many modern Italian fast food places slam-dunk pasta, rather than burgers, cheap and fast. A *tavola calda* (literally, "hot table") serves Italian-style fast food. A *rosticcería* is like a deli with great cooked food to go. Pizza places (often called Pizza Rustica) sell fresh pizza by the weight. Two hundred grams with a beer or soft drink make a good, cheap lunch. American-style fast food is just like you know it—but with better salad bars and beer.

The Italian bar is not just a place to drink. It is a local hangout serving coffee, mini-pizzas, sandwiches, cartons of milk from the cooler, and plates of fried cheese and vege-tables under the glass counter, ready to reheat, as well as alcoholic drinks. This is my budget choice, the Italian equiv-alent of English pub grub. It's cheap, friendly, local, and edi-ble. Don't be limited by what you can see. If you feel like a salad with a slice of cantaloupe and a hunk of cheese, they'll whip that up for you in a snap.

Bar procedure can be frustrating: 1) decide what you want; 2) check the price list on the wall; 3) pay the cashier; and 4) give the receipt to the bartender (whose clean fin-gers handle no dirty lire), and tell him what you want. *Panini* and *tramezzini* are sandwiches. *Da portar via* is "for the road." You'll notice a two-tiered price system. A cup of coffee at the bar is cheaper than at a table. If on a budget, don't sit without checking out the financial consequences. Decaf is *hag* or *decaff*. It's common for harried bartenders to serve your cappuccino only warm. Simply give it back with a polite *"piu caldo."*

### Picnics

In Italy picnicking saves lots of lire and is a great way to sam-ple local specialties. In the process of assembling your meal, you get to deal with the Italians in the local market scene.

On days you choose to picnic, gather supplies early. You'll probably visit several small stores or market stalls to

assemble a complete meal, and many close around noon.
While it's fun to visit the small specialty shops, a local
*alimentari* is your one-stop corner grocery store.
*Supermercados* give you decent quality with less color, less
cost, and more efficiency.

Juice lovers can get a liter of O.J. for the price of a
Coke or coffee. Look for "100% *succo* (juice)" on the label or
suffer through a sickly-sweet orange drink. Buy juice in less-
expensive liter boxes, and store what you don't drink in your
reusable water bottle for nipping between sights. Hang onto
the twist-top half-liter mineral water bottles (sold everywhere for about L1,000).

Remember, picnics can be an adventure in high cuisine.
Be daring. Try the smelly cheeses, midget pickles, presto
pesto, ugly olives, and any UFOs the locals are excited about.
Local shopkeepers are happy to sell small quantities of produce, and will even slice and stuff a sandwich for you. In a
busy market, a merchant may not want to weigh and sell
small, three-carrot-type quantities. In this case, estimate gen-
erously what you think it should cost, and hold out the lire in
one hand and the produce in the other. Wear a smile that
says, "If you take the money, I'll go." He'll grab the money.
A typical picnic for two might be fresh rolls, two tomatoes,
three carrots, 100 grams of cheese, 100 grams of meat (100
grams = about a quarter-pound, called *etto* in Italy), two
apples, a liter box of juice, and a yogurt. Total cost—$10.

## Red Tape and Business Hours

You currently need a passport but no visa and no shots to
travel in Italy. In Italy—and in this book—you'll be using the
24-hour clock. After 12:00 noon, keep going—13:00, 14:00,
and so on. For anything over 12, subtract 12 and add p.m.
(so 14:00 is 2:00 p.m.).

This book lists high-season hours for sightseeing
attractions. Off-season, roughly October through April,
generally expect shorter hours, more lunchtime breaks,
and fewer activities.

Italians arrange dates by day/month/year, so Christmas
would be 25-12-96. What we Americans call the second floor
of a building is the first floor in Europe. Commas and periods are often switched, so there are 5.280 feet in a mile, and

your temperature is 98,6. In museums art is dated with A.C. (for Avanti Cristo, or B.C.) and D.C. (for Dopo Cristo, or A.D.). O.K.?

Mail service is miserable in Italy. Postcards get last priority. It's best to tell your loved ones you're going behind the dark side of the moon for a while or keep in touch with a few phone calls. If you must have mail stops, consider a few pre-reserved hotels along your route or use American Express Mail Services. Most American Express offices in Italy will hold mail for one month. (They mail out a free listing of addresses.) This service is free to anyone using an AmExCo card or traveler's checks (and available for a small fee to others). Allow 14 days for U.S.-to-Italy mail delivery, but don't count on it. Federal Express makes two-day deliveries, for a price. Don't mail anything precious from Italy.

## Culture Shock—Accepting Italy as a Package Deal

While we think shower curtains are logical, many Italians just cover the toilet paper and let the rest of the room shower with you. When writing numbers, Italians give their "1s" an upswing and cross their "7s." If you don't adapt, your "7" will be mistaken for a sloppy "1" and you'll miss your train— and probably find a reason to be mad at the local system. Fit in!

We travel all the way to Italy to enjoy differences—to become temporary locals. You'll experience frustrations. Certain truths that we find "God-given" or "self-evident," like cold beer; ice; a bottomless cup of coffee; long, hot showers; body odor smelling bad; bigger being better; and "time is money" are suddenly not so true. One of the benefits of travel is the eye-opening realization that there are logical, civil, and even better alternatives. Travel broadens your perspective. If the beds are too short, the real problem is that you are too long. Don't look for things American on the other side of the Atlantic, and you're sure to enjoy a good dose of Italian hospitality.

## Send Me a Postcard, Drop Me a Line

If you enjoy a successful trip with the help of this book and would like to share your discoveries, please send any tips, recommendations, criticisms, or corrections to me at Europe

Through the Back Door, Box 2009, Edmonds, WA 98020. All correspondents receive a two-year subscription to our "Back Door Travel" quarterly newsletter (it's free anyway). Tips actually used get you a first-class railpass in heaven.

To update this book before your trip or to share tips, tap into our free computer bulletin board travel information service on the America Online Travel board. (From their main menu click on "Travel," then click on "Travel Forum." From there you get our info service by clicking on "Rick Steves ETBD," or you can join in our chat board by clicking: Travel Boards, List Categories, World Traveler, then ETBD. My AOL address is ricksteves@aol.com.)

Judging from the positive feedback and happy postcards I receive from travelers using this book, it's safe to assume you're on your way to a great Italian vacation—independent, inexpensive, and done with the finesse of an experienced traveler. Thanks, and *buon viaggio!*

# BACK DOOR TRAVEL PHILOSOPHY
## As Taught in *Rick Steves' Europe Through the Back Door*

*Travel is intensified living—maximum thrills per minute and one of the last great sources of legal adventure. Travel is freedom. It's recess, and we need it.*

*Experiencing the real Europe requires catching it by surprise, going casual . . . "Through the Back Door."*

*Affording travel is a matter of priorities. (Make do with the old car.) You can travel—simply, safely, and comfortably—anywhere in Europe for $60 a day plus transportation costs. In many ways, spending more money only builds a thicker wall between you and what you came to see. Europe is a cultural carnival, and time after time, you'll find that its best acts are free, and the best seats are the cheap ones.*

*A tight budget forces you to travel close to the ground, meeting and communicating with the people, not relying on service with a purchased smile. Never sacrifice sleep, nutrition, safety, or cleanliness in the name of budget. Simply enjoy the local-style alternatives to expensive hotels and restaurants.*

*Extroverts have more fun. If your trip is low on magic moments, kick yourself and make things happen. If you don't enjoy a place, maybe you don't know enough about it. Seek the truth. Recognize tourist traps. Give a culture the benefit of your open mind. See things as different but not better or worse. Any culture has much to share.*

*Of course, travel—like the world—is a series of hills and valleys. Be fanatically positive and militantly optimistic. If something's not to your liking, change your liking. Travel is addicting. It can make you a happier American, as well as a citizen of the world. Our Earth is home to nearly 6 billion equally important people. It's humbling to travel and find that people don't envy Americans. They like us, but with all due respect, they wouldn't trade passports.*

*Globe-trotting destroys ethnocentricity. It helps you understand and appreciate different cultures. Travel changes people. It broadens perspectives and teaches new ways to measure quality of life. Many travelers toss aside their hometown blinders. Their prized souvenirs are the strands of different cultures they decide to knit into their own character. The world is a cultural yarn shop. And Back Door travelers are weaving the ultimate tapestry. Come on, join in!*

# ITALY

- 116,000 square miles (the size of Arizona)
- 60 million people (477 people per square mile)
- 800 miles tall, 100 miles wide
- 1,600 lire = about U.S.$1; 1,000 lire = about 65 cents
- Country telephone code: 39; international access code: 00

*Bella Italia!* It has Europe's richest, craziest culture. If I had to choose just one, Italy's my favorite. If you take it on its own terms and accept the package deal, Italy is a cultural keelhauling that actually feels good.

Some people, often with considerable effort, manage to hate it. Italy bubbles with emotion, corruption, stray hairs, inflation, traffic jams, body odor, strikes, rallies, holidays, crowded squalor, and irate ranters shaking their fists at each other one minute and walking arm in arm the next. Have a talk with yourself before you cross the border. Promise yourself to relax and soak in it; it's a glorious mud puddle.

With so much history and art in Venice, Florence, and Rome, you'll need to do some reading ahead to maximize your experience. There are two Italys: the north is relatively industrial, aggressive, and "time-is-money" in its outlook. The Po River basin and the area between Milan, Genoa, and Torino have the richest farmland and the heavy-duty industry. The south is more crowded, poor, relaxed, farm-oriented, and traditional. Families here are very strong and usually live in the same house for many generations. Loyalties are to the family, city, region, soccer team, and country—in that order. The Apennine Mountains give Italy a rugged north-south spine, while the Alps divide Italy from France, Switzerland, and Austria in the north.

Economically, Italy has had its problems, but somehow things work out. Today Italy is the Western world's seventh-largest industrial power. Its people earn more per capita than the British. Italy is the world's leading wine producer. It is sixth in cheese and wool output. Tourism (as you'll find out) is also big business in Italy. Cronyism, which complicates my work, is an integral part of the economy.

Italy, home of the Vatican, is Catholic, but the dominant religion is life—motor scooters, football, fashion, girl-watching, boy-watching, good coffee, good wine, and *la dolce far niente* ("the sweetness of doing nothing"). The Italian character shows itself on the streets with the skilled maniac drivers and the classy dressers who star in the ritual evening stroll, or *passeggiata*.

The language is fun. Be melodramatic and move your hand with your tongue. Hear the melody, get into the flow. Fake it, let the farce be with you. Italians are outgoing characters. They want to communicate, and they try harder than any other Europeans. Play with them.

Italy, a land of extremes, is also the most thief-ridden country you'll visit. Tourists suffer virtually no violent crime—but plenty of petty purse-snatchings, pickpocketings, and shortchangings. Only the sloppy get stung. Wear your money belt! The women and children loitering around the major museums aren't there for the art.

Traditionally, Italy uses the siesta plan: people work from 8:00 or 9:00 to 13:00 and from 15:30 to 19:00, six days a week. Many businesses have adopted the government's new recommended 8:00–14:00 workday. In tourist areas, shops are open longer.

Sightseeing hours are always changing in Italy, and (especially with the expected new austerity programs promised by the new right-wing government) many of the hours in this book will be wrong by the time you travel. Use the local tourist offices to double-check your sightseeing plans.

For extra sightseeing information, take advantage of the cheap, colorful, and dry-but-informative city guidebooks sold on the streets all over. Also use the information telephones you'll find in most historic buildings. Just set the dial on English, pop in your coins, and listen. The narration is often accompanied by a brief slide show. Many dark interiors can be brilliantly lit for a coin. Whenever possible, let there be light.

Some important Italian churches require modest dress: no shorts or bare shoulders on men or women. With a little imagination (except at the Vatican), those caught by surprise can improvise something—a jacket for your knees and maps for your shoulders. I wear a super lightweight pair of long pants for my hot and muggy big-city Italian sightseeing.

While no longer a cheap country, Italy is still a hit with shoppers. Glassware (Venice), gold, silver, leather, and prints (Florence), and high fashion (Rome) are good souvenirs, but do some price research at home so you'll recognize the good values.

Many tourists are mind-boggled by the huge prices: 16,000 lire for dinner! L42,000 for the room! L126,000 for the taxi ride! That's still real money—it's just spoken of in much smaller units than a dollar. Since there are roughly L1,600 in a dollar, figure Italian prices by covering the last three zeros with your finger and taking about two-thirds of the remaining figure. That L16,000 dinner costs $10 in U.S. money; the L42,000 room, $28; and the taxi ride . . . uh-oh!

Beware of the "slow count." After you buy something, you may get your change back in batches. The salesperson (or bank teller) hopes you are confused by all the zeros and will gather up your money and say *"grazie"* before he or she finishes the count. Always do your own rough figuring beforehand and understand the transaction. Only the sloppy are ripped off. Try to enforce the local prices. It's only natural for them to inflate prices or assume you don't know what's a fair rate. Be savvy, firm, and friendly.

*La dolce far niente* is a big part of Italy. Zero in on the fine points. Don't dwell on the problems. Accept Italy as Italy. Savor your cappuccino, dangle your feet over a canal (if it smells, breathe through your mouth), and imagine what it was like centuries ago. Ramble through the rubble of Rome and mentally resurrect those ancient stones. Look into the famous sculpted eyes of Michelangelo's *David*, and understand Renaissance man's assertion of himself. Sit silently on a hilltop rooftop. Get chummy with the winds of the past. Write a poem over a glass of local wine in a sun-splashed, wave-dashed Riviera village. If you fall off your moral horse, call it a cultural experience. Italy is for romantics.

# ROME (ROMA)

Rome is magnificent and brutal at the same time. Your ears will ring, your nose will turn your hankie black, the careless will be run down or pickpocketed, you'll be frustrated by chaos that only an Italian can understand. You may even come to believe Mussolini was necessary. But Rome is required. If your hotel provides a comfortable refuge; if you pace yourself, accept and even partake in the siesta plan; if you're well-organized for sight-seeing; and if you protect yourself and your valuables with extra caution and discretion, you'll do fine. You'll see the sights and leave satisfied.

Rome at its peak meant civilization itself. Everything was either civilized (part of the Roman Empire, Latin- or Greek-speaking) or barbarian. Today Rome is Italy's political capital, the capital of Catholicism, and a splendid . . . "junkpile" is not quite the right word . . . of western civilization. As you wander, you'll find its buildings, people, cats, laundry, and traffic endlessly entertaining. And then, of course, there are its magnificent sights.

Tour St. Peter's, the greatest church on earth, and scale Michelangelo's 100-yard-tall dome, the world's largest. Learn something about eternity by touring the huge Vatican Museum. You'll find paradise—bright as the day it was painted—in the newly restored Sistine Chapel. Do the "Caesar shuffle" walk from the historic Colosseum through the ancient Forum, and over the Capitoline Hill. Then take an early evening "Dolce Vita Stroll" down the Via del Corso with Rome's beautiful people.

## Planning Your Time

For most, Rome is best done quickly. It's great, but exhausting. Time is normally short, and Italy is more charming elsewhere.

To "do" Rome in a day, consider it as a side trip from Orvieto or Florence and maybe before the night train to Venice. Crazy as that sounds, if all you have is a day, it's a great one.

**Rome in a day:** Vatican (2 hours in the museum and Sistine and 1 hour in St. Peter's), taxi over the river to the

Rome Area

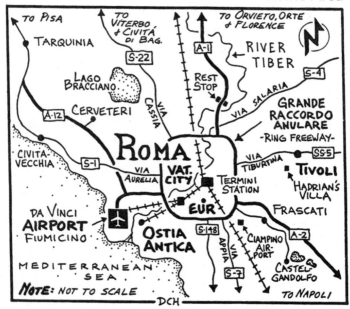

Pantheon (munch a bar snack picnic on its steps), then hike over Capitoline Hill, through the Forum, and to the Colosseum. After a dinner on Campo di Fiori, lace the top night sights (Piazza Navona, Trevi Fountain, Spanish Steps) together with a floodlit gelato-licking stroll.

**Rome in two days** (the optimal first visit): To maximize open hours, first do odd sights that close at 13:00 and finish the day with the "Caesar Shuffle" through the Forum and Colosseum. On the second day, do the Vatican (St. Peter's, climb the dome, tour the museum). After a siesta join the locals strolling from Piazza del Popolo to the Spanish Steps or from Trastevere to Campo di Fiori to the Spanish Steps.

With a third day, consider adding a side trip to Ostia and another museum.

### Orientation (tel. code: 06)

The modern sprawl of Rome is of no interest to us. Our Rome is the old core—within the triangle formed by the train station, Colosseum, and Vatican. Get a handle on

Rome by considering it in these chunks: **The ancient city** had a million people. Tear it down to size by walking through just the core. The best of the classical sights stand in a line from the Colosseum to the Pantheon. **Medieval Rome** was a little more than a hobo-camp of 50,000—thieves, mean dogs and the pope, whose legitimacy required a Roman address. The medieval city, a colorful tangle of lanes, lies between the Pantheon and the river. **Window-shoppers' Rome** twinkles with nightlife and ritzy shopping near medieval Rome, on or near Rome's main drag, the Via del Corso. **Vatican City** is a compact world of its own with two great sights: a huge basilica and the museum. And **Trastevere**, the seedy/colorful wrong-side-of-the-river neighborhood-village, is Rome at its crustiest. **Baroque Rome** is an overleaf that embellishes great squares throughout the town with fountains and church facades.

If Rome gets you down, sing the *Rawhide* theme song and remember, Romulus was gladiator.

### Tourist Information

Rome offers less tourist information per capita than any city in the First World. Most available publications are two years old, and nobody seems to know or care what is actually going on. The Ente Provinciale Per il Turismo (EPT) has three offices: at the airport, in the train station (near track #1, very crowded, the only one open on Sunday), and the central office (open 8:15–19:15, 5 Via Parigi, tel. 06/488-99255 or 488-99253). The central office is a 5-minute walk out the front of the station, near Piazza della Republica's huge fountain, less crowded and more helpful, air-conditioned, with comfortable sofas and a desk to plan on—or sit at to overcome your frustration. Ask for the free EPT city map (better than the free McDonald's version) and a quarterly periodical entertainment guide for evening events and fun. (If all you need is a map, forget the TI and pick one up at your hotel.) Fancy hotels carry a free and helpful English monthly, *Un Ospite a Roma* (A Guest in Rome). All hotels list an inflated rate to cover the hefty commission any room-finding service charges. You'll save money by booking direct.

### Rome

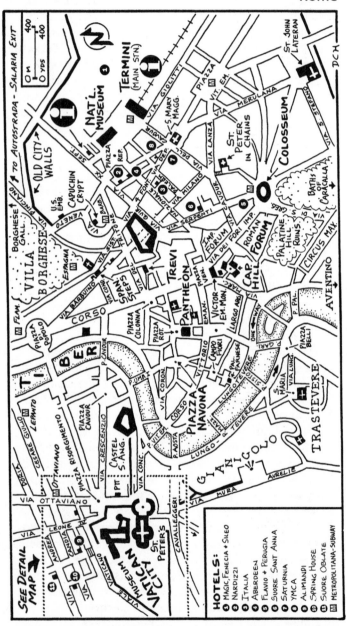

**Enjoy Rome** (8:30–13:00, 14:00–18:00, closed Saturday afternoon and on Sunday, 3 blocks northeast of the station at Via Varese 39, tel. 445-1843, English-speaking) is a free and friendly information service providing maps, museum hours, and a room-finding service (you'll get better prices going direct).

Apart from the normal big bus tours, American students in Rome lead "Secret Walks." Several 3-hour, English-only walks are given daily (L20,000 per tour or L15,000 for students, children under 15 go free, tel. 397-28728).

### Trains and Buses

The Termini train station is a minefield of tourist services: a late-hours bank, a day hotel, luggage lockers, 24-hour thievery, the city bus station, and a subway stop. Handy multilingual charts make locations very clear. La Piazza is a bright and cheery self-service restaurant (open 11:00–22:30).

### Getting Around Rome

Sightsee on foot, by city bus, or taxi. I've grouped your sightseeing into walkable neighborhoods. Public transportation is efficient, cheap, and part of your Roman experience. **Buses:** Bus routes are clearly listed at the stops. Bus #64 is particularly useful, connecting the station, Victor Emanuel Monument (near the Forum), and the Vatican. Ride it for a city overview and to watch pickpockets in action. Buy tickets at newsstands, tobacco shops, or at major bus stops but not on board (L1,500, good for 75 minutes—one Metro ride and unlimited buses, punch them yourself as you board). Buy a bunch so you can hop a bus without searching for an open tobacco shop. (Riding without a ticket, while relatively safe, is stressful. Inspectors fine even innocent-looking tourists L50,000 if found on a bus or subway without a ticket.) If you hop a bus without a ticket, locals who use tickets rather than a monthly pass can sell you a ticket from their wallet bundle. All-day bus/Metro passes cost L6,000. Learn which buses serve your neighborhood.

Buses, especially the touristic #64, and the subway, are havens for thieves and pickpockets. Assume any commotion is a thief-created distraction. Watch your pack, wear no wallet, and keep your money belt out of sight.

When it's crowded, a giggle or a jostle can be expensive. For six trips in a row, I've met a tourist who was pickpocketed. You are a target.

## Metropolitana: Rome's Subway

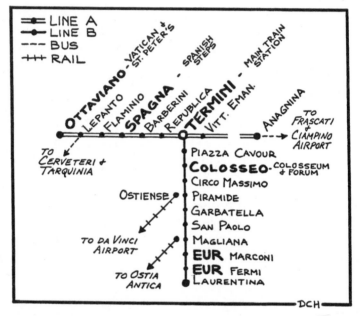

**Subway:** The Roman subway system (Metropolitana) is simple, with two clean, cheap, fast lines. While much of Rome is not served by its skimpy subway, these stops may be helpful to you: Termini (central train station, several recommended hotels, National Museum), Republica (main tourist office, several recommended hotels), Barberini (Cappuccin Crypt, Trevi Fountain), Spagna (Spanish Steps, Villa Borghese, classiest shopping area), Flaminio (Piazza del Popolo, start of the Via del Corso Dolce Vita stroll), Ottaviano (the Vatican, recommended hotels), Colosseo (the Colosseum, Roman Forum, recommended hotels), and E.U.R. (Mussolini's futuristic suburb). Buy your L1,500 subway tickets at subway ticket counters. (Attendants will try to shortchange you.)

**Taxis:** Taxis' big drop-charge (L6,400) covers you for 3 kilometers (L5,000 surcharge after 22:00). From the train station

to the Colosseo costs about L8,000, to the Vatican, about
L12,000. Three or four traveling together with more money
than time should taxi almost everywhere. Rather than wave
and wave, ask in local shops for the nearest taxi stand (*"Dové*
[DOH-vay] *una fermata dei tassi?"*). The meter is fair.

## Helpful Hints
**General Museum Hours:** 9:00–14:00, closed on Monday
(except the Vatican) and at 13:00 on Sunday. Outdoor sights
like the Colosseum, Forum, and Ostia Antica are open
9:00–19:00 (or one hour before sunset). The Capitoline Hill
museums, Rome's only nocturnal museums, are open
Tuesday and Saturday 20:00–23:00 in summer, Tuesday and
Saturday 17:00–20:00 in winter. There are absolutely no
absolutes in Italy. These hours will vary. Confirm sightseeing plans each morning with a quick L200 telephone call
asking, "Are you open today?" (*"Aperto oggi?"*) and "What
time do you close?" (*"A che ora chiuso?"*). I've included telephone numbers for this purpose. The last pages of the daily
*Messaggero* newspaper list current events, exhibits, and hours.

    **Churches:** Churches open early, close for lunch, and
reopen from about 16:00 to 19:00. Modest dress means no
bare shoulders, miniskirts, or shorts (men or women).
Kamikaze tourists maximize their sightseeing hours by visiting
churches before 9:00, seeing the major sights that don't close
for siesta (St. Peter's and the Forum) when all good Romans
are taking it cool and easy, and doing the nocturnal museums
after dark.

    **Shop Hours:** Usually 9:00–13:00 and 16:00–20:00. In
the holiday month of August, many shops and restaurants
close up for vacation—*"Chiuso per ferie"* (and "Closed for
restoration") signs decorate locked doors all over town.

    **Theft Alert:** With sweet-talking con artists, pickpockets
on buses and at the station, and thieving gangs at the ancient
sights, Rome is a gauntlet of rip-offs. Other than getting run
down, there's no great physical risk. But green tourists will be
ripped off. Thieves strike when you're distracted. Don't trust
kind strangers and keep nothing important in your pockets.
Assume you're being stalked. (Then relax and have fun.)

    **Buyer Beware:** I carefully understand the final price
before I order *anything* and I deliberately count my

change. Expect the "slow count." Wait for the last bits of your change to straggle over to you. There are legitimate extras (café prices skyrocket when you sit down, taxis get L5,000 extra after 22:00, and so on) to which paranoid tourists wrongly take offense. But the waiter who charges you L70,000 for the pizza and beer assumes you're too polite to involve the police. If you have any problem with a restaurant, hotel, or taxi, get a cop to arbitrate. Rome is trying to civilize itself.

**Siesta:** The siesta is a key to survival in summertime Rome. Lie down and contemplate the extraordinary power of gravity in the eternal city. I drink lots of cold, refreshing water from Rome's many drinking fountains (the Forum has three). If you get sick, call the International Medical Center (tel. 488-2371).

### Downtown Ancient Rome

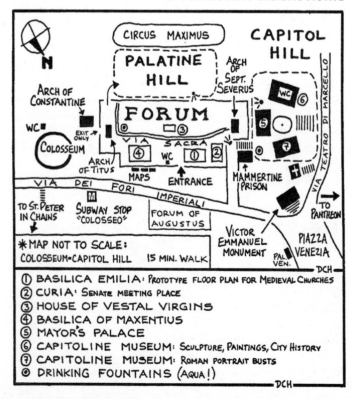

① BASILICA EMILIA: Prototype Floor Plan for Medieval Churches
② CURIA: Senate meeting place
③ HOUSE OF VESTAL VIRGINS
④ BASILICA OF MAXENTIUS
⑤ MAYOR'S PALACE
⑥ CAPITOLINE MUSEUM: Sculpture, Paintings, City History
⑦ CAPITOLINE MUSEUM: Roman portrait busts
⊙ DRINKING FOUNTAINS (Aqua!)

## Sights—Rome

(These sights are in walking order.)

▲**St. Peter-in-Chains Church (San Pietro in Vincoli)**— The original chains and Michelangelo's able-to-stand-and- toss-those-tablets *Moses* are on exhibit in an otherwise unexceptional church. Just a short walk uphill from the Colosseum (free, daily 6:30–12:30, 15:30–19:00, modest dress required).

▲▲▲**Colosseum**—This is the great example of Roman engineering, 2,000 years old. The Romans, using concrete, brick, and their trademark round arches, were able to con- struct much larger buildings than the Greeks. But in defer- ence to the higher Greek culture, notice how they finished their no-nonsense mega-structure by pasting all three orders of Greek columns (Doric, Ionic, and Corinthian) as decora- tions on the outside. The Flavian Amphitheater's popular name "Colosseum" comes from the colossal statue of Nero that used to stand in front of it.

Romans were into "big." By putting two theaters together, they created a circular amphitheater. They could fill and empty its 50,000 numbered seats as quickly and effi- ciently as we do our super-stadiums. Teams of sailors hoisted canvas awnings over the stadium to give the fans shade. This was where the ancient Romans, whose taste was nearly as violent as modern America's, enjoyed their Dirty Harry and Terminator. Gladiators, criminals, and wild animals fought to the death in every conceivable scenario. They could even flood the place to wage mock naval battles (free, not worth L8,000 to go upstairs, daily 9:00–19:00, Sunday and Wednesday 9:00–13:00, less off-season, tel. 700-4261).

▲▲▲**Roman Forum (Foro Romano)**—Ancient Rome's birthplace and civic center, the Forum was the common ground between Rome's famous seven hills. To help resur- rect this confusing pile of rubble, study the before-and-after pictures in the cheap city guidebooks sold on the streets. (Check out the small red *Rome, Past and Present* books with plastic overlays to un-ruin the ruins. They're priced at L25,000—pay no more than L14,000.)

Start at the Basilica Aemilia, on your right as you walk down the entry ramp. This ancient palace's floor plan shows how medieval churches adopted the "basilica" design. Then walk the Via Sacra, the main street of ancient Rome, running from the Arch of Septimus Severus on the right, past Basilica Aemilia, up to the Arch of Titus and the Colosseum on the left. The plain, intact brick building near the Arch of Septimus Severus was the Curia where the Roman senate sat. (Peek inside.) Only the giant barrel vault remains of the huge Basilica Maxentius, looming crumbly and weed-eaten to the left of Via Sacra as you walk to the Arch of Titus (direction: Colosseum).

As you stand in the shadow of the Bas Max, reconstruct the place in your mind. The huge barrel vaults were just side niches. Extend the broken nub of an arch out over the vacant lot and finish your imaginary Roman basilica with rich marble and fountains. People it with plenty of toga-clad Romans. Yeow.

The Arch of Titus is carved with propaganda celebrating the defeat in A.D. 70 of the Jews, beginning the Diaspora that ended only with the creation of Israel in 1947 (find the menorah).

From the Titus drinking fountain, walk up the Palatine Hill to the remains of the Imperial palaces. We get our word "palace" from this hill, where the emperors chose to live. The pleasant garden overlooks the Forum; on the far side, look down into an emperor's private stadium and then beyond at the dusty old Circus Maximus (L12,000, Forum open 9:00–19:00, Sunday 9:00–13:00, off-season 9:00–15:00, last tickets sold an hour before closing, tel. 699-0110). Just past the entry, there's a WC and a handy headless statue for you to pose behind.

▲**Thief Gangs**—If you know what to look out for, the omnipresent groups of children picking the pockets and handbags of naive tourists are no threat but an interesting, albeit sad, spectacle. Gangs of city-stained children, too young to prosecute but old enough to rip you off, troll through the tourist crowds around the Forum, Colosseum, and train and Metro stations. Watch them target tourists distracted with a video camera or overloaded with bags. The kids look like beggars and use newspapers or cardboard signs to distract their victims. Every year they get bolder, but they'll still scram like stray cats if you're onto them. A fast-fingered mother with a baby is often nearby.

▲**Mammertine Prison**—The 2,500-year-old converted cistern that once imprisoned Saints Peter and Paul is worth a look. On the walls are lists of prisoners (Christian and non-Christian) and how they were executed: Strangolati, Decapitato, Morto di Fame . . . (donation requested, daily 9:00–12:00, 14:30–17:00). At the top of the stairs leading to the Campidoglio, you'll find a refreshing water fountain. Block the spout with your fingers; it spurts up for drinking.

▲▲**Capitoline Hill (Campidoglio)**—This hill was the religious and political center of ancient Rome. It's still the home of the city's government. Michelangelo's lovely Renaissance square is bounded by two fine museums and the mayoral palace.

The Capitoline Museum (Musei Capitolini) in the Palazzo Nuovo (the building closest to the river) is the world's oldest museum (500 years old) and more important than its sister (opposite). Outside the entrance, notice the marriage announcements (and, very likely, wedding party photo ops). Inside the courtyard, have some photo fun with chunks of a giant statue of Emperor Constantine. (A rare public toilet hides near the museum ticket-taker.) The museum is worthwhile, with lavish rooms housing several great statues, including the original (500 B.C.) Etruscan Capitoline wolf and the enchanting "Commodus as Hercules." Across the square is a museum full of ancient statues—great if you like portrait busts of forgotten emperors or want to see the restored equestrian statue of Marcus Aurelius that used to sit on the pedestal in the square. (L10,000, both open Tuesday–Saturday 9:00–13:30, summer Tuesdays and Saturdays 20:00–23:00, winter Tuesdays and Saturdays 17:00–20:00, Sunday 9:00–13:00, closed Monday, tel. 671-02071.) There's a fine view of the Forum from the terrace just past the mayor's palace on the right.

To approach the great square the way Michelangelo wanted you to, walk halfway down the grand stairway toward Piazza Venezia, spin around, and walk back up. At the bottom of the stairs, look up the long stairway to your right for a good example of the earliest style of Christian church and be thankful it's not worth climbing up to see.

Way down the street on your left, you'll see a modern building actually built around surviving ancient pillars and arches. Farther ahead (toward Piazza Venezia), look into the ditch (on the right), and see how everywhere modern Rome is built on the forgotten frescoes and mangled mosaics of ancient Rome.

**Piazza Venezia** is the focal point of modern Rome. The Via del Corso, starting here, is the city's axis, surrounded by Rome's classiest shopping district. From the Palazzo di Venezia's balcony above the square (to your left with back to Victor Emanuel Monument), Mussolini whipped up the nationalistic fervor of Italy. Fascist masses filled the square screaming, "Four more years!" or something like that. (Fifteen years later, they hung him from a meat hook in Milan.)

**Victor Emanuel Monument**—This oversized monument to an Italian king loved only by his relatives and the ignorant is known to most Romans as "the wedding cake," "the type-writer," or "the dentures." It wouldn't be so bad if it weren't sitting on a priceless acre of Ancient Rome. Soldiers guard Italy's Tomb of the Unknown Soldier as the eternal flame flickers. Stand directly in front of it and see how Via del Corso bisects Rome.

▲▲▲**Pantheon**—For the greatest look at the splendor of Rome, antiquity's best-preserved interior is a must (free, normally open 9:00–18:00, Sunday 9:00–13:00, less in winter, tel. 683-00230). Walk past its one-piece granite columns and through the original bronze door. Sit inside under the glorious skylight and study it. The dome, 140 feet high and wide, was Europe's biggest until Brunelleschi's dome was built in Florence 1,200 years later. You'll understand why this wonderfully harmonious architecture was so inspirational to the artists of the Renaissance, particularly Raphael; along with Italy's first two kings, he chose to be buried here. As you walk around the outside of the Pantheon, notice the "rise of Rome"—about 15 feet since it was built.

▲**Curiosities near the Pantheon**—The only Gothic church you'll see in Rome is Santa Maria sopra Minerva. On a little square behind the Pantheon to the left, past the Bernini elephant and the Egyptian obelisk statue, it was built *sopra* (over) a pre-Christian temple of Minerva. Rome was at its low ebb, almost a ghost town through much of the Gothic period, and the little building done from this time was later redone Baroque. This church is a refreshing exception. St.

Catherine's body lies under the altar (her head is in Siena) and a little-known Michelangelo statue, *Christ Bearing the Cross*, stands to the left. Fra Angelico's tomb is in the left, or north, transept.

Exit the church via its rear door (behind the Michelangelo statue), turn left, walk to next square. On your right you'll find the **Chiesa di St. Ignazio** church, a riot of Baroque illusions. Study the fresco over the door and the ceiling in the back of the nave. Then stand on the yellow disk on the floor between the two stars. Look at the central (black) dome. Keeping your eyes on the dome, walk under and past it. Church building project runs out of money? Hire a painter to paint a fake (and flat) dome. (Both churches stay open until 19:00, take a 12:30–16:00 siesta, and welcome modestly dressed visitors.)

A few blocks away, back across Corso Victor Emanuel, is the very rich and Baroque **Gesu Church**, headquarters of the Jesuits in Rome. The Jesuits powered the Church's Counter-Reformation. With Protestants teaching that all roads to heaven didn't pass through Rome, the Baroque churches of the late 1500s were painted with spiritual road maps that said they did.

▲▲**The Dolce Vita Stroll down Via del Corso**—The city's chic and hip "cruise" from the Piazza del Popolo (Metro: Flaminio) down a wonderfully traffic-free section of the Via del Corso and up Via Condotti to the Spanish Steps each evening around 18:00. Shoppers, take a left on Via Condotti for the Spanish Steps and Gucci (shops open after siesta, 16:30–19:30). Historians, start with a visit to the Baroque Church of Santa Maria del Popolo (with Raphael's Chigi Chapel and two Caravaggio paintings, on the far side of Piazza del Popolo), continue down the Via del Corso to the Victor Emanuel Monument, climb Michelangelo's stairway to his glorious Campidoglio Square, and visit Rome's Capitoline Museum, open Tuesday and Saturday evenings. Catch the lovely view of the Forum (from past the mayor's palace on right) as the horizon reddens and cats prowl the unclaimed rubble of ancient Rome.

▲**Villa Borghese**—Rome's unkempt "Central Park" is great for people-watching (plenty of modern-day Romeos and Juliets). Take a row on the lake or visit its fine museums.

The **Borghese Gallery** has some world-class Baroque art,
including Bernini's David and his excited statue of Apollo
chasing Daphne (L4,000, 9:00–14:00, Sunday 9:00–13:00,
closed Monday, tel. 854-8577). The gallery's great painting
collection (including works by Caravaggio, Giorgioni,
Titian, and Rubens) is now in the Complesso Monumentale
San Michele a Ripa (L4,000, in Trastevere at via de San
Michele 22, 9:00–19:00, closed Monday and Sunday afternoon). Also in the Villa Borghese, the Museo di Villa Giulia
is a fine Etruscan museum (L8,000, 9:00–19:00, Sunday
9:00–13:30, closed Monday, tel. 320-1951).

▲**National Museum of Rome (Museo Nazionale
Romano delle Terme)**—Directly in front of the train station, the Palazzo Massimo houses much of the greatest
ancient Roman sculpture (L12,000, 9:00–14:00, Sunday until
13:00, closed Monday, tel. 488-0530). At the far side of the
Palace, facing Piazza Republica, the Aula Ottagona (Rotunda
of Diocletian, free, daily 10:00–13:00, 15:00–18:00) is an
impressive space decorated with fine ancient statues and
worth a quick peek.

▲▲▲**Floodlit Rome Hike: Trastevere to the Spanish
Steps**—Rome can be grueling. But a fine way to enjoy this
historian's fertility rite is an evening walk lacing together
Rome's floodlit night spots. Fine urban spaces, real-life theater vignettes, sitting close enough to the Bernini fountain to
hear no traffic, water flickering its mirror on the marble,
jostling with local teenagers to see all the gelato flavors,
enjoying lovers straddling more than the bench, jaywalking
past flak-vested *polizia*, marveling at the ramshackle elegance
that softens this brutal city for those who were born here and
can imagine living nowhere else—these are the flavors of
Rome best tasted after dark.

Taxi or ride the bus (#23 from the Vatican area) to
Trastevere, the colorful neighborhood across (*tras*) the
Tiber (*tevere*). Start your hike at Santa Maria in
Trastevere. Trastevere offers the best look at medieval-
village Rome. The action all marches to the chime of the
church bells. Go there and wander. Wonder. Be a poet.
This is Rome's Left Bank.

**Santa Maria in Trastevere,** from the third century,
(free, 8:00–12:00, 16:00–19:00) is one of Rome's oldest

churches. Notice the ancient basilica floor plan and early Christian symbols in the walls near the entry.

From the square, Via del Moro leads to the river and Ponte Sisto, a pedestrian bridge with a good view of St. Peter's dome. Cross the bridge and continue straight ahead for 1 block. Take the first left, which leads through the scary and narrow darkness to Piazza Farnese, with the imposing Palazzo Farnese. One block from there is **Campo di Fiori** (Field of Flowers), which is an affordable outdoor dining room after dark (see restaurant listings below).

If the statue (a heretic who was burned) on the square did a hop, step, and a jump forward and turned right, he'd cross the busy Corso Vittorio Emanuele and find **Piazza Navona.** Rome's most interesting night scene features street music, artists, fire-eaters, local Casanovas, ice cream, outdoor cafés (splurge-worthy if you've got time to sit and enjoy the human river of Italy), and three fountains by Bernini, the father of Baroque art. Its Tartufo "death by chocolate" ice cream (L5,000 to go) made the Tre Scalini café world famous among connoisseurs of ice cream and chocolate alike. This oblong square is molded around the long-gone stadium of Domitian, an ancient chariot racetrack that was often flooded so the masses could enjoy major water games.

Leave Piazza Navona directly across from the Tre Scalini café, go past rose peddlers and palm readers, jog left around the guarded building, and follow the yellow sign to the **Pantheon** straight down Via del Salvatore (cheap pizza place on left just before the Pantheon). From the obelisk (facing the Pantheon), head left to Casa del Caffe, then left down Via degli Orfani. At the square, pass the church on the left down Via Aquiro. At the obelisk (if it's gelato time, take a detour left behind Albergo Nazionale), turn right, walk between the Italian parliament and the huge *Il Tempo* newspaper building to the busy Via del Corso. You'll pass the huge second-century column honoring Marcus Aurelius, cross the street, and go into the lofty gallery. Take the right branch of this Y-shaped gallery and exit, continuing straight down Via de Crociferi to the roar of the water, light, and people of the Trevi fountain.

The **Trevi fountain** is an example of how Rome took full advantage of the abundance of water brought into the city by its great aqueducts. This watery Baroque avalanche was built in 1762. Romantics toss two coins over their shoulder thinking it will give them a wish and assure their return to Rome. That may sound silly, but every year I go through this touristic ritual . . . and it actually seems to work.

Take some time to people-watch (whisper a few breathy *bellos* or *bellas*) before leaving. Facing the fountain, go past it on the right down Via delle Stamperia to Via del Triton. Cross the busy street and continue to the Spanish Steps (ask, "*Dové Piazza di Spagna?*") a few short blocks and thousands of dollars of shopping opportunities away.

The **Piazza di Spagna** (rhymes with lasagna), with the very popular Spanish Steps, got its name 300 years ago when this was the site of the Spanish Embassy. It's been the hangout of many romantics over the years (Keats, Wagner, Openshaw, Goethe, and others). The Boat Fountain at the foot of the steps was done by Bernini's father, Bernini.

Facing the steps, walk to your right about a block to tour one of the world's biggest and most lavish McDonald's. About a block on the other side of the steps is the subway, or Metropolitana, which (until 23:30) will zip you home.

▲▲**Ostia Antica**—Rome's ancient seaport (80,000 people in the time of Christ, later a ghost town, now excavated), less than an hour from downtown, is the next best thing to Pompeii. Start at the 2,000-year-old theater, buy a map, explore the town, and finish with its fine little museum. To get there, take the subway's B Line to the Magliana stop, catch the Lido train to Ostia Antica (twice an hour), walk over the overpass, go straight to the end of that road, and follow the signs to (or ask for) "*scavi* Ostia Antica." Open daily from 9:00 to one hour before sunset. The L8,000 entry fee includes the museum (which closes at 14:00, tel. 565-0022). Just beyond is Rome's filthy beach (Lido).

▲▲**Vatican City**—This tiny independent country of just over 100 acres, contained entirely within Rome, has its own postal system, armed guard, helipad, mini-train station, and radio station (KPOP). Politically powerful, the Vatican is the religious capital of 800 million Roman Catholics. If you're not one already, become a Catholic for your visit. There's a helpful tourist office just to the left of St. Peter's Basilica (Monday–Saturday, 8:30–19:00, tel. 698-84466).

## Vatican City, St. Peter's, and the Museum

Check out the glossy L5,000 guidebooklet (crowded piazza on cover), which doubles as a classy souvenir. Telephone them if you're interested in their sporadic but very good tours of the Vatican grounds or the church interior, or for the pope's schedule (Sundays at noon for a quick blessing of the crowds in Piazza San Pietro from the window of his study above the square, or Wednesday mornings, when a reservation is necessary). If you don't care to see the pope, remember that the times he appears are most crowded. Handy buses shuttle visitors between St. Peter's and the Vatican Museum (L2,000, twice an hour, 8:45 until museum closes). This is far better than the exhausting 15-minute walk around the Vatican wall, and it gives you a pleasant peek at the garden-filled Vatican grounds.

### St. Peter's Basilica

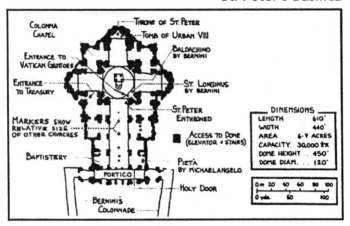

▲▲▲**St. Peter's Basilica**—There is no doubt: this is the richest and most impressive church on earth. To call it vast is like calling God smart. Marks on the floor show where the next largest churches would fit if they were put inside. The ornamental cherubs would dwarf a large man. Birds roost inside, and thousands of people wander about, heads craned heavenward, hardly noticing each other. Don't miss Michelangelo's *Pietà* (behind bulletproof glass) to the right of the entrance. Bernini's altar work and seven-story tall bronze canopy (*baldacchino*) are brilliant.

While for most the treasury (in the sacristy) is not worth the admission, the crypt is free and worth a wander. Directly under the dome, stairs will lead you down to the level of the earlier church and the tombs of many of the popes, including the very first one . . . Peter.

**The dome,** Michelangelo's last work, is (you guessed it) the biggest anywhere. Taller than a football field is long, it's well worth the sweaty climb for a great view of Rome, the Vatican grounds, and the inside of the Basilica—particularly heavenly while there is singing. The elevator (just outside the church to the right as you face it) takes you to the rooftop of the nave. From there a few steps bring you to a balcony at the base of the dome looking down into the church interior. After that the one-way (for some people claustrophobic) 300-step climb to the cupola begins. The rooftop level (below the dome) has a gift shop, WC, drinking fountain, and a commanding view (L6,000 elevator, allow an hour to go up and down).

The church strictly enforces its dress code. Dress modestly—a dress or long pants, shoulders covered. You are usually required to check any bags at a free cloakroom near the entry. St. Peter's is open daily 7:00–19:00, 18:00 in winter; ticket booths to the treasury and dome close an hour early. All are welcome to join in the mass (most days at the front altar, 17:00).

The church is particularly moving at 7:00 while tourism is still sleeping. Volunteers who want you to understand and appreciate St. Peter's give free 90-minute "Pilgrim Service" tours in English, often at 10:00 and 15:00. Check at the desk just after the dress code check as you're entering for the day's schedule. Seeing the *Pietà* is neat; understanding it is divine.

▲▲▲**The Vatican Museum**—Too often, the immense Vatican Museum is treated as an obstacle course, with four nagging miles of displays, separating the tourist from the Sistine Chapel. Even without the Sistine, this is one of Europe's top three or four houses of art. It can be exhausting, so plan your visit carefully, focusing on a few themes, and allow several hours. The museum uses a nearly-impossible-not-to-follow, one-way system.

The masterpiece here is the newly restored School of Athens, remarkable for its blatant pre-Christian Classical orientation wallpapering the apartments of Pope Julius II. Raphael honors the great pre-Christian thinkers—Aristotle, Plato, and company—who are portrayed as the leading artists of Raphael's day. The bearded figure of Plato is Leonardo da Vinci. Michelangelo broods in the foreground—supposedly added late. Apparently Raphael snuck a peek at the Sistine Chapel and decided that his arch-competitor was so good he had to put their personal differences aside and include him in this tribute to the artists of his generation. Today's St. Peter's was under construction as Raphael was working. In the School of Athens he gives us a sneak preview of the unfinished church.

Next (unless you detour through the refreshing modern Catholic art section) is the newly restored Sistine Chapel, Michelangelo's pictorial culmination of the Renaissance, showing the story of Creation with a powerful God weaving in and out of each scene through that busy week. This is an optimistic and positive expression of the high Renaissance. Later, after the Reformation wars had begun and after the Catholic army of Spain had sacked the Vatican, the reeling church began to fight back. As part of its Counter Reformation, Michelangelo was commissioned to paint the *Last Judgment* (behind the altar). Newly restored, the message is as brilliant and clear as the day Michelangelo finished it: Christ is returning, some will go to hell and some to heaven, and some will be saved by the power of the rosary.

The Vatican's small but fine collection of paintings, the Pinacoteca (with Raphael's *Transfiguration* and Caravaggio's *Entombment*), is near the entry/exit. Early Christian art is the final possible side trip before exiting via the souvenir shop. The museum clearly marks out four color-coded visits of different lengths. Rentable headphones (L8,000) give a recorded tour of the Raphael rooms and Michelangelo's Sistine masterpiece. (April, May, September, and October hours: 8:45–16:45, Saturday 8:45–14:00, closed Sunday, except last Sunday of month when museum is free; the rest of the year it's open 8:45–13:45. Last entry 45 minutes before closing. Many minor rooms close 13:45–14:45 or from 13:30 on. The Sistine Chapel is closed 30 minutes before the rest of the museum. A small door at the rear of the Sistine Chapel allows tour groups and speedy individuals to escape via St. Peter's. If you squirt out here you're done with the museum. The Pinacoteca is the only important part left. Consider doing it at the start. Otherwise, it's a 10-minute heel-to-toe slalom through the tourists from the Sistine to the entry/exit, L15,000, tel. 698-83333. The museum is closed on May 1, June 29, August 15, November 1, December 8, and on church holidays).

The museum's excellent book and card shop offers a priceless (L12,000) black-and-white photo book (by Hupka) of the *Pietà*—great for gifts. The Vatican post, with an office in the museum and one on Piazza San Pietro (comfortable writing rooms, Monday–Friday 8:30–19:00, Saturday 8:30–18:00), is the only reliable mail service in Italy. The stamps are a collectible bonus (Vatican stamps are good throughout Rome, Italian stamps are not good at the Vatican). The Vatican bank has sinful rates.

▲**Cappuccin Crypt**—If you want bones, this is it: below Santa Maria della Immaculata Concezione on Via Veneto, just off Piazza Barberini, are thousands of skeletons, all artistically arranged for the delight—or disgust—of the always wide-eyed visitor. The monastic message on the wall explains that this is more than just a macabre exercise. Pick up a few of Rome's most interesting postcards (L1,000 donation, 9:00–12:00, 15:00–18:30). A bank with long hours and good exchange rates is next door, and the American Embassy is just up the street.

▲**E.U.R.**—Mussolini's planned suburb of the future (60 years ago) is a 10-minute subway ride from the Colosseum to Metro: Magliana. From the Magliana subway stop, walk through the park uphill to the Palace of the Civilization of Labor (Pal. d. Civilta d. Concordia), the essence of Fascist architecture, with its giant, no-questions-asked, patriotic statues and its this-is-the-truth simplicity. On the far side is the Museo della Civilta Romana (history museum, Piazza G. Agnelli; Metro: E.U.R. Fermi; L5,000, 9:00–13:30, Tuesday and Thursday 15:00–18:00, closed Monday, tel. 592-6041), including a large-scale model of ancient Rome.

**Overrated Sights**—The Spanish Steps (with Italy's first, and one of the world's largest, McDonald's—McGrandeur at its greatest—just down the street) and the commercialized Catacombs, which contain no bones, are way out of the city and are not worth the time or trouble. The venerable old Villa d'Este garden of fountains near Hadrian's Villa outside of town at Tivoli is now run-down, overpriced, and disappointing.

## Sleeping in Rome
### (L1,600 = about $1, tel. code: 06)
The absolute cheapest doubles in Rome are L50,000, without shower or breakfast. You'll pay L22,000 in a sleazy dorm or hostel. A nicer hotel (L100,000 doubles), providing an oasis/refuge, makes it easier to enjoy this intense and grinding city. If you're going door-to-door, prices are soft—so bargain. Official prices that hotels list assume an agency or room-finding service kickback which, if you're coming direct, they avoid. Many hotels have high-season (mid-March through October) and low-season prices. Easter and September are the crowded times. August is too hot for

crowds. Most of my recommended hotels are small, with huge, murky entrances that make you feel like a Q-Tip. The amount of English spoken drops with the price. Most places speak some and will hold a room with a phone call. I've listed mostly places with minimal traffic noise. Many prices here are promised only to people who use no credit card, use no room-finding service, and show this book. Prices are generally guaranteed through 1996 (except for a few holiday times).

Sleep code: **S**=Single, **D**=Double/Twin, **T**=Triple, **Q**=Quad, **B**=Bath/Shower and WC, **CC**=Credit Card (Visa, MasterCard, Amex), **SE**=Speaks English (graded **A-F**). Breakfast is normally included only in the expensive places (as noted).

### Sleeping near the Train Station

The cheapest hotels in town are near the station. Avoid places on the seedy south (Colosseum) side of the station. The first two bunches of listings are closest in a safe and decent area (which gets a little weird and spooky late at night), 2 blocks northeast of the station. The next are a 5-minute walk in front of the station near the Via Nazionale.

**Via Magenta 39:** These odd ducks are about as cheap as the youth hostel and much handier (no breakfast). **Albergo Sileo** is a shiny-chandeliered ten-room place with an elegant touch that has a contract to house train conductors who work the night shift, so they offer rooms from 19:00 to 9:00 only. If you can handle this, it's a great value (D-L50,000, DB-L60,000, elevator; Via Magenta 39, fourth floor, tel. 445-0246, Allesandro and Maria Savioli, SE-D). **The Fawlty Towers** is a backpacker-type place run by the folks from Enjoy Rome. It's young, hip, and English-speaking, with a rooftop terrace and lots of information (shared triples or quads for L22,000–L25,000 per bed, D-L65,000, DB-L80,000, tel. 445-0374, reservations by credit card number).

**Via Milazzo 20: Hotel Magic** is a tiny, simple place run by a friendly mother-daughter team (Carmella and Rosanna). It's clean and high enough off the road to have no traffic problems (ten rooms, S-L50,000, D-L60,000, DB-L70,000, DBWC-L80,000, T-L90,000, TB-L100,000 with this book, no breakfast; Via Milazzo 20, third floor, 00185

Roma, tel. 495-9880, little English spoken). In the same building, also with lots of stairs: **Hotel Fenicia** (D-L80,000, DB-L85,000, DBWC-L100,000 third person pays L20,000, owner Anna promises my readers a discount, tel. 490-342). A self-serve Lavanderia is at 8 Via Milazzo (daily, 8:00–22:00, 6 kilos washed and dried for L12,000, friendly Maria Pia lets you drop off and pick up for no extra charge).

**Hotel Nardizzi Americana** (D-L100,000, DB-L120,000, T-L140,000, TB-L160,000 (also four-and-five bed rooms), including breakfast, these cash-only rates promised through 1996, in July and August they offer four nights for the price of three, CC:VMA; Via Firenze 38, 00184 Roma, elevator, tel. 488-0368, fax 488-0035, Nik, Fabrizio, and Rugero speak English) is a fine splurge in the station area. Traffic noise in the front rooms is a problem in the summer, when you'll want the window open, but it's a tranquil haven, safe, handy, central, and a short walk from the central station and Piazza Barberini on the corner of Via Firenze and Via XX Septembre. (Parking is actually work-able here. Double-park below the hotel until a space without yellow lines becomes available and grab it. The defense ministry is across the street, and you've got heavily armed guards all night.)

The nearby **Residence Adler** (D-L110,000, DB-L130,000, T-L130,000, TB-L160,000, including breakfast, CC:VMA, elevator; Via Modena 5, 00184 Roma, tel. 484-466, fax 488-0940), with wide halls, a garden patio, and 16 big, quiet, and elegant rooms in a great locale, is another worthwhile splurge.

**Hotel Pensione Italia** (SB-L85,000, DB-L130,000, TB-L180,000, with this book and cash only through 1996, including breakfast, elevator; Via Venezia 18, just off Via Nazionale, tel. 482-8355, fax 474-5550), in a busy, interest-ing, handy locale, placed safely on a quiet street next to the Ministry of the Interior, is modern, airy, bright, clean, and thoughtfully run by English-speaking Andrea.

**Hotel Aberdeen** (SB-L135,000, DB-L190,000, TB-L250,000, L30,000 less in August and winter, CC:VMA; Via Firenze 48, 00184 Roma, tel. 482-3920, fax 482-1092, SE-A, L25,000 garage), with mini-bars, phones, TVs, and showers in its modern rooms, a first-class breakfast buffet, warmly run by Anna Maria and without traffic noise, is my classiest hotel listing and a good value for Rome.

### Sleeping near the Colosseum and Elsewhere

A couple of stops on the subway from the train station, these places are out of the station sleaze and buried in a very Roman world of exhaust-stained medieval ambience.

**Hotel Flavio** (S-L60,000, D-L95,000, DB-L115,000, family rooms also, CC:VMA; hiding almost torchlit under vines on a tiny street a block toward the Colosseum from Via Cavour at Via Frangipane 34, 00184 Roma, tel. 679-7203, fax 679-6246, not much English) is a real hotel with a classy TV-lounge/lobby, an elevator, and elegant furnishings throughout in a quiet setting. Its weakness is lousy tub-showers down the hall for the five cheap doubles.

**Suore di Sant Anna** (S-L35,000, D-L70,000, including breakfast, monkish lunch, or dinner for L20,000 more; off the corner of Via dei Serpenti and Via Baccina at Piazza Madonna dei Monti 3, 00184 Roma, tel. 485-778, fax 487-1064) was built for Ukrainian pilgrims. The sisters are sweet, but the male staff doesn't seem to want your business. It's clumsy and difficult, but once you're in, you've got a comfortable home in a classic Roman village locale.

The **YWCA Casa Per Studentesse** (L32,000 per person in three- and four-bed rooms, D-L64,000, breakfast included; Via C. Balbo 4, 00184 Roma, 5 blocks toward the Colosseum from the station, tel. 488-0460, fax 487-1028) accepts women, couples, and couples with children. It's a grey and institutional place, filled with maids in white, more-colorful Third World travelers, and 75 single beds.

In old Rome but nowhere near these others, the **Albergo del Sole** (D-L100,000, DB-L140,000, no breakfast; Via del Biscione 76, 00186 Roma, tel. 688-06873, fax 689-3787) is just off the colorful Campo dei Fiori, right in the Roman thick of things. It's clean and impersonal; has 65 rooms, a roof garden, and lots of Germans; and is spoiled by its success.

**Casa di Santa Brigida** is also near the characteristic Campo di Fiori. With soft-spoken English-speaking sisters gliding down its polished hallways, and pearly gates instead of doors, this lavish convent makes the exhaust-stained Roman tourist feel like he's died and gone to heaven. If you're unsure of your destiny, this is worth the splurge (twins with all the comforts-L200,000; Piazzale Farnese 96, 00186 Roma, tel. 686-5721, fax 688-04780). Some of its 20 rooms overlook the Piazza Farnese.

### Sleeping Two Blocks from the Vatican Museum

**Pension Alimandi** (SB-L95,000, D-L105,000, DB-L130,000, third person pays L30,000, 5 percent discount off these prices with this book and cash, CC:VMA, elevator to most rooms, optional hearty L12,000 breakfast, great roof garden; just down the stairs in front of the Vatican Museum, Via Tunisi 8, 00192 Roma, tel. 397-26300, fax 397-23943, credit card by telephone or fax accepted to secure reservation, SE-A, L20,000 garage deal) is a good value, run by the friendly and entrepreneurial Alimandi brothers: Paolo, Enrico, and Luigi. From the train station follow Metro line A to last stop, Ottaviano; exit subway station to "V. le G. Cesare"; walk straight up that street 4 or 5 blocks (Via Cesare becomes Via Candia), and turn left at Via Tunisi.

    **Hotel Spring House** (DB-L150,000, DB with air-con L180,000, including breakfast, CC:VMA; Via Mocenigo 7, a block from Alimandi, tel. 397-20948, fax 397-21047) offers clean, quiet rooms with balconies, TVs, refrigerators, and a fine sixth-floor breakfast terrace.

### Sleeping in Convents near the Vatican

**Suore Oblate dell Assunzione** (Via Andrea Doria 42, 3 blocks from the Vatican Museum entrance, tel. 372-9540) and a convent across the street from the museum (Viale Vaticano 92, tel. 397-23797, fax 397-23792) are clean, peaceful and inexpensive, but no English is spoken, and it's hard to get in.

### Sleeping in Youth Hostels and Dorms

Rome has only one real youth hostel—big, institutional, not central or worth the trouble. For cheap dorm beds, consider **Pensione Ottaviano** (25 beds in two- to six-bed rooms,

L23,000 per bed with sheets, depending on the season and their mood, call from the station): free showers; no lockers but a storage room; a fun, laid-back clubhouse feel; close to the Ottaviano Metro stop (near the Vatican) at Via Ottaviano 6, tel. 397-37253 (reservations held until noon). The same slum visionaries run the dumpier **Pensione Sandy** (south of station, up a million depressing stairs, Via Cavour 136, tel. 488-4585, L22,000 beds).

## Eating in Rome

The cheapest meals in town are picnics (from *alimentari* shops or open-air markets), self-serve **rotisseries**, and stand-up or take-out meals from a **Pizza Rustica** (pizza slices sold by the weight, 100 grams is a hot cheap snack, 200 grams, or 2 *etti*, make a light meal). Most alimentari will slice and stuff your sandwich (panini) for you, if you buy the stuff there.

### Eating in Trastevere or on the Campo di Fiori

My best dinner tip is to go for Rome's Vespa street ambience and find your own place in Trastevere (bus #23 from the Vatican area) or on Campo di Fiori. Guidebooks list Trastevere's famous places, but I'd wander the fascinating maze of streets around the Piazza Santa Maria in Trastevere and find a mom-and-pop place with barely a menu, like **Da Meo Petaca** (L15,000 menu, Piazza de Mercanti 30, tel. 581-6198). For the basic meal with lots of tourists, eat amazingly cheaply at **Mario's** (three courses with wine and service for L17,000, near the Sisto bridge at via del Moro 53, tel. 580-3809, closed Sunday). For the ultimate romantic square setting, eat at whichever place looks best on Campo di Fiori: **Virgilio's** (tel. 688-02746, closed Wednesday), **Il Capitello** (tel. 656-573), and **Om Shanti** are all reasonable.

### Eating near the Pantheon

**Il Delfino** is a handy self-service cafeteria on the Largo Argentina square (7:00–21:00, closed Monday, not cheap but fast). The alimentari on the Pantheon square will make you a sandwich for a temple porch picnic.

### Eating on Via Firenze, near Hotels Nardizzi, Adler, and Aberdeen

**Lon Fon**, at #44, serves reasonably priced Chinese food with elegant atmosphere (18:30–23:00, closed Wednesday, tel. 482-5261), **Snack Bar Gastronomia** is a great local hole-in-the-wall for lunch or dinner (#34, really cheap hot meals dished up from under glass counter, tap water with a smile, open until 20:00, closed Sunday), and an alimentari (grocery store, at #54). For an air-conditioned, classier, local favorite serving traditional Roman cuisine, eat at **La Toscanella** (L20,000 menu, across from Hotel Adler, Via Modena 53, tel. 461-289, closed Sunday). Locals also love **Ristorante da Giovanni** (L22,000 menu, just off via XX Septembre at Via Antonio Salandra 1, tel. 485-950, closed Sunday). McDonald's on Piazza della Republica has free piazza seating and a L6,000 salad bar that no American fast-food joint would recognize.

### Eating near the Vatican Museum and Pension Alimandi

Viale Giulio Cesare is lined with cheap, fun eateries (such as **Cipriani Self-Service Rosticceria** near the Ottaviano subway stop at Via Vespasiano, with pleasant outdoor seating and a couple of pizzeria rustica). Don't miss the wonderful **Via Andrea Doria** open-air market in front of the Vatican Museum, two blocks between Via Tunisi and Via Andrea Doria (closed by 13:30, Monday–Saturday). Antonio's **Hostaria dei Bastioni** is a tasty and friendly place for a good sit-down meal (L9,000 pastas, L14,000 *secondi*, at the corner of the Vatican wall, Via Leone IV 29, tel. 397-23034, closed Sunday).

## Transportation Connections

**Train from Rome to: Amsterdam** (2/day, 20 hrs), **Bern** (5/day, 10 hrs), **Brindisi** (2/day, 9 hrs), **Florence** (12/day, 2 hrs), **Frankfurt** (4/day, 14 hrs), **Genova** (7/day, 6 hrs, overnight possible), **Milan** (12/day, 5 hrs, overnight possible), **Munich** (5/day, 12 hrs), **Naples** (6/day, 2–3 hrs), **Nice** (2/day, 10 hrs), **Paris** (5/day, 16 hrs), **Pisa** (8/day, 3–4 hrs), **Venice** (6/day, 5–8 hrs, overnight possible), **Vienna** (3/day, 13–15 hrs). **Città:** Take the Rome-Orvieto train (every 2 hrs, 75 min), catch the bus from Orvieto to Bagnoregio, and walk to Cività. Rome train information: tel. 4775 (call and call, wait and wait).

## Rome and Its Airport

Rome's new rail-air link connects Rome's Leonardo da Vinci (a.k.a. Fiumicino) airport with the Termini Station in 30 minutes for L13,000 (non-stop, departures last year at 7:00, 7:30, 8:10, 9:15, 10:15, and quarter after each hour until 21:15, classy lobby at track 22, tel. 65642). This is far better than the Metro link via Tiburtina. Your hotel can arrange a taxi to the airport at any hour for about L70,000. Airport information (tel. 06/65951) can connect you directly to your airline. British Air tel. 479-991. Alitalia tel. 46881.

## Driving in Rome

Greater Rome is circled by the *Grande Raccordo Anulare*. This ring road has spokes that lead you into the center (much like the strings under the skin of a baseball). Entering from the north, leave the autostrada at the Settebagni exit. Following the ancient Via Salaria (and the black-and-white "centro" signs), work your way doggedly into the Roman thick-of-things. This will take you along the Villa Borghese and dump you right on Via Veneto (where there's an Avis office). Avoid rush hour. Drive defensively: Roman cars stay in their lanes like rocks in an avalanche. Parking in Rome is dangerous. Park near a police station or get advice at your hotel. My favorite hotel is next to the Italian defense ministry— guarded by machine-gunners. You'll pay about L30,000 a day in a garage. The Villa Borghese underground garage (Metro: Spagna) is handy.

Consider this: Your car is a worthless headache in Rome. Avoid a pile of stress and save money by parking it at the huge, easy, and relatively safe lot behind the Orvieto station (follow P signs from autostrada), and catch the train to Rome (every 2 hours, 75 minutes).

# VENICE (VENEZIA)

Soak all day in this puddle of elegant decay. Venice is Europe's best-preserved big city—a car-free urban wonderland of 100 islands, laced together by 400 bridges and 2,000 alleys and doing well on the artificial respirator of tourism.

Born in a lagoon 1,500 years ago as a refuge from barbarians, Venice is overloaded with tourists and slowly sinking (unrelated facts). In the Middle Ages, after the Venetians created a great trading empire, they smuggled in the bones of St. Mark (San Marco), and Venice gained religious importance as well.

Today Venice is home to about 75,000 people in its old city, down from a peak population of around 200,000. While there are about 500,000 in greater Venice (counting the mainland, not counting tourists), the old town has a small-town feel. To see small-town Venice through the touristic flak, explore the back streets and try a Stand-Up Progressive Venetian Pub-Crawl Dinner.

## Planning Your Time

Venice is worth at least a day on even the speediest tour. Hyper-efficient train travelers take the night train in and/or out. Sleep in the old center to experience Venice at its best: early and late. For a one-day visit: cruise the Grand Canal, do the major San Marco sights (the square, Doge's Palace, St. Mark's Basilica), see the Church of the Frari for art, and wander the back streets on a pub crawl. Venice's greatest sight is the city itself. Make time to simply wander. While doable in a day, Venice is worth two. It's a medieval cookie jar, and nobody's looking.

## Orientation (tel. code: 041)

The island city of Venice is shaped like a fish. Its major thoroughfares are canals. The Grand Canal snakes through the middle of the fish, starting at the mouth where all the people and food enter, passing under the Rialto Bridge, and ending at St. Mark's Square (San Marco). Park your 20th-century perspective at the mouth, and let Venice swallow you whole.

Venice

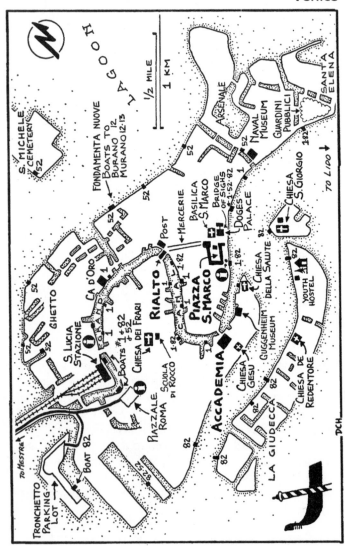

Venice is a car-less kaleidoscope of people, bridges, and odorless canals. The city has no real streets, and addresses are hopelessly confusing. There are six districts, each with about 6,000 address numbers. Luckily it's easy to find your way, since many street corners have a sign pointing you to the nearest major landmark, such as San Marco, Accademia, Rialto, and Ferrovia (the train station). To find your way, navigate by landmarks, not streets. Obedient visitors stick to the main thoroughfares as directed by these signs and miss the charm of back-street Venice.

A long causeway connects Venice to the mainland. Venice's Santa Lucia train station plops you right into the old town on the Grand Canal, an easy *vaporetto* ride or fascinating 40-minute walk from San Marco. Mestre is the sprawling mainland industrial base of Venice. While there are fewer crowds and cheaper hotels and parking lots here, Mestre has no charm. Don't stop here. Trains regularly connect Mestre with the Santa Lucia station (6/hr, 5 min). Santa Lucia is a thriving center of information, but I'd go directly to the center.

### Tourist Information

Tourist information offices are at the station (open early) and on or near St. Mark's Square (tel. 522-6356, open maybe 9:00–13:00, 14:00–16:00, closed Sunday). Pick up a city map, photocopied public transit map, and the latest museum hours, and confirm your sightseeing plans. Drop into any fancy hotel (as if you're sleeping there) and pick up the free periodical entertainment guide, *Un Ospite de Venezia* (a handy listing of events and the latest museum hours). The cheap Venice map on sale at postcard racks has much more detail than the TI map. Also consider the little sold-with-the-postcards guidebook, with a city map and explanations of the major sights.

### Parking in Venice

At Venice, the freeway ends like Medusa's head. Follow the green lights directing you to a parking lot with space. The standard place is Tronchetto (across the causeway and on the right) with a huge new multi-storied garage (L36,000 per day, half off with a discount coupon from your hotel; Hotel Guerrato has them). From there you'll find travel agencies masquerading as TIs and vaporetto docks for the boat connection (#82) to the town center. Parking in Mestre is much cheaper. Open-air lots run about L6,000 per day. There's a good L8,000-a-day garage across from the Mastre train station.

### Getting Around Venice

The public transit system is a fleet of motorized bus-boats called *vaporetti*. They work like city buses except that they never get a flat, the stops are docks, and if you get off between stops, you may drown. While route numbers change nearly yearly, for now only two lines matter: #1 is the slow boat, taking 45 minutes to make every stop along the entire length of the Grand Canal; and #82 is the fast boat down the Grand Canal, stopping only at Tronchetto (car-park), Piazza Roma (bus station), Ferrovia (train station), the Rialto Bridge, and San Marco, making the trip in 20 minutes. Buy L4,000 tickets before boarding or (for an extra fee) from a conductor on board. There are 24-hour (L15,000) and 72-hour (L30,000) passes, but I've never sailed enough to merit purchasing one (although it's fun to be able to hop on and off carelessly).

Only three bridges cross the Grand Canal, but *traghetti* (little L600 ferry gondolas, marked on better maps) shuttle locals and in-the-know tourists across the Grand Canal at seven handy locations. Take advantage of these time-savers. They can also save money. For instance, while most tourists take the L4,000 vaporetto to connect St. Mark's with Salute, a L600 traghetto also does the job.

## Helpful Hints

The Venice fly-trap lures us in and takes our money any way it can. Expect to be shortchanged by any ticket-taker. Wait through the delayed-payment-of-change trick. Count your change carefully. Accept the fact that Venice was a tourist town 400 years ago. It was, is, and always will be crowded. While 80 percent of Venice is actually an untouristy place, 80 percent of the tourists never notice. Hit the back streets.

**Get Lost:** Venice is the ideal town to explore on foot. Walk and walk to the far reaches of the town. Don't worry about getting lost. Get as lost as possible. Keep reminding yourself, "I'm on an island and I can't get off." When it comes time to find your way, just follow the directional arrows on building corners, or simply ask a local, *"Dové San Marco?"* ("Where is St. Mark's?") People in the tourist business (that's most Venetians) speak some English. If they don't, listen politely, watching where their hands point, say *"grazie"* and head off in that direction.

**Money:** Bank rates vary. I like the Banco di Sicilia a block towards San Marco from Campo San Bartolomio. AmExCo, famous for its "no commission," makes up for that with bad rates. Non-bank exchange bureaus will cost you $10 more than a bank for a $200 exchange. There's a 24-hour cash machine near the Rialto vaporetto stop that exchanges U.S. dollars and other currencies into lire at a fair rate.

**The "Rolling Venice" Youth Discount Pass:** This L5,000 pass gives anyone under 30 discounts on sights, transportation, information on cheap eating and sleeping, and a handy guidebooklet to the city—but for a short visit, it's not worthwhile (behind the American Express office at Corte Contarina 1529, Monday–Friday 9:30–13:00).

**Water:** Venetians pride themselves on having pure, safe, and tasty tap water which is piped in from the foothills of the Alps (which you can actually see from Venice on a crisp winter day).

**Pigeon Poop:** If bombed by a pigeon, resist the initial response to wipe it off immediately—it'll just smear into your hair. Wait until it dries and flake it off cleanly.

**Laundry:** A handy *lavanderia* (laundromat) near St. Mark's and most of my hotel listings is the full-service Laundry Gabriella (Monday–Friday 8:00–19:00, Rio Terra Colonne, one bridge off the Merceria near San Zulian church, down Calle dei Armeni, tel. 522-1758). Near the Rialto: Lavanderia SS. Apostoli (8:30–12:00, 15:00–19:00, closed Saturday, tel. 522-6650, on Campo SS. Apostoli). At either place you can get nine pounds of laundry washed and dried for L15,000. Drop it by in the morning, pick it up that afternoon. (Call to be sure they're open.)

**Modest dress:** If you'll be visiting St. Mark's or the other major churches, cover your knees and shoulders.

## Sights—Venice

▲▲▲**Grand Canal Tour**—Grab a front seat on boat #82 (fast, 20 minutes) or #1 (slow, 45 minutes) to cruise the entire Canale Grande from the car-park (Tronchetto) or train station (*Ferrovia*) to San Marco. While Venice is a barrage on the senses that hardly needs a narration, these notes

## Downtown Venice

LODGING:
- ❶ GUERRATO
- ❷ STURION
- ❸ CANADA
- ❹ RIVA
- ❺ SAN GALLO
- ❻ DONI
- ❼ CORONA
- ❽ PIAVE
- ❾ MASETTO
- ❿ CASA PETRARCA
- ⓫ GAMBERO
- ⓬ PAGANELLI
- ⓭ MARIN
- ⓮ ALBORETTI

give the cruise a little meaning and help orient you to this great city. Some city maps (on sale at postcard racks) have a handy Grand Canal map on the back side.

Venice, built in a lagoon, sits on pilings: pine trees driven 15 feet into the mud. More than 100 canals—about 25 miles in length—drain the city, dumping like streams into the Grand Canal.

Venice is a city of palaces. The most lavish were built fronting this canal. This cruise is the only way to really appreciate the front doors of this unique and historic chorus line of mansions from the days when Venice was the world's richest city. Strict laws prohibit any changes in these buildings, so while landowners gnash their teeth, we can enjoy Europe's best-preserved medieval city—slowly rotting. Many of the grand buildings are now vacant. Others harbor chandeliered elegance above mossy basements.

Start at Tronchetto (the bus and car-park) or the train station. FS stands for "Ferrovie dello Stato," the Italian state railway system. The bridge at the station is one of only three that cross the Canale Grande.

Vaporetto stop #4 (San Marcuola-Ghetto) is near the world's original ghetto. When this area was set aside as the local Jewish quarter in 1516, it was a kind of urban island which developed into one of the most closely knit business and cultural quarters of any Jewish community in Italy.

As you cruise, notice the traffic signs. Venice's main thoroughfare is busy with traffic. You'll see all kinds of boats: taxis, police boats, garbage, even brown-and-white UPS boats.

Venice's 500 sleek, black, graceful gondolas are a symbol of the city. They cost up to $35,000 apiece and are built with a slight curve so that one oar propels them in a straight line.

At the Ca d'Oro stop, notice the palace of the same name. For years it's been under a wooden case of scaffolding for reconstruction. Named the "House of Gold," and considered the most elegant Venetian Gothic palace on the canal, today it's an art gallery with a few important paintings. Unfortunately its interior shows nothing of its palatial origins.

Just before the Rialto Bridge, on the right, the outdoor produce market bustles with people in the morning, but is quiet with only a few grazing pigeons the rest of the day. Can you see the traghetto gondola ferrying shoppers back and forth? The huge post office, usually with a postal boat moored at its blue posts, is on the left.

A symbol of Venice, the Rialto Bridge, is lined with shops and tourists. Built in 1592, with a span of 42 meters, it was an impressive engineering feat in its day. Locals call the summit of this bridge the "icebox of Venice" for its cool breeze.

The Rialto, a separate town in the early days of Venice, has always been the commercial district, while San Marco was the religious and governmental center. Today a street called the Merceria connects the two, providing travelers with a gauntlet of shopping temptations.

Take a deep whiff of Venice. What's all this nonsense about stinky canals? All I smell is my shirt. By the way, how's your captain? Smooth dockings? To get to know him, stand up in the bow and block his view.

Notice how the rich marble facades are just a veneer covering no-nonsense brick buildings. And notice the characteristic chimneys.

After passing the British consulate, you'll see the wooden Accademia Bridge, leading to the Accademia Gallery, filled with the best Venetian paintings. The bridge was put up in 1932 as a temporary fix for the original iron one. Locals liked it, and it became permanent.

Cruising under the bridge, you'll get a classic view of the Salute Church, built as a thanks to God when the devastating plague of 1630 passed. It's claimed that more than a million trees were used for the foundation alone. Much of the surrounding countryside was deforested by Venice. Trees were needed both to fuel the furnaces of its booming glass industry and to prop up this city in the mud.

The low white building on the right (before the church) is the Peggy Guggenheim Gallery. She willed the city a fine collection of modern art.

The building on the right with the golden dome is the Dogana da Mar, a 16th-century customs house. Its two bronze Atlases hold a statue of Fortune riding the dome.

As you prepare to de-boat at stop #15—San Marco—look from left to right out over the lagoon. A wide harbor-front walk leads past the town's most elegant hotels to the green area in the distance. This is the public gardens, the only sizable park in town. Farther out is the Lido, Venice's beach. It's tempting with its sand and casinos, but its car traffic breaks into the medieval charm of Venice. The dreamy church that seems to float is the architect Palladio's San Giorgio (interesting visit, fine Tintoretto paintings, great view from its bell tower, L2,000, 9:30–12:30, 14:30–18:00 daily). And farther to the right is a residential chunk of Venice called the Guidecca.

For more vaporetto fun, ride a boat around the city and out into the Lagoon. Plenty of boats leave from San Marco for the beach (Lido), as well as speedboat tours of Burano (a quiet, picturesque fishing and lace town),

Murano (the glass blowing island), and Torcello (has the oldest churches and mosaics, but is an otherwise dull and desolate island). Boat #12 takes you to these remote points slower and cheaper.

▲▲▲**St. Mark's Square (Piazza San Marco)**— Surrounded by splashy and historic buildings, Piazza San Marco is filled with music, lovers, pigeons, and tourists from around the world by day and is your private rendezvous with the Middle Ages late at night. Europe's greatest dance floor is the romantic place to be. This is the first place to flood, has Venice's best tourist information office (rear corner or nearby), and offers fine public rest rooms (Albergo Diorno— "day hotel," WC, shower, L3,000 baggage check, between Piazza San Marco and the American Express).

With your back to the church, survey one of Europe's great urban spaces and the only square in Venice to merit the title "Piazza." Nearly two football fields long, it's surrounded by the offices of the republic. On the right are the "old offices" (16th-century Renaissance). On the left are the "new offices" (17th-century Baroque). Napoleon enclosed the square with the more simple and austere Neoclassical wing across the far end and called this "the most beautiful drawing room in Europe."

For a slow and pricey thrill, invest L10,000 (plus L4,000 if the orchestra plays) in a beer or coffee in one of the elegant cafés with the dueling orchestras. If you're going to sit awhile and savor the scene, it's worth the splurge. For the most thrills L1,500 can get you in Venice, buy a bag of pigeon seed and become popular in a flurry.

▲▲**Doge's Palace (Palazzo Ducale)**—The seat of the Venetian government and home of its ruling duke or "doge," this was the most powerful half-acre in Europe for 400 years. (L10,000, daily 9:00–19:00, last entry at 18:00, WC at exit). It was built to show off the power and wealth of the republic and remind all visitors that Venice was number one. Built in Venetian Gothic style, the bottom has pointy arches, and the top has an Eastern or Islamic flavor. Its columns sat on pedestals, but in the thousand years since they were erected, the palace has settled into the mud, and they have vanished.

Entering the palace (before the ticket booth), notice a grand staircase (with nearly naked Moses and Paul Newman at the top). Even the most powerful visitors climbed this to meet the doge. This was the beginning of an architectural power trip. The doge, the elected king of this "dictatorial republic," lived on the first floor (now used for special exhibits). It's a one-way tour through the public rooms of the top floor, finishing with the Bridge of Sighs and prison. The place is wallpapered with masterpieces by Veronese and Tintoretto. Don't worry much about the great art. Enjoy the building.

In room 12, the Senate Room, the 200 senators met, debated, and passed laws. From the center of the ceiling, Tintoretto's *Triumph of Venice* shows the city in all her glory. Lady Venice, in heaven with the Greek Gods, stands high above the lesser nations who swirl respectfully at her feet with gifts.

The Armory shows remnants of the military might the empire employed to keep the east-west trade lines open (and the local economy booming). Squint out the window at the far end for a fine view of Palladio's San Georgio church and the Lido in the distance.

After the huge brown globes, you'll enter the giant Hall of the Grand Council (180 feet long, capacity 2,000) where the entire nobility met to elect the senate and doge. Ringing the room are portraits of 76 doges (in chronological order). One, a doge who opposed the will of the Grand Council, is blacked out. Behind the doge's throne, you can't miss Tintoretto's monsterpiece, *Paradise*. At 1,700 square feet, this is the world's largest oil painting. Christ and Mary are surrounded by a heavenly host of 500 saints.

Walking over the Bridge of Sighs, you'll enter the prisons. The doges could sentence, torture, and jail their opponents secretly and in the privacy of their own homes. As you walk back over the bridge, wave to the gang of tourists gawking at you.

▲▲**St. Mark's Basilica**—For well over a thousand years, it has housed the saint's bones. The mosaic above the door at the far left of the church shows two guys carrying Mark's coffin into the church. Mark looks pretty grumpy after the long voyage from Egypt. The church has 4,000 square meters of Byzantine mosaics. The best and oldest are in the atrium (turn right as you enter and stop under the last dome). Face the piazza, gape up (it's okay, no pigeons), and study the story of Noah, the Ark, and the flood (two by two, the wicked being drowned, Noah sending out the dove, a happy rainbow, and a sacrifice of thanks). Now face the church and read clockwise the story of Adam and Eve that rings the bottom of the dome. Step inside the church (stairs on right lead to bronze horses) and notice the rolling mosaic marble floor. Stop under the central dome and look up for the Ascension. (Modest dress, no shorts or bare shoulders, free, 9:00–17:00, Sunday 14:00–17:00, tel. 522-5205, see the schedule board in the atrium listing two free English guided tours of the church each week, particularly beautiful when lit at the 18:45 mass on Saturday, 14:00–17:00 Sunday and some middays.)

Upstairs (L3,000, 9:45–17:00) you can see an up-close mosaic exhibition, a fine view of the church interior, a view of the square from the horse balcony, and (inside, in their own room) the newly restored original bronze horses. These horses, made during the days of Alexander the Great (4th century B.C.), were taken to Rome by Nero, to Constantinople by Constantine, to Venice by crusaders, to Paris by Napoleon, back "home" to Venice when Napoleon fell, and finally indoors out of the acidic air.

The treasures of the church (requiring two more L3,000 admissions) give you the best chance outside of Istanbul or Ravenna to see the glories of Byzantium. Venetian crusaders looted the Christian city of Constantinople and brought home piles of lavish loot (until the advent of TV evangelism, perhaps the lowest point in Christian history). Much of this plunder is stored in the treasury of San Marco (*tesoro*). As you view these treasures, remember most were made in A.D. 500, while western Europe was still rooting in the mud. Behind the high altar lies the body of St. Mark ("Marxus") and the Pala d'Oro, a golden altarpiece made (A.D. 1000–1300) with 80 Byzantine enamels. Each shows a religious scene set in gold and precious stones. Both of these sights are interesting and historic, but neither is as much fun as two bags of pigeon seed.

▲**Campanile di San Marco**—Ride the elevator 300 feet to the top of the bell tower for the best view in Venice. Photos on the wall inside show how this bell tower crumbled into a pile of bricks in 1902, 1,000 years after it was built. For an ear-shattering experience, be on top when the bells ring (L5,000, daily 9:00–19:00). The golden angel at its top always faces into the wind.

**Clock Tower**—From Piazza San Marco you can see the bronze men (Moors) swing their huge clappers at the top of each hour. Notice the world's first "digital" clock on the tower facing the square (with dramatic flips every 5 minutes).

▲▲**Galleria dell' Accademia**—Venice's top art museum is packed with the painted highlights of the Venetian Renaissance (Bellini, Giorgione, Veronese, Tiepolo, and Canaletto). It's just over the wooden Accademia Bridge (L12,000, 9:00–19:00, Sunday and Monday 9:00–14:00; expect delays, as they allow only 180 visitors at a time, tel. 522-2247).

▲**Museo Civico Correr**—The interesting city history museum offers dusty bits of Venice's glory days and fine views of Piazza San Marco. Entry is on the square opposite the church (L8000, 10:00–17:00, closed Tuesday).

▲▲▲**Chiesa dei Frari**—This great Gothic Franciscan church, an artistic highlight of Venice featuring three great masters, offers more art per lira than any other Venetian sight. Freeload on English-language tours to get the most out of the Titian *Assumption* above the high altar. Then move one chapel to the right to see Donatello's wood carving of St. John the Baptist almost live. And for the climax, continue right through an arch into the sacristy to sit before Bellini's *Madonna and the Saints*. Perhaps the greatest Venetian painter, Bellini's genius is obvious in the pristine clarity, believable depth, and reassuring calm of this three-paneled altarpiece. Notice the rich colors of Mary's clothing and how good it is to see a painting in its intended setting. For many, these three pieces of art make a visit to the Accademia Gallery unnecessary (or it may whet your appetite for more). Before leaving, check out the Neoclassical pyramid-shaped tomb of Canova and (opposite that) the grandiose tomb of Titian, the Venetian. Compare the carved marble Assumption behind his tombstone portrait with the painted original above the high altar (L1,000, 9:00–12:00, 14:30– 18:00, Sunday 15:00–18:00).

▲**Scuola di San Rocco**—Next to the Frari church, another lavish building bursts with art, including some 50 Tintorettos. The best paintings are upstairs, especially the *Crucifixion* in the smaller room. View the neck-breakingly splendid ceiling paintings with one of the mirrors (*specchio*) available at the entrance (L8,000, daily 9:00–17:30, last entrance 17:00). For lots of Tiepolo (14 stations of the cross), drop by the nearby Church of San Polo.

▲**Peggy Guggenheim Collection**—This popular collection of far-out art, including works by Picasso, Chagall, and Dali, offers one of Europe's best reviews of the art styles of the 20th century (L10,000, 11:00–18:00, closed Tuesday).

**Ca' Rezzonico**—This 18th-century Grand Canal palazzo is now open as the Museo del '700 Veneziano, offering a good look at the life of Venice's rich and famous in the 1700s (L5,000, 10:00–16:00, closed Friday, tel. 522-4543, at a vaporetto stop by the same name).

▲**Gondola Rides**—A rip-off for some, but a traditional must for romantics; gondoliers charge about L100,000 for a 40-minute ride (less during the day). You can divide the cost— and the romance—by up to six people (some take seven if you beg and they're hungry). Glide through nighttime Venice with your head on someone else's shoulder. Follow the moon as it sails past otherwise unseen buildings. Silhouettes gaze down from bridges, while window glitter spills onto the black water. You're anonymous in the city of masks as the rhythmic thrust of your striped-shirted gondolier turns old crows into songbirds. For cheap gondola thrills, stick to the L600 1-minute ferry ride on a Grand Canal traghetti, or hang out on a bridge along the gondola route and wave at (or drop left-over pigeon seed on) romantics.

▲**Glassblowing**—Don't go all the way to Murano Island to see glassblowing demonstrations. A demo's a demo. For the handiest show, wait by one of several glassworks near St. Mark's Square and follow any tour group into the furnace room for a fun and free 10-minute show. You'll usually see a vase and a "*leetle orse*" made from molten glass. The commercial that always follows in the showroom is actually entertaining. Prices around St. Mark's have a sizable

tour-guide commission built in. Serious glass-shoppers buy
at small shops on Murano Island.

**Santa Elena**—For a pleasant peek into a completely
untouristy residential side of Venice, catch the boat from San
Marco to the neighborhood of Santa Elena (at the fish's tail).
This 100-year-old suburb lives as if there were no tourism.
You'll find a kid-friendly park, a few lazy restaurants, and
great sunsets over San Marco.

▲▲**Evening: The Stand-Up Progressive Venetian Pub-
Crawl Dinner**—Venice's residential back streets hide plenty
of characteristic bars with countless trays of interesting
toothpick munchie food (*cicheti*). Partaking in the *giro di
ombre* (pub crawl) tradition is a great way to mingle and have
fun with the Venetians. Real cicheti pubs are getting rare in
these fast-food days, but locals can point you in the right
direction or you can follow the plan below. As always, the
best way to find a landmark is to ask locals, "*Dové . . . ?*" and
go where they point.

Italian cicheti wait under glass in bars. Try fried mozzarella cheese, blue cheese, calamari, artichoke hearts, and
anything ugly on a toothpick. Ask for a *piatto misto* (mixed
plate). Drink the house wines. A small glass of house red or
white wine (*ombre rosso* or *ombre bianco*) or a small beer (*bir-
rino*) costs about L1,000. Meat and fish munchies are
expensive; veggies are around L4,000 for a meal-sized
plate. A good last drink is the local sweet red wine called
Fragolino. To be safe you might give each pub L20,000 (or
whatever) for your group and explain you want to eat and
drink until it's *finito*. A liter of wine costs around L7,000.
Bars don't stay open very late, and the cicheti selection is
best early, so start your evening by 18:30. (I'd appreciate
any feedback on this plan.)

**First course:** Start on Campo San Bartolomeo near the
Rialto Bridge. If the statue walked backwards 20 yards,
turned left and went under a passageway, he'd hit Rosticceria
San Bartolomeo. This isn't really a pub, but they have a like-
ably surly staff, great fried *mozzarella e prosciutto* (L1,800) and
L800 glasses of wine. Continue over a bridge to Campo San
Lio (landmark), take a left past Hotel Canada, and walk
straight over another bridge and into Alberto's Osteria,
called simply Osteria on Calle Malvasia. This fine local-style

bar has plenty of snacks and cicheti. Say "hi" to Alberto, order with your best Italian (and by pointing), then sit or stand for the same price (9:00–15:00, 17:30–21:00, closed Sunday, tel. 522-9038). Alberto will make a fine L10,000 piatto misto with wine.

**Second course:** Leaving Alberto's, turn left on Calle Malvasia and go basically straight with a jog to the left through a couple of squares to Campo Santa Maria di Formosa. (Ask, *"Dové Santa Maria di Formosa?"*) You could split a pizza with wine on the square (Piero's Bar all' Orologio, opposite the canal, has best setting.) *Capriciosa* means the house specialty. You can get "pizza to go" on the square from Cip Ciap Pizza Rustica (over the bridge behind the SMF gelateria on Calle del Mondo Novo, open until 21:00, closed Tuesday).

**Third course:** Fresh fruit and vegetables from the stand on the square next to the water fountain (open until about 20:00).

**Fourth course:** More cicheti and wine. From Bar all' Orologio (on Campo S.M. di Formosa), with your back to the church (follow yellow sign to SS Giov e Paolo), head down the street to Osteria Mascaron (Gigi's bar, best selection by 19:30, closes at 23:00 and on Sunday).

**Fifth course:** Gigi also runs **Enoteca Mascareta**, another good bar 30 yards further down the street (#5183, tel. 523-0744). The piano sounds like they dropped it in the canal, but the wine was saved. If you're feeling like the painting of Bacchus on the wall looks, it's time for . . .

**Sixth course:** Gelato. The unfriendly but delicious gelateria on Campo di Formosa closes at about 20:00 and on Thursday. (The owner, Mario, promised me that even if you buy a cone for the L1,000 take-away price, you can sit on his chairs for 5 minutes.) Or head toward San Marco where the gelaterias stay open later (the best is opposite the Doge's Palace, by the two columns, on the bay). There's also a good late-hours gelateria (L1,000 small cones) midway between Campo San Bartolomeo and the Rialto Bridge.

You're not a tourist, you're a living part of a soft Venetian night . . . an alley cat with money. Streetlamp halos, live music, floodlit history, and a ceiling of stars make St. Mark's magic at midnight. Shine with the old lanterns on the gondola piers where the sloppy Grand Canal splashes at

the Doge's Palace . . . reminiscing. Comfort the four fright-
ened tetrarchs (ancient Byzantine emperors) under the moon
near the Doge's Palace entrance. Cuddle history.

**Rialto pub crawl:** There are also a lot of cicheti bars
around the Rialto market (between the bridge, Campo San
Polo, Chiesa di San Cassiano, and recommended Hotel
Guerrato). You could track down: Do Mori, Cantina Do
Spade, Vini da Pinto, All' Arco, Osteria Antico Dolo, and
Osteria Enoteca Vivaldi (all within a block or two of each
other, most closed on Sunday). You'll notice the same local
crowd popping up at each of these characteristic places.

## Sights—Venice's Lagoon

Several interesting islands hide out in the Venice Lagoon.
**Burano**, famous for its lace-making, is a sleepy island with a
sleepy community—village Venice without the glitz. Lace
fans enjoy Burano's Scuola di Merletti (L3,000, 10:30–12:30,
14:00–17:00, closed Monday, tel. 730-034). **Torcello,**
another lagoon island, is dead except for its church, which
claims to be the oldest in Venice (L2,000, 10:00–12:30,
14:00–17:00, tel. 730-084). It's impressive for its mosaics,
but not worth a look on a short visit unless you really have
your heart set on Ravenna but can't make it there. The
island of **Murano**, famous for its glass factories, has the
Museo Vetrario, which displays the very best of 700 years
of Venetian glassmaking (L5,000, 10:00–16:00, closed
Wednesday, tel. 739-586). The islands are reached easily
but slowly by vaporetto (catch at the Fondamente Nove
dock). Four-hour speedboat tours of these three lagoon
destinations leave twice a day from the dock near the
Doge's Palace.

## Sleeping in Venice
### (L1,600 = about $1, tel. code: 041)

Finding a room in Venice is easy. Simply call one of my recommendations a few days in advance, reconfirm by telephone
the morning of your arrival day, and arrive by mid-afternoon.
While many stay in a nearby less-crowded place and side-trip
to Venice, I can't imagine not sleeping downtown. If you
arrive on an overnight train, your room may not be ready.
Drop your bag at the hotel and dive right into Venice.

## Venice Lagoon

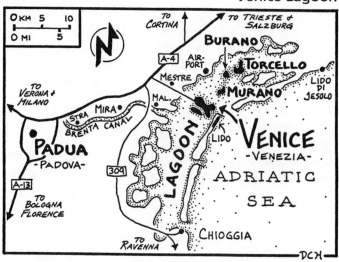

Baths (*bagno*) are more expensive than showers (*doccia*). A toilet in the room knocks the price up. Don't book through the tourist office (which pockets a L15,000-per-person "deposit"). The prices I've listed here are for those who book direct (mention that you have this book and insist on the listed price through 1996). Prices may be cheaper (or soft), especially off-season. If on a budget, ask for a cheaper room or a discount. I've let location and character be my priorities. Rooms are clean, quiet, and generally stark, with high ceilings, dim lights, bare floors, and rickety freestanding furniture.

Sleep code: **S**=Single, **D**=Double/Twin, **T**=Triple, **Q**=Quad, **B**=Bath/Shower and toilet unless "BWC" price is given, **WC**=Toilet, **CC**=Credit Card (**V**isa, **M**asterCard, **A**mex), **SE**=Speaks English (graded **A-F**); breakfast is included unless otherwise noted. I never met an elevator in a Venetian hotel.

### Sleeping near the Rialto Bridge

**Albergo Guerrato**, near a handy and colorful produce market, 1 minute from the Rialto action, is run by English-speaking Roberto and Piero Caruso. Their 800-year-old building is Old World simple, airy, and wonderfully

characteristic (D-L80,000, DB-L90,000, DBWC-L110,000,
T-L108,000, TB-L122,000, TBWC-L150,000,
Q-L136,000, QB-L153,000, QBWC-L180,000, including a
big breakfast and city map, prices promised through 1996
with this book, CC:VM; walk over the Rialto away from
San Marco, go straight about 3 blocks, turn right on Calle
drio la Scimia, and you'll see the red sign, Calle drio la
Scimia 240a, Rialto, tel. and fax 522-7131 or 528-5927,
SE-A). My tour groups completely book this place for 40
nights each year. Sorry.

   **Locanda Sturion** (DB-L200,000 to 230,000,
QB-L300,000 to 420,000 with canal view, CC:VMA, miles
of stairs; S. Polo, Rialto, Calle Sturion 679, 30125 Venezia,
tel. 523-6243, fax 522-8378, SE-A), with air-con and all the
modern comforts, is pricey because it overlooks the Grand
Canal. Telephone reservations are fine until 16:00 with no
deposit; 100 yards from the Rialto Bridge (opposite the
vaporetto dock).

   **Hotel Canada** (two D with adjacent bath-L140,000,
DB-L175,000, CC:VM; Castello San Lio 5659, 30122
Venezia, tel. 522-9912, fax 523-5852, SE-B) has 25 small
bright rooms, all with private showers, WC, and phones. In a
"typical noble Venetian home," it's ideally located on a quiet
square, between the Rialto and San Marco. (See directions to
Alberto's under Pub Crawl Evening, above.)

### Sleeping near St. Mark's Square (zip code: 30124)

**Hotel Riva** (two fourth-floor view D with adjacent showers-
L95,000, DB-L120,000; Ponte dell' Angelo, 5310, Venezia,
tel. 522-7034), with gleaming marble hallways and bright
modern rooms, is romantically situated on a canal along the
gondola serenade route. You could actually dunk your breakfast rolls in the canal (but don't). Sandro will hold a corner
(*angolo*) room if you ask. It's behind San Marco where the
canals Rio di San Zulian and Rio del Mondo Nouvo hit Rio
Canonica o Palazzo.

   **Hotel San Gallo** (SB-L100,000, DB-L180,000,
TB-L240,000; San Marco 1093/A, 30124 Venice, tel. 522-
7311 or 528-9877, fax 522-5702, SE-C; Luca and Franco
promise these prices to those with this book, air-con rooms)

is about 100 yards off Piazza San Marco (with back to the church, take the second-to-last archway right off St. Mark's Square). Breakfast is on a chirpy, breezy roof garden.

**Albergo Doni** (D-L90,000, T-L120,000; Riva Schiavoni, San Zaccaria N. #4656 Calle del Vin, tel. 522-4267, SE-B, easy telephone reservations) is a dark, hardwood, clean, and quiet place with 12 dim-but-classy rooms run by a likable smart-aleck named Gina, who promises my readers one free down-the-hall shower each a day. It's two bridges behind San Marco, or walk east along the San Marco waterfront (Riva Degli Schiavoni), over two bridges, take the first left (Calle del Vin), and follow the signs.

**Albergo Corona** is a squeaky-clean, confusing Old World place with nine basic rooms (D-L60,000, breakfast L8,000 extra, showers L3,000; find Campo SS Filippo e Giacomo behind San Marco, go down Calle Sacristia, take first right then go left on Calle Corona to #4464, tel. 522-9174, lots of stairs, SE-F).

**Locanda Piave**, with 12 fine rooms above a bright and classy lobby, is a rare value (S-L65,000, D-L95,000, T-120,000, five public showers, CC:VMA; from Campo Santa Maria Formosa, go behind the church, over a bridge and down Parrocchia di San Zaccaria to the first corner on right, Ruga Giuffa 4838/40, 30122 Venezia, tel. 528-5174, fax 523-8512, SE-D).

**Alloggi Masetto**, incredibly well-located with four dirt-cheap rooms, is a homey place filled with birds, goldfish, and stacks of magazines, and run by Irvana Artico, a crusty landlady who surprises you with pretty good English (D-L45,000, DB-L50,000, T-L60,000, TB-65,000, no breakfast; just off San Marco; from AmExCo head toward San Marco, first left, first left again through "Contarina" tunnel, follow yellow sign to Commmune di Venezia, jog left again and see her sign, Sotoportego Ramo Contarina, Frezzeria, San Marco 1520 A, tel. 523-0505).

**Locanda Casa Petrarca**, wicker-cozy and bubbling jazz, hangs like an ivy-framed painting over a dead-end alley. Nelli is a friend as well as a host (seven rooms, D-L85,000, DB-L105,000, with this book in 1996; no breakfast; Calle Schiavone #4386. With your back to St. Mark's, take last right off square. From Campo San Luco, go down Calle dei

Fuseri, take left before red "restorante" sign, fake left, look right, tel. and fax 520-0430, SE-A).

**Locanda Gambero,** with 30 rooms, is the biggest one-star hotel in the San Marco area. (S-L61,000, D-L100,000, DB-L110,000, DBWC-L125,000, T-L135,000, TB-L148,000, TBWC-L168,000, CC:VM; a straight shot down Calle dei Fabbri from the Rialto vaporetto #1 dock; from Piazza San Marco walk down Calle dei Fabbri, over one bridge to #4685, tel. 522-4384, fax 520-0431, SE-B). Gambero runs "La Bistrot," a user-friendly French/Italian eatery with a pleasant art-deco ambiance and good L7,000 pasta specials with no extra charges.

**Albergo Paganelli,** rubbing drainpipes with Venice's most expensive hotels, is on the broad promenade running from the Doge's Palace along the Grand Canal toward the "tail of the fish" (DB-160,000 to 180,000, TB-L240,000, request *"con vista"* for a grand canal view; CC:VMA; at the S. Zaccaria vaporetto stop, Riva Schiavoni 4182, Campo S. Zaccaria 4687, 30122 Venezia, tel. 522-4324, fax 523-9267). With spacious rooms, carved and gilded headboards, chandeliers, and hairdryers, this very hotelesque place is a good value. Half of their rooms are in a less interesting *dependencia* a block off the canal.

### Sleeping in Other Parts of Venice

**Hotel Marin** is 3 minutes from the train station but completely out of the touristic bustle of the Lista di Spagna (D-L90,000, DB-L115,000, T-L120,000, TB-L150,000, Q-L150,000, QB-L180,000, CC:VMA; from the train station, cross the bridge and go behind the big green domed church. From the bridge go right, left, right, and right to San Croce 670b, tel. and fax 718-022). Cozy, plain, and cheery, it will seem like a 19-bedroom home the moment you cross the threshold. It's family-run by helpful, English-speaking Bruno, Nadia, and son Samuel (they have city maps).

**Hotel Agli Alboretti** is a cozy, family-run place in a quiet neighborhood a block behind the Accademia Museum (25 rooms, DB-L170,000 to 190,000, CC:VMA; 100 yards from the Accademia vaporetto stop at 884 Accademia, tel. 523-0058, fax 521-0158). The rooms are homey and thoughtfully appointed, and you'll have breakfast in a shady patio.

**Foresteria della Chiesa Valdese,** warmly run by a Protestant church, offers dorm beds at youth-hostel prices in a handier location (halfway between San Marco and Rialto). This rundown but charming old palace has elegant paintings on the ceilings (L22,000 dorm beds or L50,000 doubles with sheets and breakfast, more expensive for one-night stays, with some larger "apartments" for small groups; from Campo Santa Maria Formosa, walk past the Orologio bar to the end of Calle Lungo and cross the bridge, Castello 5170, tel. 528-6797, closed 13:30–18:00).

The **Venice youth hostel** (L22,000 beds with sheets and breakfast in ten- to 18-bed rooms, membership required; on Giudecca Island, tel. 523-8211; boat #82 from station or San Marco to Zittele) is crowded, cheap, and newly remodeled (desk open 7:00–9:30, 13:00–23:00). Their budget cafeteria welcomes non-hostelers (nightly 18:00–21:00).

## Eating in Venice

For low-stress (but not necessarily low-price) meals, you'll find plenty of self-service restaurants (*self-service* in Italian). One is right at the Rialto Bridge. Pizzerias are cheap and easy. Those that sell take-out by the slice or gram are cheapest. Menus should clearly explain the *coperto* (cover charge) and *servicio* (service charge).

You'll pay a premium to eat in the tourist center. For reasonable Grand Canal-side meals, try the places along the canal opposite the Rialto vaporetto stop.

A key to cheap eating in Venice is bar snacks, especially stand-up mini-meals in out-of-the-way bars. Order by pointing. *Panini* (sandwiches) are sold fast and cheap at bars everywhere. My favorite Venetian dinner is the pub crawl (described above under Sights). Any of the listed bars would make a fine one-stop, sit-down dinner.

The **produce market** that sprawls for a few blocks just past the Rialto Bridge (best 8:00–13:00, closed Sunday) is a great place to assemble a picnic. The nearby street, Ruga Vecchia, has good bakeries and cheese shops. Side lanes in this area are speckled with fine little hole-in-the-wall munchie bars.

The **Mensa DLF** (to the right of the train station as you face the tracks, 12:30–13:30, 18:00–21:00, closed

Saturday, Sunday, and during lunch on Tuesday and
Thursday, tel. 716-242), the public transportation workers'
cafeteria, is cheap and open to the public.

### *Eating near Campo San Bartolomeo*

While these places aren't worth hiking to, they're handy,
near the central Campo San Bartolomeo (a block toward San
Marco from the Rialto Bridge). Directions start from the
statue in this square's center.

The very local, hustling **Rosticceria San Bartolomeo/
Gislon** (Calle della Bissa 5424, 20 yards behind the statue to
its left, under a passageway, tel. 522-3569, 9:30–14:30,
17:00–21:00, closed Monday) is a cheap—if confusing—
self-service restaurant on the ground floor (L6,000 pasta,
L800 wine, prices listed at door, no cover or service charge,
stools along the window). While old "example" dishes are
left on display, the kitchen whips up fine pastas. Good but
pricier meals are served at the full-service restaurant upstairs.
Get a take-out meal to eat on a nearby bridge or *campo*.

If the statue on the square were to jump off his
pedestal, walk ahead 50 yards and down a narrow alley to
the left, he'd find the **Devil's Forest Pub**, with English
decor and self-service Italian food (L7,000 pasta, no cover,
open very late). Across the lane, **Pizzeria Bora Bora** has a
fun inexpensive menu, noisy local crowd, and lousy service.

**Ristorante Pizzeria da Nane Mora** (behind the
statue, past PTT, over the bridge, and right at the red
Santuario Madonna della Grazie church, on a tiny triangular square, open at 19:00, tel. 522-8028) has good pizza and
indoor/outdoor seating.

**Antiche Cantine Ardenghi de Lucia and Michael** is
a truly local hangout. From Campo S. Giovanni e Paolo,
pass the church-looking hospital (notice the illusions painted on its facade), go over the bridge to the left, and take the
first right to #6369 under the red telephone (no sign for tax
reasons, open until 21:00, closed Sunday, tel. 523-7691).
Michael speaks English and serves a good L20,000 meal.

## Transportation Connections

**Trains from Venice to: Bern** (4/day, change in Milan, 8 hrs),
**Brindisi** (3/day, 11 hrs), **Florence** (4/day, 3 hrs, ideally to

## Temptations: Venice to Milan

Santa Maria Novella station), **Milan** (12/day, 3–4 hrs), **Munich** (5/day, 8 hrs), **Naples** (2/day, 6 hrs), **Paris** (3/day, 11 hrs), **Rome** (5/day, 4–7 hrs, overnight possible), **Verona** (12/day, 1½ hrs), **Vienna** (4/day, 9 hrs). **To the Dolomites**: train from Venice to Bolzano (8/day, 4 hrs with one change) and catch a bus into the mountains from there. Train and couchette reservations (L24,000) are easily made at the American Express office near San Marco. Venice train info: tel. 041/715-555.

## NEAR VENICE: PADUA, VICENZA, VERONA, AND RAVENNA

While the Italian region of Veneto has much more to offer than Venice, few venture off the lagoon. Five important towns and possible side trips, in addition to the lakes and the Dolomites, make zipping directly from Venice to Milan (3-hr trip, hrly departures) a route strewn with temptation.

### Planning Your Time

The towns of Padua, Vicenza, Verona, and Ravenna are all, for various reasons, reasonable stops. But none are essential parts of the best three weeks Italy has to offer. Of the towns discussed below, only Ravenna (2½ hours from Padua or Florence) is not on the main train line. Each town gives the visitor a low-key slice of Italy compared with Venice/Florence/Rome. While an overnight could be pleasant, only 3 or 4 hours are needed for a quick first visit.

High-speed town-hopping between Venice and Bolzano or Milan (with three-hour stops at Padova, Vicenza, and Verona) is a good day. Trains run frequently enough to allow flexibility and little wasted time.

## PADUA (PADOVA)

Living under Venetian rule for four centuries seemed only to sharpen Padua's independent spirit. Nicknamed "the brain of Veneto," Padua has a prestigious university (founded 1222) and was called home by smart guys like Galileo, Dante, and Petrarch.

The old town is a colonnaded time-tunnel experience, and Padua's museums and churches hold their own in Italy's artistic big league. You'll see Giotto's well-preserved cycle of more than 30 frescoes in the **Chapel of the Scrovegni** (L10,000, daily 9:00–19:00). Don't miss Donatello's *Crucifixion*, with statues of Mary and Padua's six patron saints on the high altar of the Basilica di Sant'Antonio, and his great equestrian statue (the first since ancient Roman times) of the Venetian mercenary General Gattamelata on Piazza del Santo outside the Basilica. For work by Mantegna, see the important (but devastated by WWII bombs) frescoes in the Church of the Hermits (Chiesa degli Eremitani).

The tourist information office is in the train station (tel. 049/875-0655). **Hotel Piccolo Vienna** (D-L46,000, DB-L65,000; Via Beato Pellegrino 133, tel. 049/871-6331) is small and near the station. **Hotel Verdi** (D-L48,000; bus #10 from the station to Teatro Verdi; Via Dondi dell'Orologio 7, tel. 049/875-5744), in the old center, is very friendly and accommodating. The well-run **Ostello Citta di Padova** (L18,000 per bed with sheets and breakfast; bus #3, #8, #12, or #18 from the station; Via Aleardi 30, tel. 875-2219) has four-, eight-, and 12-bedded rooms. Many budget travelers enjoy making this hostel a low-stress, low-price home base from which to tour Venice. I'd rather flip-flop it—sleeping in Venice and side-tripping to Padua, 30 minutes away by train.

## VICENZA

To many architects, Vicenza is a pilgrimage site. Entire streets look like the back of a nickel. This is the city of Palladio, the 16th-century Renaissance architect who gave us the "Palladian" style so influential in Britain (countless country homes) and the U.S.A. (Thomas Jefferson's Monticello was inspired by Palladio's Rotonda, a private but sometimes tourable Palladian residence on the edge of Vicenza.)

For the casual visitor, a quick stop offers plenty of Palladio. From the train station, catch nearly any bus (L1,200) to Piazza Matteotti, where you can visit the tourist office (Piazza Matteotti 12, tel. 0444/544-122, pick up a map). From there, see the Olympic Theater, Palladio's last work (and one of his greatest). This oldest indoor theater in Europe is still used and is considered one of the world's best.

From the Olympic Theater, begin your stroll down Vicenza's main drag, a steady string of Renaissance palaces and Palladian architecture peopled by Vicenzans who keep their noses above the tourist trade and are considered by their neighbors to be as uppity as most of their colonnades.

After a few blocks, you'll see the huge Basilica standing over the Piazza dei Signori, which has been the town center since Roman times. It was young Palladio's proposal to redo the dilapidated Gothic palace of justice in his neo-Greek style that established him as Vicenza's favorite architect. The rest of his career was a one-man construction boom. Notice the 13th-century, 280-foot-tall tower and the Loggia del Capitanio (opposite the basilica), one of Palladio's last works.

If you stay in Vicenza, **Hotel Vicenza** (D-L65,000, DB-L80,000; Piazza dei Signori at Stradella dei Nodari, tel. and fax 0444/321-512) is a rare, reasonable place in the Palladian center of things.

Finish your Corso Palladio stroll by walking to Piazzale Gasperi (where the PAM supermarket is a handy place to grab a picnic for the train ride) and walk 5 minutes down Viale Roma back to the station. Trains leave about every half-hour toward Milan/Verona and Venice (less than an hour away).

## VERONA

Romeo and Juliet made Verona a household word. But, alas, a visit here has nothing to do with those two star-crossed lovers. You can pay to visit the house falsely claiming to be Juliet's, with an almost believable (but slathered-with-tour-groups) balcony, take part in the tradition of rubbing the breast of Juliet's statue in the courtyard to ensure finding a lover (or picking up the sweat of someone who can't), and even make a pilgrimage to what isn't "La Tomba di Giulietta" (but the town has been an important crossroads for 2,000 years and is therefore packed with genuine history). R and J fans will take some solace in the fact that two real feuding families, the Montecchi and the Capellos, were the models for Shakespeare's Montagues and Capulets. And, if R and J had existed and were alive today, they would recognize much of their "home town."

Verona's main attraction is its wealth of Roman ruins, the remnants of its 13th- and 14th-century political and cultural boom, and its 20th-century, quiet, pedestrian-only ambience. After Venice's festival of tourism, Veneto's second city (in population and in artistic importance) is a cool and welcome sip of pure Italy. If you like Italy but don't need great sights, this town is a joy.

### Orientation (tel. code: 045)

The most enjoyable core of Verona is along Via Mazzini between Piazza Brà and Piazza Erbe, Verona's medieval market square. Head straight for Piazza Brà. In front of the station buy a L1,300 ticket (stamp it on bus, good for an hour) and ride bus #11, #12, #13, or #51 under Porta Nuova arch and down boring Corso Porta Nuova to Piazza Brà (the big green square with important-looking buildings). The station-Piazza Brà walk is miserable. Taxis pick up only at taxi stands and cost about L8,000 to the center or the river. All the sights of importance are within an easy walk through the old town, which is defined by a bend in the river. You can rent a bike on Piazza Brå (L20,000 per day).

### Tourist Information

Tourist Information offices are at the station (tel. 800-0861, 8:30–19:30, closed Sunday) and in the center (to the right of the Arena on the side of the big yellow building with columns at Via Leoncino 61, tel. 045/592-828, open 8:00–20:00, Sunday 8:30–13:30).

### Parking in Verona

Drivers will find lots of free parking at the stadium or cheap long-term parking near the train station. The most central lot is behind the Arena on Piazza Cittadella (guarded, L10,000/day). The town center is closed to regular traffic.

## Sights—Verona

**Verona's Arena,** on Piazza Brå, dates from the firstcentury A.D. This elliptical, 140-by-120-meter amphitheater, the third largest in the Roman world, is well-preserved and looks great in its pink marble. Over the centuries, crowds of up to 25,000 spectators have cheered Roman gladiator battles, medieval executions, and modern plays (including a popular opera/ballet festival every July and August). Climb to the top for a fine city view (L6,000, 8:30–18:30, closed Monday).

**Piazza Brå, down Via Mazzini, to Piazza Erbe**—For me, the highlight of Verona is the evening *passeggiata* (stroll) from the elegant cafés of Piazza Brå, through the old town on Via Mazzini—one of Europe's many "first pedestrian-only streets"—to the bustling and colorful medieval market square, Piazza Erbe. Piazza Erbe is a photographer's delight, with pastel buildings corralling the stalls, fountains, pigeons, and people that have come together here for centuries.

The bogus **House of Juliet** is a block off Piazza Erbe (detour right to Via Cappello #23). The tiny, admittedly romantic courtyard is a spectacle in itself, with Japanese posing from the balcony, Nebraskans polishing Juliet's bronze breast, and amorous graffiti everywhere. The info boxes (L500 for two) offer a good history. ("While no documentation has been discovered to prove the truth of the legend, no documentation has disproven it either.") The "museum" is only empty rooms and certainly not worth the L5,000 entry fee.

**From Piazza Erbe to the Roman Bridge:** From the center of the square, continue toward the river on Via della Costa (walking under the "arch of the whale's rib"—look up). Poke around Piazza dei Signori, with its statue of Dante wondering why all the tourists choose Juliet over him. Exit at the end opposite Piazza Erbe, where you'll find the strange and very Gothic tombs of the Scaligeri family, who were to Verona what the Medici family was to Florence.

Walking further, you'll come to the river. Turning right (past two important churches: Sant Anastasia and the Duomo; Verona's historic churches are all open 9:00–18:00 and charge L4,000, there's a L9,000 combo ticket covering all), you come to the Ponte Pietra (a Roman bridge that survived until WWII). Just across the river, built into the hill above the Ponte Pietra, is Verona's Roman Theater, which stages Shakespeare plays every summer (only a little more difficult to understand in Italian than in Olde English). You can climb the stairs behind the theater for a great town view. From the Duomo, if you hike upstream, you'll pass the well-preserved first-century Roman gateway, the Porta Borsari. Then, just before the castle, is the Roman triumphal arch, the Arco dei Gavi. The medieval castle, the Castelvecchio, is now an art museum (fine 16th- to 18th-century paintings, L5,000, 8:30–18:30, closed Monday). Finally, a few blocks farther up the river, you'll find the 12th-century Church of San Zeno Maggiore. This offers not only a great example of Italian Romanesque, but also a set of 48 paneled 11th-century bronze doors that are nicknamed "the poor man's Bible" (pretend you're an illiterate medieval peasant and do some reading), and Mantegna's San Zeno Triptych.

## Sleeping in Verona (L1,600 = about $1, zip code: 37100, tel. code 045)

Several fine, family-run places are in the quiet streets just off Piazza Brà and within 200 meters of the bus stop. Tiny

**Albergo Ristorante Ciopeta**, more *ristorante* than *albergo*, offers the best budget beds I could find (five rooms, S-L60,000, D-L85,000, T-L110,000, with breakfast; Vicolo Teatro Filarmonico 2, tel. 800-6843, fax 803-3722, Sr. Cristofoli speaks *un poco* English).

Two classier places just off Piazza Brå toward the river are **Hotel Cavour** (DB-L125,000, TB-L165,000, without breakfast, prices go soft in the off-season, modern showers, air-conditioned; Vicolo Chiodo 4, tel. and fax 590-508, Patricia speaks English) and not quite so quiet and atmospheric **Albergo Al Castello** (DB-L95,000, one L70,000 D, without breakfast, CC:VM; Corso Cavour 43, tel. 800-4403, Katia speaks English). For sleek, modern comfort in the same great neighborhood, consider **Hotel Europa** (DB-L175,000 with breakfast, L150,000 in slower times, call a day ahead to check for discounts, CC:VMA; Via Roma 8, 37121 Verona, tel. 800-2882, fax 800-1852).

**Hotel Catullo** is a cheaper, quiet, quirky, and paranoid place deeper in the old town, with good basic rooms up three flights of stairs (D-L60,000, DB-L80,000; left off Via Mazzini onto Via Catullo, down an alley between 1D and 3A at Via Valerio Catullo 1, tel. 800-2786).

The **Verona youth hostel** is one of Italy's best hostels (L15,000 beds with breakfast; bus #72 from the station, over the river beyond Ponte Nuovo at Salita Fontana del Ferro 15, tel. 590-360).

## Transportation Connections
**Trains from Verona to: Florence** (10/day, 3 hrs), **Milan** (hrly, 90 min), **Rome** (6/day, 6 hrs), **Bolzano** (hrly, 90 min). Town-hopping between **Verona, Padua, Vicenza** and **Venice** couldn't be easier: all towns are 30 minutes apart on the (hrly, 3 hr) Venice-Milan line. Verona train info: tel. 045/590-688.

## RAVENNA
Ravenna is on the tourist map for one reason—its 1,500-year-old churches decorated with best-in-the-west Byzantine mosaics. Briefly a capital of eastern Rome during its fall, Ravenna was taken by the barbarians. Then in A.D. 539, the Byzantine emperor Justinian made the city Byzantium's lieutenant in the west. Ravenna was a light in the Dark Ages.

Two hundred years later, the Lombards booted Byzantine out, and Ravenna melted into the backwaters of medieval Italy and stayed out of historical sight for a thousand years. Today the city booms with a big chemical industry, the discovery of offshore gas deposits, and the construction of a new ship canal. It goes busily on its way, while busloads of tourists slip quietly in and out of town for the best look at the glories of Byzantium this side of Istanbul.

While not worth an overnight, it's only a 90-minute detour from the main Venice-Florence train line, and worth the effort for those interested in old mosaics. While all agree that Ravenna has the finest mosaics in the West, many will find their time better spent taking a careful look at the good but not as sublime Byzantine-style mosaics in Venice.

## Orientation (tel. code: 0544)

Central Ravenna is quiet, with more bikes than cars and a pedestrian-friendly core. For a quick stop, I'd see the basilicas, mausoleum, covered market, and Piazza del Popolo.

Before you leave the train station, if you're day-tripping to Ravenna, jot down when the next few trains depart for Ferrara (to go to Venice) or Bologna (to get to Florence).

## Sights—Ravenna

**Orientation Walk**—A visit to Ravenna can be as short as a 2-hour loop from the train station. From the station, walk straight down Viale Farini to Piazza del Popolo. A right on Via IV Novembre takes you a block to the colorful covered market (Mercato Coperto, open for picnic fixings 7:00–13:30, closed Sunday). Get a map at the tourist office a block away (daily 9:00–13:00, 15:00–18:00, Via Salara 8, tel. 35404). Ravenna's two most important sights, Basilica di San Vitale and the Mausoleum of Galla Placidia, are 2 blocks away down Via San Vitale. On the other side of Piazza del Popolo is the Church of Sant'Apollinare Nuovo, also worth a look. From there you're about a 5-minute walk back to the station. (Sights open 9:00–19:00, until 16:30 October–March.)

▲▲**Basilica di San Vitale**—It's impressive enough to see a 1,400-year-old church. But to see one decorated in brilliant mosaics that still convey the intended feeling that "this peace and stability was brought to you by your emperor and God" is rare indeed. Study each of the scenes: the arch of apostles with a bearded Christ at their head; the lamb on the twinkly ceiling; the beardless Christ astride a blue earth behind the altar; and the side panels featuring Emperor Justinian, his wife Theodora (an aggressive Constantinople showgirl who used all her charms to gain power with—and even over—her emperor husband), and their rigid and lavish courts. San Vitale can be seen as the last of the ancient Roman art and the first of the Christian era. This church was the prototype for Constantinople's *Hagia Sophia* built ten years later, and it inspired Charlemagne to build the first great church in northern Europe in his capital of Aix-la-Chapelle (present-day Aachen).

▲▲**Mausoleum of Galla Placidia**—Just across the court-yard is the humble-looking little mausoleum with the old-est—and to many, the best—mosaics in Ravenna. The little light that sneaks through the thin alabaster panels brings a glow and a twinkle to the very early Christian symbolism (Jesus the Good Shepherd, Mark's lion, Luke's ox, John's eagle, the golden cross above everything) that fills the little room. Cover the light of the door with your hand to see the beardless Christ as the Good Shepherd. This was a popular scene with the early church.

▲**Basilica of St. Apollinare Nuovo**—This austere sixth-century church, in the typical early Christian basilica form, has two huge and wonderfully preserved side panels. One is a pro-cession of haloed virgins, each bringing gifts to the Madonna and the Christ Child. Opposite, Christ is on his throne with four angels, awaiting a solemn procession of 26 martyrs.

**Church of Sant' Apollinare in Classe**—Featuring great Byzantine art, this church is generally considered a must among mosaic pilgrims (3 miles out of town, easy bus and train connections, closed from 12:00–14:00, tel. 527-004).

**Overrated Sights**—The nearby beach town of Rimini is an overcrowded and polluted mess.

### Sleeping in Ravenna
**(L1,600 = about $1, tel. code 0544)**
Two cheap hotels near the station are **Al Giaciglio** (D-L45,000, DB-L58,000; Via R. Brancaleone 42, tel.

39403) and **Hotel Ravenna** (D-L60,000, DB-L75,000; Via Varoncelli 12, tel. 212-204). The **youth hostel** is a 10-minute walk from the station (follow the signs for Ostello Dante, Via Nicolodi 12, tel. 420-405).

## Transportation Connections
**Ravenna by train to Venice:** 3 hrs with a change in Ferrara (Ravenna-Ferrara, every 2 hrs, 60 min; Ferrara-Venice hrly, 100 min). **To Florence:** 4 hrs with a change in Bologna (Ravenna-Bologna, 8/day, 1½ hrs; Bologna-Florence, hrly, 1½ hrs). Train information: tel. 36450.

# FLORENCE (FIRENZE)

Florence, the home of the Renaissance and birthplace of our modern world, is a "supermarket sweep," and the groceries are the best Renaissance art in Europe.

Get your bearings with a Renaissance walk. Florentine art goes beyond paintings and statues—there's food, fashion, and handicrafts. You can lick Italy's best gelato while enjoying Europe's best people-watching.

## Planning Your Time

If you're in Europe for three weeks, Florence deserves a well-organized day. Siena, a convenient hour away by bus, has none of the awesome sights but is a more enjoyable home base. For a day in Florence, see Michelangelo's *David*, tour the Uffizi gallery (best Italian paintings), tour the underrated Bargello (best statues), and do the Renaissance ramble (explained below). Art lovers will want to chisel another day out of their itinerary for the many other cultural treasures Florence offers. Shoppers and ice cream lovers may need to do the same. Plan your sightseeing hours carefully. Get an early start. Mondays and afternoons can be sparse. You may very likely lose an hour or two in lines. If the line at *David* depressed you, remind yourself that people think nothing of waiting an hour at Disneyland to see Captain Io.

## Orientation (tel. code: 055)

The Florence we're interested in lies mostly on the north bank of the Arno River. Everything is within a 20-minute walk of the train station, cathedral, or Ponte Vecchio (Old Bridge). The less awesome but more characteristic Oltrarno (south bank) area is just over the bridge. Orient yourself by the huge red-tiled dome of the cathedral (the Duomo) and its tall bell tower (Giotto's Tower). This is the center of historic Florence.

### Tourist Information

Normally overcrowded, under-informed, and understaffed, the train station's tourist information office is not worth a stop if you're a good student of this book. If there's no line, pick up a

Florence Area

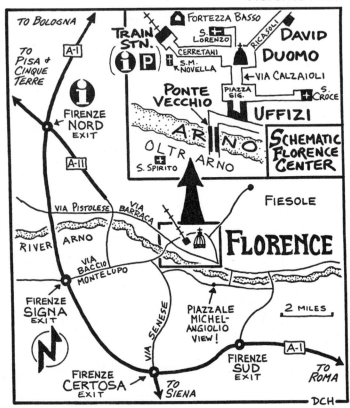

map, a current museum-hours listing, and the periodical entertainment guide or tourist magazine (daily in summer 9:00–
21:00, tel. 282-893 or 219-537). The free monthly *Florence
Concierge Information* magazine lists the latest museum hours,
markets, bus and train connections, and events; it's stocked by
the expensive hotels (pick one up, as if you're staying there).

### Getting Around Florence
Taxis are expensive. A L1,400 ticket gives you 60 minutes
on the buses, L1,900 gives you two hours, and L5,500 gets
you 24 hours (tickets not sold on bus, buy in tobacco shop,
validate on bus). If you organize your sightseeing with some
geographic logic, you'll do it all on foot.

## Helpful Hints

**Museums and Churches:** See everyone's essential sight, *David*, right off. In Italy a masterpiece seen and enjoyed is worth two tomorrow; you never know when a place will unexpectedly close for a holiday, strike, or restoration. The Uffizi has 1- to 2-hour lines on busy days. Lunchtime is better than 14:00. By 16:00, lines (and heat) are normally gone. Many museums close at 14:00 and stop selling tickets 30 minutes before that. Most close Monday and at 13:00 or 14:00 on Sunday. (The *Concierge Information* magazine thoughtfully lists which sights are open afternoons, Sundays, and Mondays.) Churches usually close 12:30– 15:00 or 16:00. Hours can change radically and no one knows exactly what's going on tomorrow. Local guidebooks are cheap and give you a map and a decent commentary on the sights.

**Addresses:** Street addresses list businesses in red and residences in black or blue (color-coded on the actual street number, and indicated by a letter following the number in printed addresses: n=black, r=red). *Pensioni* are usually black, but can be either.

**Theft Alert:** Florence has particularly hardworking thief gangs. They specialize in tourists and hang out where you do . . . near the train station and major sights. Older tourists are the easiest targets.

**Parking:** The cheapest central car-park is at Fortezza Basso (clearly signposted).

## Sights—Florence

▲▲▲**A Florentine Renaissance Walk**—Even during the Dark Ages, people knew they were in a "middle time." It was especially obvious to the people around here—sitting on the rubble of Rome—that there was a brighter age before them. The long-awaited rebirth, or "Renaissance," happened in Florence for good reason. Wealthy for its cloth industry, trade, and banking; powered by a fierce city-state pride (locals would pee into the Arno with gusto, knowing rival city-state Pisa was downstream); and fertile with more than its share of artistic genius (imagine guys like Michelangelo and Leonardo attending the same high school); Florence was a natural home for this cultural explosion.

**Florence**

| | | | | | |
|---|---|---|---|---|---|
| ❶ | CASA RABATTI | ❼ | PENSIONE CENTRALE | ⓭ | SORELLE BANDINI |
| ❷ | HOTEL ENZA | ❽ | PENS. BURCHIANTI | | RESTAURANTS: |
| ❸ | HOTEL UNIVERSO | ❾ | PENSIONE MAXIM | ⓮ | TRAT. CASALINGA |
| ❹ | HOTEL VISCONTI | ⓾ | PENS. BRETAGNA | ⓯ | TRAT. CONTADINO |
| ❺ | HOTEL ELITE | ⓫ | PENS. ALESSANDRA | ⓰ | GROTTA DI LEO |
| ❻ | PENSIONE SOLE | ⓬ | HOTEL SCALETTA | ⓱ | IL LATINI |

Take a walk through the core of Renaissance Florence by
starting at the Accademia (home of Michelangelo's *David*) and
cutting through the heart of the city to the Ponte Vecchio on
the Arno River. (A ten-page, self-guided tour of this walk is
outlined in my museum guidebook, *Mona Winks*. Otherwise,
you'll find brief descriptions below.)

At the Accademia you'll look into the eyes of Renaissance
man—humanism at its confident peak. Then walk to the

Cathedral (Duomo) to see the dome that kicked off the architectural Renaissance. Step inside the Baptistery to see a ceiling
covered with preachy, flat, 2-D, medieval mosaic art. Then, to
see what happened when art met math, see the realistic 3-D
reliefs on the doors. The painter, Giotto, designed the bell
tower—an early example of how a Renaissance genius was
broad and well-rounded. Continue toward the river on
Florence's great pedestrian mall, Via de' Calzaioli (or "Via
Calz"), which was part of the original grid plan given the city
by the ancient Romans. Down a few blocks, compare medieval
and Renaissance statues on the exterior of the Orsanmichele
Church. Via Calz connects the cathedral with the central
square (Piazza della Signoria), the city palace (Palazzo
Vecchio), and the Uffizi Gallery containing the greatest collection of Italian Renaissance paintings in captivity. Finally,
walk through the Uffizi courtyard, a statuary think-tank of
Renaissance greats, to the Arno River and the Ponte Vecchio.

▲▲▲The Accademia (Galleria dell' Accademia)—This
museum houses Michelangelo's *David* and powerful (unfinished) *Prisoners*. Eavesdrop as tour guides explain these masterpieces. More than any other work of art, when you look
into the eyes of *David*, you're looking into the eyes of
Renaissance man. This was a radical break with the past.
Man was now a confident individual, no longer a plaything
of the supernatural. And life was now more than just a prepa-
ration for what happens after you die.

The Renaissance was the merging of art and science. In
a humanist vein, *David* is looking at the crude giant of
medieval darkness and thinking, "I can take this guy." Back
on a religious track (and speaking of veins), notice David's
large and overdeveloped right hand. This is symbolic of the
hand of God that powered David to slay the giant . . . and, of
course, enabled Florence to rise above its crude neighboring
city-states.

Beyond the magic marble are two floors of interesting
pre-Renaissance and Renaissance paintings, including a couple
of dreamy Botticellis (Via Ricasoli 60, L12,000, 9:00–19:00,
Sunday 9:00–14:00, closed Monday, tel. 238-8609).

Behind the Accademia, the Piazza Santissima Annunziata features lovely Renaissance harmony. Brunelleschi's
Hospital of the Innocents (Spedale degli Innocenti, not

worth going inside), with terra-cotta medallions by della Robbia, was built in the 1420s and is considered the first Renaissance building.

▲▲**Museum of San Marco**—One block north of the Accademia on Piazza San Marco, this museum houses the greatest collection anywhere of medieval frescoes and paintings by the early Renaissance master Fra Angelico. You'll see why he thought of painting as a form of prayer and couldn't paint a crucifix without shedding tears. Each of the monks' cells has a Fra Angelico fresco. Don't miss the cell of Savonarola, the charismatic monk who rode in from the Christian right, threw out the Medici, turned Florence into a theocracy, sponsored "bonfires of the vanities" (burning books, paintings, and so on), and was finally burned himself when Florence decided to change channels (L8,000, 9:00–14:00, closed Monday).

▲▲**The Duomo**—Florence's mediocre Gothic cathedral has the third-longest nave in Christendom (free, daily, 9:00–18:00, with an occasional lunch break). The church's noisy neo-Gothic facade from the 1870s is covered with pink, green, and white Tuscan marble. Since nearly all of its great art is stored in the Museo dell' Opera del Duomo, behind the church, the best thing about the inside is the shade. The inside of the dome is decorated by what must be the largest painting of the Renaissance, a huge (and newly restored) *Last Judgment* by Vasari and Zuccari. The cathedral is capped by Brunelleschi's magnificent dome—the first Renaissance dome and the model for domes to follow (ascent L5,000). When planning St. Peter's in Rome, Michelangelo said, "I can build a dome bigger, but not more beautiful, than the dome of Florence."

**Giotto's Tower**—Climbing Giotto's Tower (Campanile, L5,000, daily 9:00–16:30, maybe later in summer) beats climbing the neighboring Duomo's dome because it's 50 fewer steps, faster, not so crowded, and offers the same view plus the dome.

▲▲**Museo dell' Opera del Duomo**—The underrated cathedral museum, behind the church at #9, is great if you like sculpture. It has masterpieces by Donatello (a gruesome wood carving of Mary Magdalene clothed in her matted hair, and the *cantoria*, the delightful choir loft bursting with happy children) and Luca della Robbia (another choir loft, lined with the dreamy faces of musicians praising the Lord); a late Michelangelo *Pietà* (Nicodemus, on top, is a self-portrait); Brunelleschi's models for his dome; and the original restored panels of Ghiberti's doors to the Baptistery. To get the most out of your sightseeing hours, remember that this is one of the few museums in Florence that stays open late (9:00–19:30, closed Sunday, L8,000, tel. 230-2885).

▲**The Baptistery**—Michelangelo said its bronze doors were fit to be the gates of Paradise. Check out the gleaming copies of Ghiberti's bronze doors facing the Duomo, and the famous competition doors around to the right. Making a breakthrough in perspective, Ghiberti used mathematical laws to create the illusion of 3-D on a 2-D surface. Go inside Florence's oldest building and sit and savor the medieval mosaic ceiling. Compare that to the "new, improved" art of the Renaissance (free, interior open 13:30–16:30, Sunday 9:00–13:00, bronze doors are on the outside so always "open"; original panels are in the Museo dell' Opera del Duomo).

▲**Orsanmichele**—Mirroring Florentine values, this was a combination church-granary. The best L200 deal in Florence is the machine which lights its glorious tabernacle. Notice the grain spouts on the pillars inside. Also study the sculpture on its outside walls. You can see man stepping out of the literal and figurative shadow of the church in the great Renaissance sculptor Donatello's *St. George*. (On Via Calzaioli, free, 8:00–12:00, 15:00–18:00. If closed, try going through the back door.)

▲**Palazzo Vecchio**—The interior of this fortified palace, which was once the home of the Medici family, is worthwhile only if you're a real Florentine art and history fan (L12,000, 9:00–19:00, Sunday 8:00–13:00, closed Thursday, handy public WC inside on ground floor). Until 1873, Michelangelo's *David* stood at the entrance, where the copy is today. While the huge statues in the square are important only as the whipping boys of art critics and as pigeon roosts, the nearby Loggia dei Lanzi has several important statues. Notice Cellini's bronze statue of Perseus (with the head of Medusa). The plaque on the pavement in front of the fountain marks the spot where Savonarola was burned.

▲▲▲**Uffizi Gallery**—The greatest collection of Italian painting anywhere is a must, with plenty of works by Giotto, Leonardo, Raphael, Caravaggio, Rubens, Titian, and Michelangelo, and a roomful of Botticellis, including his *Birth of Venus*. There are no official tours, so buy a book on the street before entering (or follow *Mona Winks*). The long entrance line is a reasonable cost for an interior with no Louvre-style mob scenes. The museum is nowhere near as big as it is great: few tourists spend more than 2 hours inside. The paintings are displayed (behind obnoxious reflective glass) on one comfortable floor in chronological order from the 13th through 17th century.

Essential stops are (in this order): the Gothic altar-pieces (narrative, pre-realism, no real concern for believable depth); Giotto's altarpiece in the same room progresses beyond "totem pole angels;" Uccello's *Battle of San Romano*, an early study in perspective (with a few obvious flubs); Fra Lippi's cuddly Madonnas; the Botticelli room, filled with masterpieces including a pantheon of classical fleshiness and the small *La Calumnia*, showing the glasnost of Renaissance free-thinking being clubbed back into the darker age of Savonarola; two minor works by Leonardo; the octagonal classical sculpture room with an early painting of Bob Hope and a copy of Praxiteles' *Venus de Medici*, considered the epitome of beauty in Elizabethan Europe; Michelangelo's only surviving easel painting, the round *Holy Family*; Raphael's noble *Madonna of the Goldfinch*; Titian's voluptuous *Venus of Urbino*; and views from the café terrace at the end (L12,000, 9:00–19:00, Sunday 9:00–14:00, closed Monday, last ticket sold 45 minutes before closing, go very late to avoid crowds and heat, there's an elevator for the frail and exhausted).

Enjoy the Uffizi square, full of artists and souvenir stalls. The surrounding statues honor the earthshaking: artists, plus philosophers (Machiavelli), scientists (Galileo), writers (Dante), explorers (Amerigo Vespucci), and the great patron of so much Renaissance thinking, Lorenzo (the Magnificent) de Medici.

▲▲▲**Bargello (Museo Nazionale)**—The city's underrated museum of sculpture is behind the Palazzo Vecchio (4 blocks from the Uffizi) in a former prison that looks like a mini-

Palazzo Vecchio. It has Donatello's *David* (the very-influential first male nude to be sculpted in a thousand years), works by Michelangelo, and much more (Via del Proconsolo 4; L8,000, 9:00–14:00, closed Monday). Dante's house, across the street and around the corner, is interesting only to his Italian-speaking fans.

▲**Medici Chapel (Cappelle dei Medici)**—This chapel, containing two Medici tombs, is drenched in incredibly lavish High Renaissance architecture and sculpture by Michelangelo (L8,000, 9:00–14:00, closed Monday). Behind San Lorenzo on Piazza Madonna, it's surrounded by a lively market scene that, for some reason, I find more interesting. Don't miss a wander through the huge double-decker central market.

**Science Museum (Museo di Storia della Scienza)**—This is a fascinating collection of Renaissance and later clocks, telescopes, maps, and ingenious gadgets. One of the most talked-about bottles in Florence is the one here containing Galileo's finger. English guidebooklets are available. It's friendly, comfortably cool, never crowded, and just down-stream from the Uffizi (L10,000, Monday, Wednesday, and Friday 9:30–13:00, 14:00–17:00, Tuesday and Thursday 9:30–13:00, closed Sunday, Piazza dei Giudici 1).

▲**Michelangelo's Home, Casa Buonarroti**—Fans enjoy Michelangelo's house, which has some of his early, much-less-monumental works (L8,000, 9:00–13:30, closed Tuesday, Via Ghibellina 70).

▲**The Pitti Palace**—Across the river, the gargantuan Pitti Palace has five separate museums. The Galleria Palatina collection has works by many of the great masters (especially Raphael, L12,000). The Galleria d'Arte Moderna (upstairs) is also enjoyable. Behind the palace, the huge semi-landscaped Boboli Gardens offer a cool refuge from the city heat (museums open 9:00–14:00, closed Monday, the gardens cost L4,000 and are open 9:00–17:30, except on Monday).

▲**Brancacci Chapel**—For the best look at the early Renaissance master Masaccio, see his restored frescoes here (L5,000, 10:00–17:00, holidays 13:00–17:00, closed Tuesday; across the Ponte Vecchio and turn right a few blocks to Piazza del Carmine).

▲**Piazzale Michelangelo**—Across the river overlooking the city (look for the huge statue of David), this square is worth the half-hour hike or the drive for the view. After dark it's packed with local schoolkids sharing slices of watermelon with their dates. Just beyond it is the stark and beautiful, crowd-free, Romanesque San Miniato church). (Bus #13 from the train station).

**Scenic City Bus Ride**—For a candid peek at a Florentine suburb, ride bus #7 (from near the station) for about 20 minutes through neighborhood gardens, vineyards, orchards, and large villas. It ends at a plaza with small eateries and good views of Florence and the nearby hills.

**▲▲Gelato**—Gelato is a great Florentine edible art form. Italy's best ice cream is in Florence. Every year I repeat my taste test. And every year Vivoli's wins (on Via Stinche, see map, 8:00–24:00, closed Mondays, the last three weeks in August, and January). Festival del Gelato and Perche Non!, just off Via Calz, are also good. That's one souvenir that can't break and won't clutter your luggage. Get a free sample of Vivoli's *riso* (rice, my favorite) before ordering.

**Siena Evening Side Trip**—Connoisseurs of peace and small towns, who aren't into art or shopping (and who won't be seeing Siena otherwise), should consider riding the bus (75 min) to Siena for the evening. Florence has no after-dark magic. Siena *is* after-dark magic.

**Shopping**—Florence is a great shopping town. Busy street scenes and markets abound, especially near San Lorenzo (closed Sunday and Monday), on the Ponte Vecchio, and near Santa Croce. Leather, gold, silver, art prints, and tacky plaster "mini-*Davids*" are most popular.

## Sleeping in Florence
### (L1,600 = about $1, tel. code: 055)

The hotel scene in generally crowded and overpriced Florence isn't bad. With good information and a phone call ahead, you can find a stark, clean, and comfortable double with breakfast for L80,000, with a private shower for L100,000. You get roof-garden elegance for L140,000. All places listed are old and rickety. I can't imagine Florence any other way. The prices listed here are guaranteed through 1996 only if you call direct. Don't use the tourist office, which costs your host and jacks up the price. Except for Easter and Christmas, there are plenty of rooms in

Florence. Budget travelers can call around and find soft prices. If you're staying for three or more nights, ask for a discount. The technically optional and overpriced breakfast can be used as a bargaining chip. Call ahead. I repeat, *call ahead*. Places will happily hold a room until early afternoon. If they say they're full, mention you're using this book.

Sleep code: **S**=Single, **D**=Double/Twin, **T**=Triple, **Q**=Quad, **B**=Bath/Shower and Toilet (unless followed by a BWC listing), **CC**=Credit Card (**V**isa, **M**asterCard, **A**mex). Unless otherwise noted, breakfast is included. English is generally spoken.

### Sleeping East of the Train Station

**Casa Rabatti** (four rooms, D-L55,000, DB-L70,000, L25,000 per bed in shared quad or quint, no breakfast, 6 blocks from station; Via San Zanobi 48 black, 50129 Florence, tel. 212-393) is the ultimate if you always wanted to be a part of a Florentine family. Simple, clean, friendly, and run by Marcella and Celestino (who don't speak English), this is my best rock-bottom listing.

**Hotel Enza** (S-L55,000, SB-L60,000, D-L75,000, DB-L95,000, T-L100,000, TB-L120,000, family loft, ask about a discount for three nights, no breakfast; 6 blocks from station, Via San Zanobi 45 black, 50129 Florence, tel. 490-990) has 16 clean and cheery rooms, run by English-speaking Eugenia who clearly enjoys her work. While Eugenia's chihuahua, Tricky, is tiny, her singles are particularly spacious.

Other guidebooks rave about the same places 2 blocks from the station on Via Faenza. The street is filled with English-speaking tourists and sleepable L60,000 doubles. Number 56 is an English-speaking slumber mill: **Albergo Azzi** (L70,000 doubles, L30,000 per bed in shared quads and quints, no breakfast; Via Faenza 56, tel. 213-806). Not quite as good are **Merlini** (tel. 212-848), **Paola** (tel. 213-682), and **Armonia** (tel. 211-146).

**Hotel Loggiato dei Serviti**, at the most prestigious address in Florence on the most Renaissance (traffic-free) square in town, gives you Renaissance romance with a place to plug in your hair-dryer (L250,000 doubles with everything, CC:VMA; Piazza SS. Annunziata 3, Firenze, tel. 289-592, fax 289-595). Stone stairways lead you under open-beam ceilings through this 16th-century monastery's elegantly appointed public rooms. The cells, with air conditioning, TVs, mini-bars, and telephones, wouldn't be recognized by their original inhabitants.

A handy modern Launderette is just off via Cavour at via Guelfa 22r (daily 8:00–22:00, 12 pounds wash and dry for L10,000).

### Sleeping South of the Station near Piazza Santa Maria Novella

From the station, follow the underground tunnel to Piazza Santa Maria Novella, a pleasant square by day and only a little sleazy after dark. (Thief alert where the tunnel surfaces.) It's handy: 3 blocks from the cathedral, near a good laundromat (**La Serena**, 8:30–20:00, closed Sunday; Via della Scala 30 red; L18,000 for 11 pounds), cheap restaurants (on Via della Scala and via Palazzuolo, see below), the bus and train station. There's a great Massaccio fresco (*The Trinity*) in the church on the square (free).

**Hotel Universo** (D-L80,000, DB-L100,000, TB-L135,000, QB-L170,000, to get these discounted prices—promised through 1996—you must show this book, CC:VMA, elevator, English spoken; right on Piazza S. M. Novella at #20, 50123 Florence, tel. 281-951, fax 292-335), a big group-friendly hotel with stark concrete hallways but fine rooms, is warmly run by a group of gentle men.

**Hotel Visconti** (D-L80,000, DB-L94,000, elevator, TV room, peaceful and sunny roof garden; 20 meters off the square opposite the church at Piazza Degli Ottaviani 1, tel. and fax 213-877) artfully decorated by English-speaking and very mellow Manara, is like living in a relaxing blue-and-white cameo. In the same building, up one floor, the simple, threadbare, a little bit musty but tidy **Pensione Ottaviani** rattles in its spaciousness (D-L65,000, DB-L80,000, with this book, tel. 239-6223, fax 293-355, English spoken).

**Hotel Pensione Elite** (SB-L85,000, SB-L95,000, DB-L90,000, DBWC-L120,000; at end of square with back to church, go right to Via della Scala 12, second floor, tel. 215-395) has eight comfortable rooms. With none of the backpacking flavor of Via Faenze, it's a good basic value; run warmly by Maurizio and Nadia.

**Pensione Sole** (S-L45,000, D-L65,000, DB-L85,000, TB-L115,000, no breakfast; Via del Sole 8, third floor, no lift but lots of stairs, tel. and fax 239-6094, Anna speaks no English), a clean, cozy, family-run place with seven bright rooms, is well-located just off S. M. Novella toward the river.

**Pensione Centrale** (D-L115,000, DB-L145,000 with an "American" breakfast, CC:VMA; near the Duomo at Via dei Conti 3, 50123 Florence, tel. 215-216, fax 287-750) is run by Marie Therese Blot, who is a wealth of information and makes you feel right at home.

**Pensione Burchianti** (DB-L90,000, DBWC-L110,000, L30,000 to L40,000 for extra bed, prices promised with this book; midway between the station and the Duomo at Via del Giglio 6, tel. 212-796, fax 475-387) is a spacious old noble house. Each of its 11 rooms has a bit of old Florence surviving on its walls or ceilings.

**Pensione Maxim** (D-L95,000, DB-L115,000, T-L120,000, TB-135,000, with this book through 1996, CC:VMA; Via dei Medici 4, with an elevator at Via dei Calzaiuoli 11, 50123 Florence, tel. 217-474, fax 283-729) is big, basic, and as close to the sights as possible, yet quiet.

### Sleeping on the River Arno

**Pensione Bretagna** (S-L65,000, SB-L75,000, D-L100,000, DB-L115,000, DBWC-L135,000, including optional L10,000 breakfast, CC:VMA; west of the Ponte Vecchio, just past Ponte San Trinita, at Lungarno Corsini 6, 50123 Firenze, tel. 289-618, fax 289-619, e-mail: A.Castaldini@agora.stm.it), a classy, Old World-elegant place with thoughtfully appointed rooms, is run by English-speaking Antonio. Imagine breakfast under a painted, chandeliered ceiling overlooking the Arno river.

**Pensione Alessandra** (D-L110,000, DB-L140,000, CC:VMA, Borgo SS. Apostoli 17, tel. 283-438, fax 210-619) is a big, serious, and professional old place with 25 rooms on a quiet street a block off the river near the Ponte Vecchio.

### Sleeping in Oltrarno, South of the River

Across the river in the Oltrarno area, between the Pitti Palace and the Ponte Vecchio, you'll still find small traditional crafts shops; neighborly piazzas hiding a few offbeat art treasures;

family eateries; two distinctive, moderately priced hotels; two student dorms; and a youth hostel. Each of these places is only a few minutes' walk from the Ponte Vecchio.

**Hotel La Scaletta** (D-L100,000, DB-L140,000, T-L140,000, TB-L170,000, CC:VM, 8 percent discount for cash, 10 percent for cash and flowers; elevator, English spoken; Via Guicciardini 13 black, 50125 Firenze, straight up the street from the Ponte Vecchio, next to the AmExCo, tel. 283-028, fax 289-562, easy telephone reservations, call several days in advance) is elegant, friendly, and clean, with a dark, cool, labyrinthine floor plan and lots of Old World lounges. Owner Barbara and her children, Manfredo, Bianca, and Diana, elevate this well-worn place with brute charm. Your journal becomes poetry when written on the highest terrace of La Scaletta's panoramic roof garden (cheap drinks). If Manfredo is cooking dinner, eat here.

**Pensione Sorelle Bandini** (D-L110,000, DB-L140,000; Piazza Santo Spirito 9, 50125 Firenze, tel. 215-308, fax 282-761) is a ramshackle 500-year-old palace on a perfectly Florentine square, with cavernous rooms, museum warehouse interiors, a musty youthfulness, a balcony lounge-loggia with a view, and an ambience that, for romantic bohemians, can be a highlight of Florence. Mimmo or Sr. Romeo will hold a room until 16:00 with a phone call.

**Institute Gould** (D-L60,000, DB-L64,000, L26,000 beds in shared doubles and quads; 49 Via dei Serragli, tel. 212-576; office open Monday–Friday 9:00–13:00, 15:00–19:00, Saturday 9:00–13:00) is a Protestant Church-run place with 72 beds in 27 rooms and clean, modern facilities. Since you must arrive during their office hours, you can't check in on Sunday.

The Catholic-run **Pensionato Pio X-Artigianelli** (L20,000 beds in doubles and triples, L3,000 extra if you want a single; Via dei Serragli 106, tel. 225-044) is more freewheeling and ramshackle, with 44 beds in 20 rooms.

**Ostello Santa Monaca** (L18,000 beds with sheets, no breakfast; 6 Via Santa Monaca, a few blocks past Ponte Alla Carraia, tel. 268-338, fax 280-185), and the classy **Villa Camerata IYHF hostel** (tel. 601-451), on the outskirts of Florence, should be last alternatives.

# Eating in Florence

### Eating South of the River
There are several good and colorful restaurants in Oltrarno near Piazza Santo Spirito. **Trattoria Casalinga** (just off Piazza Santo Spirito, near the church at 9 Via dei Michelozzi, tel. 218-624, closed Sunday) is an inexpensive and popular standby, famous for its home cooking. Good values but more expensive are **Trattoria Sabitino** on Borgo S. Frediano and **Osteria del Cinghiale Bianco** at Borgo S. Jacopo 43 (closed Tuesday and Wednesday). For a splurge, **Trattoria Oreste** (on Piazza S. Spirito at #16), with a renowned cook and on-the-piazza ambience, may have the best L50,000 dinner in the area. The **Ricchi** bar on the same square has fine homemade gelati and a particularly pleasant interior.

### Eating near Santa Maria Novella
**Trattoria il Contadino** (Via Palazzuolo 69 red, a few blocks south of the train station, 12:00–14:30, 18:00–21:30, closed Sunday, tel. 238-2673) and **Trattoria da Giorgio** (Via Palazzuolo 100 red, 12:00–15:00, 18:30–22:00, closed Sunday) each offer a L14,000 hearty family-style, fixed-price menu with a bustling working-class/budget-Yankee-traveler atmosphere. Get there early or be ready to wait. **La Grotta di Leo** (Via della Scala 41 red, tel. 219-265, closed Wednesday) has a cheap, straightforward menu and decent food.

    **Il Latini** is an internationally famous but popular-with-the-locals traditional Florentine eatery. You'll share a large table under hanging hams. There's no menu. The wine's already on the table. Just order as you go. This isn't cheap, but it can provide a memorable evening's experience, not to mention a wonderful dinner (Via del Palchetti 6, just off Moro between S.M. Novella and the river, tel. 210-916, open from 19:30, closed Monday).

### A Quick Lunch near the Sights
I keep lunch in Florence fast and simple, eating in one of countless self-service places, Pizza Rusticas (holes-in-walls selling pizza by weight), or just picnicking (juice, yogurt,

cheese, roll: L8,000). For mountains of picnic produce or just a cheap sandwich and piles of people-watching, visit the huge multi-storied **Mercato Centrale** (7:00–14:00, closed Sunday) in the middle of the San Lorenzo street market. Behind the Duomo, **Snack** (15 Pronconsolo) serves decent cheap lunches. For a reasonably priced pizza with a Medici-style view, try one of the pizzerias on Piazza della Signori. Next to Santa Croce, **Osteria/Pizzeria BaldoVino** (via San Giuseppe 22r, tel. 241-773, closed Tuesday) makes budget travelers feel welcome. And near my first two hotel listings, **Trattoria San Zanobi** serves a good L20,000 menu (via San Zanobi 33r, tel. 475-286).

### Eating in Fiesole

Many locals enjoy catching the bus to the breezy hill town of Fiesole for dinner, a sprawling Florence view, and a break from the city heat. **Ristorante La Romagnola** (Via A. Gramsci 43, closed Monday) serves fine meals and inexpensive pizza. City buses make the 20-minute trip regularly.

## Transportation Connections

**Trains from Florence to: Assisi** (10/day, 2½ to 3 hrs), **Brindisi** (3/day, 11 hrs with change in Bologna), **Frankfurt** (3/day, 12 hrs), **La Spezia** (for the Cinque Terre, 2/day direct, 2 hrs, or change in Pisa), **Milan** (12/day, 3–5 hrs), **Naples** (2/day, 4 hrs), **Orvieto** (6/day, 2 hrs), **Paris** (1/day, 12 hrs overnight), **Pisa** (2/hr, 1 hr), **Rome** (hourly, 2½ hrs), **Venice** (7/day, 3 hrs), **Vienna** (4/day, 9–10 hrs). Florence train information: tel. 055/24334 (9:30–18:00 with a lunch break).

**Buses from Florence:** The SITA bus station is a block from the Florence train station (bus info: tel. 483-651, some schedules in Florence's *Concierge* magazine). **Siena** (L10,000, hourly, 75-min fast buses or 2-hr slow buses, faster than the train and drops you at San Domenico near the sights rather than at the train station), **San Gimignano** (L8,000, hourly buses, 1¾ hrs).

## Driving Florentine

Arriving in Florence, follow signs to Centro and Fortezza di Basso. After driving and trying to park in Florence, you'll understand why Leonardo never invented the car. Cars flatten the charm of Florence. Get near the *centro* and park where you can. Garages charge around L30,000 a day. The big underground lot at the train station charges L2,000 per hour. The cheapest and biggest garage is at Fortezza di Basso (L20,000 per day). Borgo Ognissanti 96, near the Amerigo Vespucci bridge, is reasonable and closer to the center. White lines are free, blue are not. I got towed once in the town of Michelangelo—an expensive lesson.

## PISA

Pisa was a regional superpower in her medieval heyday (11th, 12th, and 13th centuries), rivaling Florence and Genoa. Its Mediterranean empire, which included Corsica and Sardinia, helped make it a wealthy republic. But the Pisa fleet was beaten (1284, by Genoa) and its port silted up, leaving the city high and dry with only its Piazza of Miracles (and its university) keeping it on the map.

Pisa's three important sights (the cathedral, baptistery, and bell tower) float regally on the best lawn in Italy. Even as the church was being built, the Piazza del Duomo was nicknamed the Campo dei Miracoli, or "Field of Miracles," for the grandness of the undertaking. The style throughout is Pisa's very own "Pisan Romanesque" (surrounded by what may be Italy's tackiest ring of souvenir stands). This spectacle is tourism at its most crass. Wear gloves.

### Planning Your Time

Pisa is a touristy quickie. By train it's a joy. By car it's a headache. Train travelers may be changing trains in Pisa anyway. Hop on the bus and see the tower. Since you can't climb the tower, a look doesn't take very long and is worthwhile even after (or before) hours. Sophisticated sightseers stop more for the Pisano carvings in the cathedral and baptistery than for a look at the tipsy tower. There's nothing wrong with Pisa, but I'd stop only to see the "Piazza of Miracles" and get out. By car it's a 45-minute detour from the freeway.

### Orientation (tel. code: 050)

To get to the Leaning Tower, follow signs to the Duomo or the Piazza dei Miracoli. This is on the north edge of town. Drivers (coming from the Pisa Nord autostrada exit) don't have to mess with the city (although you will mess with some terrible traffic). There's no option better than the L1,500-per-hour pay lot just outside the town wall near the Duomo.

Train travelers bus easily from the station in the center, over the Arno River, and to the Duomo. Bus #1 (for Duomo) leaves from the bus circle to the right of the station every 10 minutes. Buy your L1,100 ticket from the magazine kiosk in the station's main hall.

Seeing the tower and the Square and wandering through the church are 90 percent of the Pisan thrill. The Pisa tourist board has a scheme to get you into its neglected secondary sights. The overpriced Baptistery ticket includes your choice of another sight. And a five-in-one ticket "saves" you even more money on sights most people wouldn't see even if they were free.

For a quick lunch, the pizzeria/trattoria **La Buca** (near tower at Via S. Maria and Via G. Tassi) is a decent value.

### Tourist Information
Tourist Information offices are at the train station (open daily, 9:00–18:00, Sunday 9:00–12:00, tel. 050/560-464) and at the Leaning Tower (tel. 42291). Train information: tel. 41385.

### Sights—Pisa
▲▲**Leaning Tower**—This most famous example of "Pisan Romanesque" architecture was leaning even before its completion. Notice how the architect, for lack of a better solution, kinked up the top section. The 294 tilted steps to the top are closed while engineers work to keep the bell tower from toppling. The formerly clean and tidy area around the tower is now a construction zone. Steam pipes drying out the subsoil and huge weights are working together to stop the leaning (but not straighten out the tower).

▲▲**Cathedral**—The huge "Pisan Romanesque" cathedral (L2,000, 10:00–19:40, Sunday 13:00–19:40), with its richly carved pulpit by Giovanni Pisano, is artistically more important than its more famous bell tower.

**Baptistery**—The baptistery (biggest in Italy, in front of the cathedral, L10,000, 8:00–20:00), with a pulpit by Nicolo Pisano (1260) which inspired Renaissance art to follow, is interesting for its great acoustics. If you ask nicely and leave a tip, the doorman uses its echo power to sing haunting harmonies with himself. Notice that even the baptistery leans about 5 feet. (The Nicolo Pisano pulpit and carvings in Siena were just as impressive to me—in a more enjoyable atmosphere.)

**Other Sights**—Pisa, of course, is more than the Campo dei Miracoli. Walking from the station to the Duomo shows you a classy old-world town with an Arno-scape much like its rival upstream. But for most, Pisa is just a cliché that needs to be seen and a chance to see the Pisano pulpits. For more Pisan art, see the Museo dell' Opera del Duomo (behind the tower) and the Museo Nazionale di San Matteo (on the river near Piazza Mazzini). The cemetery bordering the cathedral square is not worth the admission, even if its "Holy Land dirt" does turn a body into a skeleton in a day.

## Transportation Connections
**Trains from Pisa to: Florence** (hrly, 60 min), **La Spezia** (hrly, 60 min, milk-run from there into coastal villages), **Siena** (change at Empoli: Pisa-Empoli, hrly, 30 min; Empoli-Siena, hrly, 60 min). Even the fastest trains stop in Pisa, and you'll very likely be changing trains here whether you plan to stop or not.

## Driving in Pisa
Drivers will see the Leaning Tower as they approach Pisa from the north. There's a large parking lot right at the sights, just outside the wall on the north end of town, so those coming in by freeway don't actually have to drive into Pisa.

**To Florence and Siena:** The drive from Pisa to Florence is that rare case where the non-autostrada highway (free, more direct, and at least as fast) is a better deal than the autostrada. When departing for Florence, San Gimignano, or Siena, follow the blue "superstrada" signs (green signs are for the autostrada) for the SS road (along the city wall east from the tower—away from the sea) for Florence (and later Siena).

**To the Cinque Terre:** From Pisa, catch the Genova-bound autostrada. The white stuff you'll see in the mountains as you approach La Spezia isn't snow—it's Carrara marble, Michelangelo's choice for his great art. From Pisa to La Spezia takes about an hour.

# HILL TOWNS OF CENTRAL ITALY

Break out of the Venice-Florence-Rome syndrome. There's more to Italy! Experience the slumber of Umbria, the texture of Tuscany, and the lazy towns of Lazio. For starters, here are a few of my favorites.

Siena seems to be every Italy connoisseur's pet town. In my office whenever Siena is mentioned, someone moans, "Siena? I *luuuv* Siena!" San Gimignano is the quintessential hill town, with Italy's best surviving medieval skyline. Assisi—visited for its hometown boy, St. Francis, who made very good—twinkles after dark. Orvieto, one of the most famous hill towns, is best used as a springboard for trip to tiny Cività. Stranded alone on its pinnacle in a vast canyon, Cività's the most lovable.

## Planning Your Time

Siena, the must-see town, has the easiest train and bus connections. With three weeks for Italy, I'd spend three nights in

## Hill Towns of Central Italy

Siena (with a whole-day side trip into Florence and a day to relax and enjoy Siena). Whatever you do, enjoy a sleepy medieval evening in Siena. After an evening in Siena, its major sights can be seen in half a day. San Gimignano is a sterile, pint-sized Siena. Don't rush Siena for San Gimignano.

Città di Bagnoregio is the awesome pinnacle town. A night in Bagnoregio (via Orvieto bus) with time to hike to the town and spend three hours makes the visit worthwhile. Two nights and an entire day is a good way to keep your pain/pleasure ratio in order.

Assisi is the third most visit-worthy town. It has half a day of sightseeing and another half a day of wonder. While a zoo by day, it's magic at night.

## SIENA

Seven hundred years ago, Siena was a major military power in a class with Florence, Venice, and Genoa. The town was weakened by a disastrous plague in 1348. In the 1550s her bitter rival Florence really salted her, making Siena forever a non-threatening backwater. Siena's loss became our sightseeing gain, as its political and economic irrelevance pickled it purely Gothic. (Siena's population is 60,000 compared to Florence's 420,000.)

Siena is the hill-town equivalent of Venice. Traffic-free red-brick lanes cascade every which way. Siena's thriving historic center offers Italy's best Gothic city experience. While most people do Siena, just 30 miles south of Florence, as a day trip, it's best experienced after dark. In fact, it makes more sense to do Florence as a day trip from Siena. While Florence has the blockbuster museums, Siena has an easy-to-enjoy soul. Right off the bat, Siena becomes an old friend.

For those who dream of a Fiat-free Italy, this is it. Sit at a café on the red-bricked main square. Take time to savor the first European city to eliminate automobile traffic (1966), and then, just to be silly, wonder what would happen if they did it in your city.

## Orientation (tel. code: 0577)

Siena lounges atop a hill, stretching its three legs out from Il Campo. This main square is the historic meeting point of Siena's neighborhoods. The entire center is pedestrians-only,

Siena

**① Locanda Garibaldi**   **④ Hotel Duomo**   **⑦ Pension Bernini**
**② Piccolo Hotel Etruria**   **⑤ Hotel Cannon**   **⑧ Alma Domus**
**③ Pension La Perla**   **⑨ ⑩ Lea+Liberty**
DCH

no buses and no cars. Everything I mention is within a 15-minute walk of the square. Navigate by landmarks, following the excellent system of streetcorner signs. The average visitor sticks to the San Domenico–Il Campo axis.

## Tourist Information

Pick up the excellent and free topographical town map from the main TI on Il Campo (#56, look for the yellow Change sign, 8:30–19:30, closed Sunday, less off season, tel. 280-551). The small hotel-information office at San Domenico is in cahoots with local hotels and charges for maps.

## Getting Around Siena

From Siena's train station, buy a L1,200 bus ticket from the yellow machine near the exit, cross the square, and board any orange city bus heading for Piazza Gramsci (GRAHM-shee) or Via Tozzi. Your hotel is probably within a 5-minute walk of Piazza Gramsci. Buses from Florence (or other cities) drop you at Siena's San Domenico church, a 10-minute walk from the center square (go left of the church following signs to Il Campo).

## Sights—Siena

Siena is one big sight. Its essential individual sights come in two little clusters: the square, with the museum in the city hall and its tower; and the cathedral, its baptistery, and the cathedral's museum with its surprise viewpoint. Check these sights off, and you're free to wander.

▲▲▲**Il Campo**—Siena's great central piazza is urban harmony at its best. Like a people-friendly stage set, its gently tilted floor fans out from the tower and city hall backdrop. It's the perfect invitation to loiter. Built in 1347, Il Campo was located at the historic junction of Siena's various competing districts, or *contrada*, on the old marketplace. The brick surface is divided into nine sections, representing the council of nine merchants and city bigwigs who ruled medieval Siena. Don't miss the Fountain of Joy at the square's high point, with its pigeons politely waiting their turn to gingerly tightrope down slippery snouts to slurp a drink, and with the two naked guys about to be tossed in. At the base of the tower, the Piazza's chapel was built in 1348 as a thanks to God for ending the Black Plague (after it killed more than a third of the population).

▲**Museo Civico**—The Palazzo *Pubblico* (City Hall at the base of the tower) has a fine and manageable museum housing a good sample of Sienese art. You'll see, in the following order, the Sala Risorgimento with dramatic scenes of Victor Emmanuel's unification of Italy (surrounded by statues that don't seem to care); the chapel with impressive inlaid wood chairs in the choir; and the Sala del Mappamondo, with Simone Martini's *Maesta* (Enthroned Virgin) facing the faded Guidoriccio da Fogliano (a mercenary providing a more concrete form of protection). Next is the Sala della Pace, which has two interesting frescoes showing "The Effects of Good and Bad Government." Notice the whistle-while-you-work happiness of the utopian community ruled by the utopian government (in the best-preserved fresco) and the fate of a community ruled by politicians with more typical values (in a terrible state of repair). Later you'll see a particularly gruesome *Slaughter of the Innocents*. The big stairs lead to a loggia with a nothing-special view (L6,000, daily 9:00–19:00, Sundays and winter closing at 13:30, tel. 292-111).

▲**Torre del Mangia (the city tower)**—Siena gathers around its city hall, not its church. It was a proud republic and its "declaration of independence" is the tallest secular medieval tower in Italy, the tall-as-a-football-field Torre del Mangia (named after a watchman who did more eating than watching; his statue is in the courtyard, to the left as you enter). Its 300 steps get pretty skinny at the top, but the reward is one of Italy's best views (L5,000, 10:00–18:00 or 19:00, limit of 30 towerists at a time, avoid the midday crowd).

**The Palio**—The feisty spirit of each of Siena's 17 contrada lives on. These neighborhoods celebrate, worship, and compete together. Each even has its own historical museum. Contrada pride is evident any time of year in the colorful neighborhood banners and parades. (If you hear distant drumming, run to it for the medieval action). But contrada pride is most visible twice a year (July 2 and August 16), when they have their world-famous Palio di Siena. Ten of the 17 neighborhoods compete (chosen by lot), hurling themselves with medieval abandon into several days of trial races and traditional revelry. On the big day, Il Campo is stuffed to the brim with locals and tourists, as the horses charge wildly around the square in this literally no-holds-barred race. Of course, the winning neighborhood is the scene of grand celebrations afterward. The grand prize: simply proving your contrada is *numero uno*. All over town, sketches and posters depict the Palio. The TI has a free scrapbook-quality Palio brochure with English explanations. While the actual palio really packs the city, you could side-trip in from Florence to see horse-race trials each of the three days before the big day (usually at 9:00 and 19:45).

▲▲▲**The Duomo**—Siena's cathedral is as Baroque as Gothic gets. The striped facade is piled with statues and ornamentation, and the interior is decorated from top to bottom. From the heads of 172 popes peering down from the ceiling to the fine inlaid art on the floor, this is one busy interior.

To orient yourself in this *panforte* of Italian churches, stand under the dome with the altar at high noon: you'll find the *Slaughter of the Innocents* on the floor at 10:00, Pisano's pulpit at 11:00, Bernini at 3:00, Michelangelo (snacks, shop, and WC) at 7:00, the library at 8:00, and Donatello at 9:00. Take some time with the floor mosaics in the front. Nicolo Pisano's wonderful pulpit is crowded but delicate Gothic storytelling from 1268. Bernini's sumptuous *Cappella della Madonna del Voto* (the last work in the cathedral, from 1659) is enough to make a Lutheran light a candle. Step inside and look back at the two Bernini statues: St. Jerome playing the crucifix like a violinist lost in beautiful music, and Mary Magdalene in a similar state of spiritual ecstasy. The Piccolomini altar is most interesting for its two Michelangelo statues (the big ones). Paul, on the left, may be a self-portrait. Peter, on the right, looks somewhat like Michelangelo's more famous statue of Moses. Originally contracted to do 15, Michelangelo left the project early (1504) to do his great *David* in Florence. The library (L2,000), brightly frescoed with scenes glorifying the works of a pope from 500 years ago, contains some intricately decorated or "illuminated" music scores and a Roman copy of three Greek graces. Donatello's statue of St. John the Baptist is being restored (free, 7:30–19:30, until 18:30 off-season, modest dress required).

▲**Baptistery**—Siena is so hilly that there wasn't enough flat ground to build a big church on. What to do? Build a big church and prop up the overhanging edge with the baptistery. This dark and quietly tucked away cave of art is worth a look (and L2,000) for the bronze carvings of Donatello (the six women, or angels) and Ghiberti on the baptismal font and for its cool tranquility.

▲▲**The Opera Metropolitana (cathedral museum)**—
Siena's most enjoyable museum, on the Campo side of the
church (look for the yellow signs), was built to house the
cathedral's art. The ground floor is filled with the cathedral's
original Gothic sculpture by Pisano (who spent ten years
here doing and orchestrating the carved decoration of the
cathedral in the late 1300s) and a fine Donatello *Madonna
and Child*. Upstairs to the left awaits a private audience with
Duccio's *Maesta* (Enthroned Virgin). Pull up a chair and
study one of the great pieces of medieval art. What was the
flip side of the *Maesta* (displayed on the opposite wall), with
26 panels—the medieval equivalent of pages—shows scenes
from the passion of Christ. At the end of the top floor, a little sign directs you to the "panorama." Climb to the first
landing, then take the skinnier second spiral for Siena's surprise view. Look back over the Duomo, then consider this:
when rival republic Florence began its grand cathedral,
proud Siena decided to build the biggest church in all
Christendom. The existing cathedral would be used as a
transept. You're atop what would have been the entry. The
wall below you, connecting the Duomo with the museum of
the cathedral, was as far as Siena got before a plague killed
the city's ability to finish the project. Were it completed,
you'd be looking straight down the nave (L5,000,
9:00–19:30, closing at 18:30 in shoulder months, and 13:30
off-season, tel. 283-048).

**Church of San Domenico**—This huge brick church, a
landmark for those arriving by bus or car, is worth a quick
look. The simple, bland interior fits the austere philosophy
of the Dominicans. Walk up the steps in the rear of the
church for a look at various paintings from the life of Saint
Catherine, patron saint of Siena and, since 1939, of all Italy.
Halfway up the church on the right, you'll find her head
(free, 7:00–13:00, 15:00–17:30, less in winter).

**Sanctuary of Saint Catherine**—A few downhill blocks
toward the center from San Domenico (follow signs to the
Santuario di Santa Caterina), step into the cool and peaceful
site of Catherine's home. Siena remembers its favorite
hometown girl, a simple, unschooled, but almost mystically
devout girl who, in the mid-1300s, helped get the pope to
return from France to Rome. Pilgrims have come here since

1464. Wander around to enjoy art depicting scenes from her life. Her room is downstairs (free, 9:00–12:30, 15:30–18:00, via Tiratoio).

▲**The Pinacoteca (National Picture Gallery)**—Siena was a power in Gothic art. But the average tourist, wrapped up in a love affair with the Renaissance, hardly notices. This museum takes you on a walk through Siena's art, chronologically from the 12th through 15th centuries. For the casual sightseer, the Sienese art in the city hall and cathedral museums is adequate. But art fans enjoy this opportunity to trace the evolution of Siena's delicate and elegant art. (From the Campo, walk out Via di Citta to Piazza di Postierla and go left on San Pietro, L8,000, 8:30–19:00 July–September, afternoon admittance only at set times, closes around 14:00 on Monday, Sunday, and off-season; because of staff problems, call to confirm these unreliable times, tel. 281-161.)

## Sleeping in Siena
### (L1,600 = about $1, tel. code: 0577, zip code: 53100)

Most visitors daytrip in from Florence, but finding a room can be tough, especially if you arrive during Easter or for the Palio in early July and mid-August. Call ahead, as Siena's few budget places are listed in all the budget guidebooks. Most places are accustomed to holding telephone reservations until 17:00, if you can get the message across in Italian. While tour groups turn the town into a Gothic amusement park in midsummer, Siena is basically yours in the evenings and off-season.

Nearly all listed hotels lie between Il Campo and the church of San Domenico (the intercity bus stop) and Piazza Gramsci (where the bus from the train station drops you). Have breakfast on Il Campo or in a nearby bar.

Sleep code: **S**=Single, **D**=Double/Twin, **T**=Triple, **Q**=Quad, **B**=Bath/Shower and Toilet, **CC**=Credit Card (Visa, MasterCard, Amex), **SE**=Speaks English (graded **A-F**).

### *Sleeping near Il Campo*
Each of these first listings is just a horse-wreck away from one of Italy's most wonderful civic spaces.

**Locanda Garibaldi** (D-L65,000, T-L85,000; half a block downhill off the square to the right of the tower at Via Giovanni Dupre 18, tel. 284-204, fax . . . what's that? SE-D, disdains taking reservations, call only a few days in advance) is a dying breed. In this modest, very Sienese restaurant-albergo, gentle Marcello wears two hats, running a busy restaurant with seven doubles upstairs. This is a fine place for dinner.

**Piccolo Hotel Etruria** (SB-L60,000, DB-L90,000, TB-L122,000, QB-L153,000, CC:VMA; with back to the tower, leave Il Campo to the right, Via Donzelle 1-3, tel. and fax 288-088, SE-D) is a good bet for a real hotel with all the comforts, just off the square.

**Albergo Tre Donzelle** (S-L34,000, D-L57,000, DB-L72,000; Via Donzelle 5, tel. 280-358, Sra. Iannini SE) is a plain, institutional, but decent place next door that makes sense only if you think of Il Campo as your terrace.

**Pension La Perla** (DB-L80,000, tiny box showers in the DB rooms; a block off the square opposite the tower on Piazza Independenza at Via della Terme 25, tel. 47144) is a funky, jumbled place with a narrow maze of hallways, forgettable rooms, and a laissez-faire environment, run by English-speaking Paolo.

**Hotel Duomo** (SB-L130,000, DB-L170,000, TB-L235,000, including breakfast; CC:VMA; follow Via di Citta, which becomes Via Stalloreggi, to #38 Via Stalloreggi; tel. 289-088, fax 43043, SE-B) is the best in-the-old-town splurge, a truly classy place with spacious, elegant rooms. Don't ask for room #62.

A few blocks up Via Banchi di Sopra, a block off Piazza Matteotti, is the spacious, group-friendly **Hotel Cannon d'Oro** (SB-L70,000, DB-L95,000, CC:VMA; Via Montanini 28, tel. 44321, fax 280-868, SE-B).

### Sleeping Closer to the Bus Stop and San Domenico Church

These hotels (listed in order of closeness to Il Campo—max 10 minutes' walk) are ideal for those arriving by car or bus and wanting to minimize luggage-lugging. The first two enjoy fine views of the old town and cathedral (which sits floodlit before me as I type).

**Pension Bernini** (SB-L65,000, D-L80,000, DB-L90,000, prices drop for drop-ins; on the main San Domenico-Il Campo drag at Via Sapienza 15, tel. 289-047, SE-D but has fun trying) is the place to stay if you want to join a Sienese family in a modest, clean home with a few immaculate and comfortable rooms. The bathrooms are down the hall, the upholstery is lively, and the welcome is warm. The friendly owners, Nadia and Mauro, who welcome you to picnic on their spectacular view terrace for breakfast or dinner, get the "we try hardest in Siena" award. The parrot actually says "*ciao*" as you come and go from the terrace.

**Alma Domus** (S-L35,000, SB-L45,000, DB-L75,000, TB-L95,000, QB-L115,000; from San Domenico, walk downhill toward the view, turn right then left down Via Camporegio; make a U-turn at the little chapel down the brick steps to Via Camporegio 37, tel. 44177 and 44487, fax 47601, SE-F) is ideal, unless nuns make you nervous or you plan on staying out past the 23:00 curfew. This quasi-hotel (not a convent) is run with firm but angelic smiles by sisters who offer clean, quiet, rooms for a steal and save the best views for the foreigners. Bright lamps, quaint balconies, fine views, grand public rooms, top security, and a friendly atmosphere make this the best deal in town for the lire. The checkout time is a strict 10:00, but they have a *deposito* for luggage.

**Hotel Chiusarelli** is a proper hotel in a fine location (S-L55,000, SB-L80,000, DB-L116,000; just outside the old town, across from San Domenico and overlooking the stadium at Viale Curtone 15, tel. 280-562, fax 271-177, CC:VMA, SE-A).

For a Sienese villa experience in a classy residential neighborhood a few blocks away from the center (past San Domenico), with easy parking on the street, consider **Albergo Lea** (S-L60,000, DB-L105,000, TB-L140,000 with breakfast, CC:VMA; Viale XXIV Maggio 10, tel. and fax 283-207, SE-A; they have a Hertz desk in their lobby), and if you're traveling with rich relatives who want sterility near the action, the **Hotel Villa Liberty** has big bright and comfortable rooms (DB-L150,000 to L190,000 with breakfast, CC:VMA; facing the fortress at Viale V. Veneto 11, elevator, air-con, TVs, mini-bars, etc., tel. 44966, fax 44770, SE-A).

The tourist office has a list of private homes that rent rooms for around L25,000 per person. Many require a stay of several days, but some are central and a fine value. Siena's **Guidoriccio Youth Hostel** (L19,000 beds in doubles, triples, and dorms with sheets and breakfast, cheap meals; bus #15, #10, or #3 from Piazza Gramsci or the train station to Via Fiorentina 89 in the Stellino neighborhood, open 7:00–9:00, 15:00–23:30, tel. 52212, SE-B) has 120 cheap beds, but given the hassle of the bus ride and the charm of downtown Siena at night, I'd skip it.

## Eating in Siena

Restaurants are reasonable by Florentine and Venetian standards. Don't hesitate to pay a bit more to eat pizza on Il Campo (**Pizzeria Spadaforte**, mediocre pizza, great setting, the tables are steeper than the price, 12:00–16:00, 19:00–22:00, tel. 281-123). The ambience is a classic European experience. **Ristorante Gallo Nero** (3 blocks down Via del Porrione from the Campo at #65, tel. 284-356) is a friendly and inexpensive "grotto" for authentic Tuscan cuisine. This "black rooster" serves a mean Ribollita (L7,000, hearty Tuscan bean soup) and charges only L3,000 for a half-liter of Chianti. For authentic Sienese dining at a fair price, eat at the **Locanda Garibaldi** (down Via Giovanni Dupre a few steps from the square, closed Saturday, open at 19:00, arrive early to get a table, L23,000 menu). Marcello does a nice L5,000 *piatto misto dolce* with sweet wine for a little of several local sweets. For a peasant's dessert, take your last glass of Chianti (borrow the *bicchiere* for *dieci minuti*) with a chunk of bread to the square, lean against a pillar, and sip Siena Classico. Picnics any time of day are royal on the Campo.

**Osteria la Chiacchera** (just below Pension Bernini at Costa di San Antonio 4, tel. 280-631, 12:00–15:00, 19:00–24:00) is a wonderfully medieval, tasty, and affordable hole-in-the-wall. **Osteria della Artista** (1 Via Stalloreggi) is popular with locals for a cheap meal. **Rosticceria/Pizzeria 4 Cantoni** (near Hotel Duomo at Piazza di Postierla 5, tel. 281-067, closed Wednesday) is cheap, easy, and away from the tourism. And **Pizza Rustica** places, scattered throughout Siena, serve up cheap pizza sold by the gram to go.

For a chance to enjoy a snack on a balcony overlooking the Campo, stop by the **Gelateria Artigiana La Costarella** (ice cream), **Bar Barbero** (*panforte* and cappuccino, best balcony) or **Par Paninoteca** (sandwiches, messy balcony), each just off the square on Via di Citta.

Siena's claim to caloric fame is its panforte, a rich, chewy concoction of nuts, honey, and candied fruits that impresses even fruitcake-haters (although locals I met prefer a white cookie called *Ricciarelli*). All over town Prodotti Tipici shops sell Sienese specialties. Don't miss the evening passeggiata (peak time is 19:00) along Via Banchi di Sopra with gelato in hand (**Nannini's** at Piazza Salimbeni has fine gelato).

## Transportation Connections

**Trains from Siena to Florence:** While most trains take longer and require a change (in Empoli), *rapido* SITA buses go regularly between downtown Florence and Siena's San Domenico church, nonstop by autostrada (L10,000, 70 min, tel. 204-245, buy ticket before boarding at the *biglietteria*, or ticket office). Don't confuse the blue (intercity) and orange (city) buses. The milk-run bus from Florence to Siena is most scenic, offering an interesting glimpse of small-town and rural Tuscany. From Siena there's one bus a day to Rome (3 hrs, L20,000) and to Viterbo (for Città). Rome trains: 8/day, 3½ hrs including a 20-minute connection in Chiusi.

**Arriving by car:** From the autostrada, take the Porta S Marco exit and follow the Centro, then Stadio signs (stadium, soccer ball). The soccer-ball signs take you to the stadium lot (L700 per hour) right at the huge bare-brick San Domenico church. To park free, find any white-striped car stall on the streets behind Hotel Villa Liberty (and note the L200,000 tow fee incentive to know your days of the week in Italian).

## SAN GIMIGNANO

The epitome of a Tuscan hill town with 14 medieval towers still standing (out of an original 72!), San Gimignano is a perfectly preserved tourist trap so easy to visit and visually pleasing that it's a good stop. Remember, in the 13th century, back in the days of Romeo and Juliet, towns were run by feuding noble families. And they'd periodically battle things out from the protective bases of their respective family towers. Skylines like San Gimignano's were the norm in medieval Tuscany. Florence had hundreds of towers.

## Orientation (tel. code: 0577)

While the basic three-star sight here is the town itself, there are a few worthwhile stops. From the town gate, shop straight up the traffic-free town's cobbled main drag to the Piazza del Cisterna (with its 13th-century well). The town sights cluster around the adjoining Piazza del Duomo. Tourist Information office is in the old center on the Piazza Duomo (daily, 9:00–13:00, 15:00–19:00, tel. 940-008).

## Sights—San Gimignano

The **Collegiata** (free, with the round windows and wide steps) is a Romanesque church filled with fine Renaissance frescoes. In Palazzo del Popolo (facing the same piazza), you'll find the city museum and San Gimignano's tallest tower. The **Museo Civico** (L7,000, daily 9:30–19:30) has a classy little painting collection with a 1422 altarpiece by Taddeo di Bartolo honoring Saint Gimignano. You can see him with the town in his hands surrounded by events from his life. You can climb the 180-foot-tall **Torre Grossa** for L7,000 (daily 9:30–19:30) but the free **Rocco** (castle), a short climb behind the church, offers a better view and a great picnic perch, especially at sunset. Thursday is market day (8:00–13:00), but for local merchants, every day is a sales frenzy.

## Transportation Connections

**San Gimignano to Florence:** From Florence, take a bus to San Gimignano (regular departures, 75 min, change in Poggibonsi) or catch the train to Poggibonsi, where frequent buses shuttle tourists to San Gimignano (20 min). Buses also connect San Gimignano with **Siena** (16/day, 1½ hr) and **Volterra** (6/day, 2 hrs). Bus tickets are sold at the bar just inside the town gate. San Gimignano has no baggage check service.

You can't drive within the walled town of San Gimignano, but a car-park awaits just a few steps from the town gate.

## ASSISI

Around the year 1200, a simple monk from Assisi challenged the decadence of church government and society in general with a powerful message of nonmaterialism, simplicity, and a "slow down and smell God's roses" lifestyle. Like Jesus, Francis taught by example. A huge monastic order grew out of his teachings, which were gradually embraced (some would say co-opted) by the church. Clare, St. Francis's partner in poverty, founded the Order of the Poor Clares. Catholicism's purest example of Christlike simplicity is now glorified in beautiful churches. In 1939, Italy made Francis and Clare its patron saints.

Any pilgrimage site will be commercialized, and the legacy of St. Francis is Assisi's basic industry. In summer the town bursts with splash-in-the-pan Francis fans and Franciscan knickknacks. Those able to see past the tacky monk mementos can actually have a "travel on purpose" experience. Francis' message of love and simplicity and sensitivity to the environment has a broad appeal.

### Orientation (tel. code: 075)

Assisi, crowned by a ruined castle, is beautifully preserved and has a basilica nearly wallpapered by Giotto. Most visitors are day-trippers. Assisi after dark is closer to a place Francis could call home.

The Tourist Information office is on Piazza della Comune (open 8:00–14:00, 15:30–18:30, less on Saturday, closed on Sunday, tel. 812-534). Buses connecting Assisi's train station (near Santa Maria degli Angeli) with the old town center (L1,200, 2/hr, 5 km) stop at Piazza Unita d'Italia (Basilica di San Francisco), Largo Properzio (Sta. Clare) and Piazza Matteotti (top of old town).

### Sights—Assisi

▲▲▲**The Basilica of St. Francis**—In 1230, at his request, Saint Francis was buried outside of his town with the sinners on the "hill of the damned." Now called the "Hill of Paradise," this is one of the artistic highlights of medieval Europe. It's frescoed from top to bottom by Cimabue, Giotto, Simone Martini, and the leading artists of the day. The three-part basilica (upper and lower

Assisi

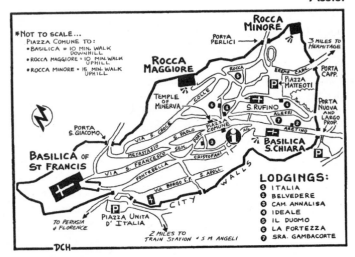

*NOT TO SCALE...
PIAZZA COMUNE TO:
• BASILICA = 10 MIN. WALK DOWNHILL
• ROCCA MAGGIORE = 10 MIN. WALK UPHILL
• ROCCA MINORE = 15 MIN. WALK UPHILL

LODGINGS:
❶ ITALIA
❷ BELVEDERE
❸ CAM. ANNALISA
❹ IDEALE
❺ IL DUOMO
❻ LA FORTEZZA
❼ SRA. GAMBACORTE

churches built over the saint's tomb) is a theological work of genius—but difficult for the 20th-century tourist/pilgrim to appreciate. Since the basilica is the reason most visit Assisi and the message of St. Francis has even the least devout blessing the town Vespas, I've designed a *Mona Winks*-type tour with the stress on the theology of the place rather than the art history.

Enter the church from the parking lot at the lower level. At the doorway look up and see Saint Francis who (sounding a bit like John Wayne) greets you with the Latin inscription saying, "Slow down and be joyful, pilgrim. You've reached the Hill of Paradise and this church will knock your spiritual socks off." Start with the tomb (turn left into the nave and go down the "Cripta" stairs). Grab a pew in front of His tomb.

**The message:** Francis' message caused a stir. He traded a life of power and riches for one of obedience, poverty, and chastity. The Franciscan existence (Brother Sun, Sister Moon, and so on) is a space where God, man, and the natural world frolic harmoniously. In an Italy torn by fighting between towns and families, Francis promoted peace and the restoration of order. (He set an example by reconstructing a crumbled chapel.) While the Church was waging bloody Crusades, Francis pushed ecumenism and understanding. Even today, the leaders of the world's great religions meet for summits here in Assisi.

This rich building seems to contradict the teachings of the poor monk it honors. But it was built as an act of religious and civic pride to remember the hometown saint. It was also designed and still functions as a pilgrimage center and a splendid classroom.

**The tomb:** Holy relics were the "ruby slippers" of medieval Europe. They gave you power—got your prayers answered and helped you win wars—and ultimately helped you get back to your eternal Kansas. For obvious reasons of security, you didn't flaunt your relics. In fact Francis' tomb was hidden until 1818, when this crypt was opened to the public. The saint's remains are above the altar in the stone box with the iron ties. His four best friends are buried in the corners of the room. On your way out, notice the remains of Francis' rich Roman patron, Jacopa dei Settesoli, in an urn behind the black metal grill in the back of the room (up four steps).

**The lower basilica** is appropriately Franciscan, subdued and Romanesque. The nave was frescoed with parallel scenes from the lives of Christ and Francis—connected by a ceiling of stars. Unfortunately after the church was built and decorated, the popularity of the Franciscans meant side chapels needed to be built. Huge arches were cut out of the scenes, but some scenes survive. The first panels show Jesus being stripped of his clothing opposite the famous scene of Francis stripping off his clothes in front of his father. In the third fresco on the right wall, Christ is being taken down from the cross (just half his body can be seen) and it looks like the story is over. Defeat. But in the opposite fresco we see Francis preaching to the birds, reminding the faithful that through baptism, the message of the Gospel survives.

These stories directed the attention of the medieval pilgrim to the altar where, through the sacraments, he met God. The church was thought of as a community of believers sailing toward God. The prayers coming out of the nave (*navis*, or ship) fill the triangular sections of the ceiling—called *vele*, or sails—with spiritual wind. With a priest for a navigator and the altar for a helm, faith propelled the ship.

Stand behind the altar (toes to the bottom step) and look up. The three scenes are "Obedience" (Francis wearing a yoke), "Chastity" (in a tower of purity held up by two angels), and, straight ahead, "Poverty." Here, Jesus blesses the marriage as

Francis slips a ring on Lady Poverty. In the foreground, two "self-sufficient" merchants (the new rich of a thriving North Italy) are throwing sticks and stones at the bride. But Poverty, in her patched wedding dress, is fertile and strong, and even those brambles blossom into a rosebush crown.

Putting your heels to the altar and bending back like a drum major, look up at Francis, who traded a life of earthly simplicity for glory in heaven. Turn to the right and march . . .

Saint Francis's patched robe is on display in the right transept. This guy brought the message of God to the people. Franciscan friars, known as the "Jugglers of God," were a joyful part of the community. Look around at the painted scenes in this transept. Back in 1300, this was radical art—believable homespun scenes, landscapes, trees, real people. Check out the crucifix (by Giotto) with the eight sparrow-like angels. For the first time, holy people are expressing emotion—one angel turns her head sadly at the sight of Jesus; another scratches her hands down her cheeks, drawing blood. The up-until-now-in-control Mary has fainted in despair. The Franciscans, with their goal of bringing God to the people, found a natural partner in Europe's first modern painter, Giotto.

Francis' friend, "Sister Death," was really not all that terrible. In fact Francis would like to introduce you to her now (to the right of the door leading into the bright courtyard). Go ahead, block the light and meet her. I'll wait for you in the courtyard.

From the courtyard you can enter the bookshop and the skipable Museum-Treasury (Gothic fine arts and paintings, no English explanations, L3,000). Monks in robes are not my idea of easy-to-approach people, but the Franciscans are still God's Jugglers (and most of them speak English). Climb the stairs to the upper basilica.

**The Upper Basilica**, built later than the lower, is brighter and Gothic. It's a gallery of frescoes by Giotto and his assistants showing 28 scenes from the life of St. Francis. Follow the great events of Francis' life, starting at the altar and working clockwise. Immediately to the right of the altar, the first panel shows God looking over 20-year-old Francis, a dandy imprisoned in his selfishness. A medieval pilgrim, fluent in symbolism, would understand this because the Temple of Minerva (which you'll see today on Assisi's Piazza del Comune) was a prison then. The rose window never existed but symbolizes the eye of God. Next, Francis offers his cape to a stranger. Later, he's visited by the Lord in a dream and told to leave the army and go home. Next is the sad scene of Francis giving his dad his clothes, his credit cards, and even his time-share condo on Capri. Naked Francis is covered by the bishop, symbolizing his transition from a man of the world to a man of the church. Later is a vision the pope had of a simple man propping up his teetering church. This led to the papal acceptance of the Franciscan reforms.

Skip to the other side (fourth panel from the door). Here, Christ appears to Francis being carried by a seraph (six-winged angel). For the strength of his faith, Francis is given the marks of his master, the "battle scars of love" . . . the stigmata. Throughout his life, Francis was interested in chivalry; now he's joined the spiritual knighthood. The weeds in the foreground were an herb which, in olden days, "drove away sadness and made men merry and joyful." Pilgrims smiled.

Turning to leave, notice the scene to the right of the door. Here Francis (sans seraph) is preaching to the birds. Francis was more than a nature lover. Notice that the birds are of different species. They represent the diverse flock of humanity and nature—all created and loved by God and worthy of each other's love.

This is the message that the basilica hopes the pilgrim will take home. Stepping out the door you see the Latin *Pax* (peace) and the Franciscan Tau cross in the grass. Tau, the last letter in the Hebrew alphabet, is symbolic of faithfulness to the end. Francis signed his name with this simple character. Tau and Pax. (For more pax, take the high lane back to town, up to the castle or into the countryside.)

The church is free, open 7:00–19:00, sometimes closed for lunch or mass. Tours are limited to 9:00–12:00 and 14:00–17:00—times you may want to avoid. The modest dress code is strictly enforced. Info: tel. 812-238. Much of the above is from the excellent little *The Basilica of Saint Francis—A Spiritual Pilgrimage* by Goulet, McInally and Wood, L3,500 in the bookshop.

▲**Basilica di Santa Chiara (Saint Clare)**—Dedicated to the founder of the order of the Poor Clares, this Umbrian Gothic church (1265, with the huge buttresses added in the next century) is simple, in keeping with the Poor Clares' dedication to a life of contemplation. The interior's fine frescoes were whitewashed in the baroque days. The Chapel of St. George on the right (actually an earlier church incorporated into this one) has the crucifix which supposedly spoke to St. Francis, leading to his conversion in 1206. In the back of that chapel are some important Franciscan relics, including Clare's robe. Stairs lead from the nave down to the tomb of Saint Clare. The attached cloistered community of the Poor Clares has flourished for 700 years (church open 7:00–12:00, 14:00–18:30). For a change of pace, cross the street behind the church at the arch and dip into the goofy mechanical and water-powered Biblical world of Silvano Gianbolina.

**Piazza del Comune**—This square (straight up Via San Francesco from the basilica) is the center of town. You'll find the Roman temple of Minerva, a Romanesque tower, banks, the post office, the Pinacoteca (pathetic art gallery, not worth the admission), and the tourist information office. For a look at Assisi's Roman roots, tour the **Roman Forum** (Foro Romano, L4,000, 10:00–13:00, 15:00–19:00) which is actually under the Piazza del Comune. The floor plan is sparse, and the odd bits and pieces obscure, but it's well explained in English, and it is ancient.

▲**The Rocca Maggiore** (big castle, L5,000, 10:00–19:00) offers a good look at a 14th-century fortification and a fine view of Assisi and the Umbrian countryside. If you're counting lire, the view is just as good from outside the castle and the interior is pretty bare—except for a model of a guillotine with an interesting history in English. Inside, for an extra fee, there is a Torture Museum with four rooms filled with gruesome examples of medieval creativity—explained almost joyously in English. For a picnic with the same birds and views that inspired St. Francis, leave all the tourists and hike to the Rocca Minore (small castle) above Piazza Matteotti.

▲▲**Santa Maria degli Angeli**, a huge Baroque church towering above the buildings below Assisi, was built around the tiny but historic Porziuncola chapel. St. Francis took Jesus literally when he told him to "go and restore my house." Twenty-four-year-old Francis put the ruined and abandoned chapel back together. It was in this chapel that Francis heard the command to organize his following into an order. As you enter St. Mary of the Angels, notice the sketch on the door showing the original little chapel with the monks' huts around it, and Assisi before it had its huge basilica. Francis lived here after he founded the Franciscan Order in 1208, and this was where he consecrated St. Clare as the Bride of Christ. The other "sights" in the church (a chapel on the spot where Francis died, the rose garden, a museum which has a few monastic cells upstairs) are not very interesting.

## Sleeping in Assisi
### (L1,600 = about $1, tel. code: 075, zip code: 06081)

The town accommodates large numbers of pilgrims on religious holidays. Finding a room any other time should be easy.

**Albergo Italia** (D-L50,000, DB-L75,000, CC:VM; just off the Piazza del Comune's fountain at Vicolo della Fortezza, tel. 812-625, fax 804-3749, SE-B) is clean and simple with great beds. Some of its 13 rooms overlook the town square.

**Hotel Belvedere** (D-L60,000, DB-L90,000; 2 blocks past St. Clare's church at Via Borgo Aretino 13, tel. 812-460, fax 816-812) offers comfortable rooms and good views, and is run by friendly, English-speaking Enrico and his American wife, Maria Maddalena.

**Camere Annalisa Martini** (S-L30,000, D-L55,000, T-L70,000, Q-L90,000, six rooms sharing three bathrooms; just below the Piazza del Comune at Via S. Gregorio 6, tel. 813-536) is a cheery home swimming in vines, roses, and bricks in the town's medieval core. Annalisa speaks English and enthusiastically accommodates her guests with a picnic garden, washing machine, refrigerator and homey, lived-in feeling rooms.

**Hotel Ideale** (SB-L65,000, DB-L95,000, CC:VMA; Piazza Matteotti 1, tel. 813-570, fax 813-020) is on the far edge of town with a peaceful garden, free parking, view balconies, all the modern comforts, and an English-speaking welcome.

**Albergo Il Duomo** (nine rooms, D-L46,000 to L55,000, DB-L63,000 to L70,000, CC:VM; Vicolo S. Lorenzo 2, tel. 812-742, fax 812-284, Carlo SE) is tidy and quiet on a stairstep lane at the top end of town between the castle and Piazza Matteotti.

**Hotel La Fortezza** is small, clean, subdued, modern, comfortable (DB-85,000, CC:VMA; just up the lane from the Piazza del Comune at Vicolo della Fortezza 19b, tel. 812-993, fax 812-418), and runs a good restaurant.

**Sra. Gambacorte** rents several decent rooms on a quiet lane just above St. Clare's with a roof terrace (S-L30,000, D-L60,000, T-L90,000; 9 via Sermei, tel. 815-206 or 812-454).

Francis probably would have bunked with the peasants in Assisi's **Ostello della Pace** (L17,000 beds with breakfast, in four- to six-bed rooms; a 15-minute walk below town at via di Valethye, at the San Pietro stop on the station-town bus, tel. 816-767).

## Transportation Connections
**Trains from Assisi to: Rome** (9/day, 2½ hrs with a change in Foligno), **Florence** (10/day, 2½ hrs, sometimes changing at Terontola-Cortona). **Siena** (5/day, 4 hrs), **Orvieto** (4/day, 2–3 hrs). Train info: tel. 817-789. One or two buses a day to Rome and Florence.

## ORVIETO
Umbria's grand hill town, while no secret, is still worth a quick look. Just off the freeway, with three popular gimmicks (its ceramics, cathedral, and Classico wine), it's loaded with tourists by day—quiet by night.

## Orientation (tel. code: 0763)
A handy funicular/bus shuttle takes visitors quickly from the train station and car-park to the top of the town (4/hr, L1,400 ticket includes connecting Piazza Cahen-Piazza Duomo minibus transfer, where you'll find everything that matters). From the top of the funicular, walk right onto the waiting orange bus. Drivers park at the base of the hill at the huge, free lot behind the Orvieto train station (follow the "P" and *funicolare* signs). A pedestrian tunnel leads under the train tracks to the funicular (across from the train station). The shuttle bus drops you at the tourist office (#24 Piazza Duomo, tel. 0763/41772, 8:00–14:00, 16:00–19:00, weekends from 10:00) on the cathedral square.

Ride the back streets into the Middle Ages. The town sits majestically on tufa rock. Streets lined with buildings

## Orvieto Area

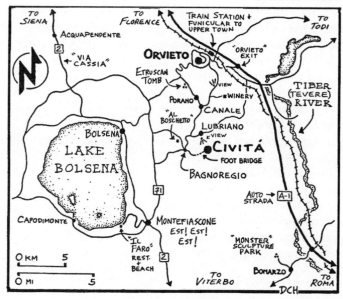

made of the exhaust-stained volcanic stuff seem to grumble Dark Ages. Piazza Cahen is only a transportation hub at the entry to the hilltop town. It has a ruined fortress with a garden, a commanding view, and a popular well which is an impressive (but overpriced) double helix carved into tufa rock.

### Sights—Orvieto

The Orvieto **Duomo** (cathedral) has Italy's most striking facade. Grab a gelato from the gelateria to the left of the church and study this fascinating mass of mosaics and sculpture. In a chapel to the right of the altar, you'll find some great Signorelli frescoes (7:00–13:00, 14:30–18:30).

Surrounding the striped cathedral are a fine **Etruscan Museum** (L4,000, 9:00–13:30, 14:30, Sunday 9:00–13:00), a great gelati shop, and unusually clean public toilets (down the stairs from the left transept). Drinking a shot of wine in a ceramic cup as you gaze up at the cathedral lets you experience all of Orvieto's claims to fame at once.

**Underground Orvieto Tours** weaves a good archeological history into an hour-long look at about 100 meters of caves (L10,000, tours twice daily at 11:00 and 16:00 from the TI, tel. 301-091 or the TI). Orvieto is honeycombed with Etruscan and medieval caves. You'll see only the remains of an old olive press, two impressive 40-meter-deep Etruscan well shafts, and the remains of a primitive cement quarry, but if you want underground Orvieto, this is the best place to get it.

Orvieto Classico wine is justly famous. For a homey peek into a local winery, visit **Tanuta Le Velette**, where English-speaking Corrado and Cecilia Bottai welcome those who'd like a look at their winery and a taste of the final product (8:00–12:00, 14:00–17:00, closed Sunday, tel. 0763/29090 or 29144). At their sign (5 minutes past Orvieto at the top of the switchbacks just before Canale, on the Bagnoregio road) cruise down the long tree-lined drive and park at the striped gate. Call first to be sure they're home and have a moment to show you around.

## Sleeping in Orvieto
### (L1,600 = about $1, tel. code: 0763, zip code: 05018)

Here are four places in the old town, one in a more modern neighborhood near the station, and one on a local farm.

**Hotel Corso** (DB-L90,000; on the main street up from the funicular toward the Duomo at Via Cavour 343, tel. 42020) is small, clean, and friendly, with comfy modern rooms.

**Hotel Duomo** (D-L50,000, DB-L78,000; a block from the Duomo, behind the gelateria at Via di Maurizio 7, tel. 41887) is a funky, brightly colored, Old World place with simple rooms and a great location.

**Albergo Posta** (D-L58,000, DB-L78,000; Via Luca Signorelli 18, tel. 41909) is a 5-minute walk from the cathedral into the medieval core. It's a big, old, formerly elegant, but well-cared-for-in-its-decline building with a breezy garden, a grand old lobby, and spacious, clean, plain rooms with vintage rickety furniture and springy beds.

**Bar Ricci** (D-L40,000; via Magalotti 22, tel. 41119, ES-F) serves up dumpy cheap rooms and cheap pasta.

**Albergo Picchio** (D-L44,000, DB-L60,000, TB-L78,000; Via G. Salvatori 17, 05019 Orvieto Scalo, tel. 301-144 or 90246) is a shiny, modern, concrete-and-marble place, more comfortable but with less character, and family-run by Marco and Picchio. It's in the lower, ugly part of town, 300 yards from the train station.

    **Agriturismo Pomonte** (Canino N. 1 Corbara, Orvieto, house on a hilltop at curve in road 3 km from Corbara, tel. 0763/304080, Cesari family) is a great farm-and-family experience.

## Transportation Connections

**Trains from Orvieto to: Rome** (14/day, 70 min, only take trains going to Rome's Termini Station where the subway takes day-trippers conveniently to the major sights; consider leaving your car at the large car-park behind the Orvieto station). **Florence** (12/day, 2 hrs); **Siena** (5 day, 2–3 hrs, with change in Chiusi). **Bagnoregio** is a 40-minute, L2,000 bus ride (6:25, 7:50, 9:10, 12:40, 13:55, 15:45, 17:35, and 18:35 from Orvieto's Piazza Cahen and from its train station daily except Sunday, buy tickets from the "cafe snack bar" at the station, get return times from the conductor). If the bus is empty, develop a relationship with your driver. He may let you jump out in Lubriano for a great photo of distant Civitá.

## CIVITÀ DI BAGNOREGIO

Perched on a pinnacle in a grand canyon, this is Italy's ultimate hill town. Immerse yourself in the traffic-free village of Civitá. Curl your toes around its Etruscan roots.

    Civitá is terminally ill. Only 15 residents remain as, bit by bit, it's being purchased by rich big-city Italians who escape to their villas here. Apart from its permanent (and aging) residents and those who have weekend villas here, there is a group of Americans (mostly Seattle-ites), introduced to the town through a small University of Washington architecture program, who have bought into the rare magic of Civitá. When the program is in session, 15 students live with residents and study Italian culture and architecture.

    Civitá is connected to the world and the town of Bagnoregio by a long donkey path. While Bagnoregio lacks the pinnacle-town romance of Civitá, it rings true as a pure bit of small-town Italy. It's actually a healthy, vibrant community (unlike Civitá, the suburb it calls "the dead city"). Get a

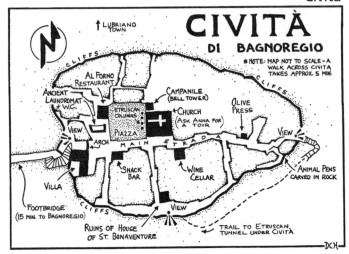

haircut, sip a coffee on the square, walk down to the old laundry (ask, "*Dové la lavanderia vecchia?*"). From Bagnoregio, yellow signs direct you along its long and skinny spine to its older neighbor, Cività. Enjoy the view as you head up the long donkey (and now, Vespa) path to Cività and its main (and only) square. A shuttle bus runs from the base of the Cività bridge to Bagnoregio and maybe to Al Boschetto (see Sleeping, below) about hourly in season (L1,000).

**Al Forno** (green door on main square, open daily, June–October only, tel. 0761/793-586), run by the Mostarde family, is the only restaurant in town and serves up a decent pasta-and-wine lunch or dinner.

At the church on the main square, Anna will give you a tour (tip her and buy your postcards from her). Around the corner, on the main street, is a cool and friendly wine cellar with a dirt floor and stump chairs, where Domenica serves local wine—L1,000 a glass and worth it, if only for the atmosphere. Step down into her cellar and note the traditional wine-making gear and the provisions for rolling huge kegs up the stairs. Tap on the kegs in the cool bottom level to see which are full. Most village houses are connected to cellars like this which often date from Etruscan times.

Down the street is Victoria's **Antico Mulino** (L1,500), an atmospheric homemade museum of old olive-presses. Her grandson toasts delicious bruschetta on weekends. Just down the way, Maria (for L1,000) will show you through her garden with a fine view (**Maria's Giardino**). Continuing through the town, the main drag peters out and a trail leads you down and around to the right to a tunnel that has cut through the hill under the town since Etruscan times. The "Marchesa," who married into the Ferrari family, owns the house at the town gate—complete with Città's only (for now) hot-tub.

Evenings on the town square are a bite of Italy. The same people sit on the same church steps under the same moon, night after night, year after year. I love my cool late evenings in Città. Listen to the midnight sounds of the valley from the donkey path.

Whenever you visit, stop halfway up the donkey path and listen to the sounds of rural Italy. Reach out and touch one of the monopoly houses. If you know how to turn the volume up on the crickets, do so. If you visit in the cool of the early morning, have cappuccino and rolls at the small café on the town square.

## Sleeping and Eating near Città
### (L1,600 = about $1, tel. code: 0761)

When you leave the tourist crush, life as a traveler in Italy becomes easy and prices tumble. Room-finding is easy in small-town Italy.

Just outside Bagnoregio is **Al Boschetto**. The Catarcia family speaks no English; they don't need to. Have an English-speaking Italian call for you from Venice or Florence (D-L60,000, DB-L75,000, breakfast L5,000, CC:V; Strada Monterado, Bagnoregio/Viterbo, Italy, tel. 792-369, walking and driving instructions below). Most rooms have private showers (no curtains, slippery floors—be careful not to flood the place; sing in search of your shower's resonant frequency).

The Catarcia family (Angelino, his wife Perina, sons Gianfranco and Dominico, daughter-in-law Giuseppina, and the grandchildren) is wonderful. Splurge for good country cookin' at Al Boschetto (L35,000 for a full-blown dinner from bruschetta through desert with sweet wine). Bunny is the house specialty. Everything at Angelino's is deliciously homegrown—

figs, fruit, wine, rabbit, pasta. This is traditional rural Italian cuisine at its best. Share a table with fellow Americans to maximize the cuisine experience. If the mood is right, the boys will take you down deep into the gooey, fragrant bowels of the cantina. Music and vino melt the language barrier in the wine cellar. Maybe Angelino or his sons will teach you their theme song, "Trinka, Trinka, Trinka." The lyrics are easy (see previous sentence). Warning: Angelino is Bacchus squared, and he's taught his boys well. Descend at your own risk. There are no rules unless the female participants set them. (For every three happy reports I get, I receive one angry postcard requesting I drop these guys from my book.) If you're interested in savoring small-town Italy, it doesn't get any better than Bagnoregio, Cività, and Al Boschetto.

The Orvieto bus drops you at the town gate. (Remember, no service at all on Sunday.) Al Boschetto is a 15-minute walk out of town past the old arch (follow Viterbo signs), turn left at the pyramid monument, and right at the first fork (follow Montefiascone sign). Cività is a pleasant 45-minute walk (back through Bagnoregio) from Al Boschetto. If you plan to leave Al Boschetto early in the morning, get them to leave the *chiave* (kee-ah-vee) in the front door, or you're locked in.

**Hotel Fidanza** (DB-L80,000; Via Fidanza 25, Bagnoregio [Viterbo], tel. and fax 793-444, decent dinners), comfortable, right in Bagnoregio town, and with incredibly low blood pressure, is the only other hotel in town. Rooms 206 and 207 have views of Cività.

For more information about a two-bedroom, fully furnished/equipped Cività apartment with terrace and cliffside garden, rentable May through October ($600/week, $2,000/month, 1 week minimum), call Carol Watts in Kansas at (913) 539-0815, evenings.

## Transportation Connections

Cività is a 30-minute walk from **Bagnoregio**. A shuttle bus zips to and from the base of the Cività bridge every hour or so. Public buses connect Bagnoregio to the rest of the world via Orvieto (for connections, see Orvieto, above). While there's no official baggage-check service in Bagnoregio, I've arranged with Laurenti Mauro, who runs the Bar Enoteca just outside the Bagnoregio old town gate (near the bus station), to let you leave your bags there (open 6:00–24:00 with a short lunch break). Pay him L2,000 per bag or buy breakfast there (better than Al Boschetto's).

**Driving from Orvieto to Bagnoregio:** Orvieto overlooks the autostrada (and has its own exit). The shortest way to Città from the freeway exit is to turn left (away from Orvieto) and follow signs to Lubriano and Bagnoregio. The more winding and scenic route takes 20 minutes longer: From the freeway, pass under hill-capping Orvieto (on your right, signs to Lago di Bolsena, on Viale I Maggio), take the first left (direction: Bagnoregio), winding up past great Orvieto views, the Orvieto Classico vineyard (see below), through Canale, and through farms and fields of giant shredded wheat to Bagnoregio, where the locals (or rusty old signs) will direct you to Angelino Catarcia's Al Boschetto, just outside town. Either way, just before Bagnoregio, follow the signs left to Lubriano and pull into the first little square by the church on your right for a breathtaking view of Città. Then return to the Bagnoregio road. Drive through Bagnoregio (following yellow Città signs) and park at the base of the steep donkey path up to the traffic-free, 2,500-year-old, canyon-swamped pinnacle town of Città di Bagnoregio.

## Still Not Satisfied?

Italy is spiked with hill towns. Perugia is big and reeks with history. Cortona is smaller with a fine youth hostel (tel. 0575/601-765). Todi is nearly untouristed. Pienza (Renaissance planned town) and Montepulciano (dramatic setting) are also worth the hill-town lover's energy and time. Sorano and Pitigliano have almost no tourism. Bevagna (near Assisi) is as dazed as its town fool who stands between the twin dark Romanesque churches on its main square. Paranoid Orte filled its tufa perch so completely that there's no room for charm, and traffic circulates on a single skinny one-way lane. You'll see Orvieto's poor cousin—which must be the densest town in Italy—from the freeway, 30 minutes north of Rome. Train travelers often use the town of Chiusi as a home base for the hill towns. The region's trains (to Siena, Orvieto, Assisi) go through or change at this hub, and there are several reasonable pensioni near the station.

# THE CINQUE TERRE

The Cinque Terre, a remote chunk of
the Italian Riviera, is the traffic-free, low-
brow, underappreciated alternative to the
French Riviera. There's not a museum in
sight. Just sun, sea, sand (well, pebbles), wine,
and pure unadulterated Italy. Enjoy the villages, swimming,
hiking, and evening romance of one of God's great gifts to
tourism, the Cinque Terre (CHEENK-wa TAY-Ray). For a
home base, choose among five villages, each filling a ravine
with a lazy hive of human activity. Vernazza is my favorite.

## Planning Your Time

The ideal minimum stay is two nights and a completely uninterrupted day. The Cinque Terre is served by the milk-run
train from Genoa and La Spezia. Speed demons arrive in the
morning, check their bag in La Spezia, take the 5-hour hike
through all five towns, laze away the afternoon on the beach
or rock of their choice, and zoom away on the overnight train
to somewhere back in the real world. Each town has its own
character, and all are a few minutes apart by an hourly train.
There's no checklist of sights or experiences; just the hike,
the towns, and your fondest vacation desires.

For a good Cinque Terre day consider this: Pack your
beach and swim gear, wear your walking shoes, and catch the
train to town #1: Riomaggiore. (Since I still get the names
mixed up, I think of the five Cinque Terre towns by number.) Walk the cliff-hanging Via dell' Amore to Manarola
(#2) and buy food for a picnic, then hike to Corniglia (#3) for
a rocky but pleasant beach. Swim here or in the more resorty
Monterosso (#5, a 10-minute train ride away). From #5, hike
or catch the boat home to Vernazza (#4).

If you're into *la dolce far niente* (the sweetness of doing
*nada*) and don't want to hike, you could enjoy the blast of
cool train-tunnel air that announces the arrival of every
Cinque Terre train and go directly to Corniglia or
Monterosso to maximize beach time.

If you're a hiker, hike from Riomaggiore all the way
to Monterosso al Mare, where a sandy "front door"-style
beach awaits.

## Orientation

### *Getting Around the Cinque Terre*

The city of La Spezia is the gateway to the Cinque Terre. In La Spezia's train station, the milk-run Cinque Terre train schedule is posted at window #5. Take the L2,000 half-hour train ride into the Cinque Terre town of your choice.

**Cinque Terre Train Schedule:** The schedule changes with the seasons. Since the train is the Cinque Terre lifeline, any shop or restaurant posts the current schedule (La Spezia train info: tel. 0187/714-960).

Trains leave La Spezia for the Cinque Terre villages (last year's June–September schedule) at 6:25, 7:14, 8:30, 10:04, 11:00, 12:20, 13:12, 13:47, 14:17, 14:46, 15:22, 16:28, 17:48, 18:17, 19:06, 19:49, 21:10, 22:36, and 23:55. Pick up a current schedule. Trains often run a few minutes late.

While you can hike or catch the irregular boats, the easy way to zip from town to town is by train. These *locale* trains (that's Italian for "milk-run") are so tiny they don't even register on the Thomas Cook train timetable. But they go nearly hourly and are cheap. To orient yourself, remember that directions are "*per* (to) *Genoa*" or "*per La Spezia*," and virtually any train that stops at one of the five villages will stop at all five. The five towns are just minutes apart by train. Know your stop. After leaving the town before your destination, move down to the door. Since the stations are small and the trains are long, you may need to get off the train deep in a tunnel and you may need to open the door yourself.

Since a one-town hop costs the same as a five-town hop (L2,000), and every ticket is good all day with stopovers, you can save money by exploring the region in one direction on one ticket.

## Cinque Terre Experiences

▲**Swimming**—Wear your walking shoes and pack your swim gear. Each beach has showers that may work better than your hotel's. (Bring soap and shampoo.) Monterosso's beaches, immediately in front of the train station, are by far the best (and most crowded). It's a sandy resort with everything rentable . . . lounge chairs, umbrellas, paddle boats, and usually even beach access (L2,000). Vernazza has a sandy children's cove, sunning rocks by a little waterfall, and showers by the breakwater. The tiny "Acque Pendente" (waterfall) cove that locals call their *laguna blu* between Vernazza and Monterosso is accessible only by small hired boat. Forget Manarola or Riomaggiore for beaches. I do my CinqueTerre swimming on the pathetic but peaceful manmade beach below the Corniglia station. Unfortunately, much of it has washed away and it's almost nonexistent when the surf's up. It has a couple of buoys to swim to, and is clean and less crowded than the Monterosso beach. The beach bar has showers, drinks, snacks, and goils. The nude Guvano (GOO-vah-noh) beach (between Corniglia and Vernazza, 30- to 45-minute hike or hire a boat) made headlines in Italy in the 1970s, as clothed locals in a makeshift armada of dinghies and fishing boats retook their town beach. But big-city nudists still work on all-around tans in this remote setting.

▲▲▲**Hiking**—All five towns are connected by good trails. Experience the area's best by hiking from one end to the other. The entire hike can be done in about 3 hours, but allow 5 for dawdling. While you can detour to hilltop sanctuaries, I'd keep it simple by following the easy blue-and-white-marked low trails between the villages. A good L5,000 hiking map (sold in all the towns, not necessary for this described walk) covers the expanded version of this hike from Porto Venere through all the five Cinque Terre towns to Levanto.

**Riomaggiore-Manarola (20 min):** From the Riomaggiore (town #1) station the Via del' Amore affords a film-gobbling promenade (wide enough for baby strollers) down the coast to Manarola. While there's no beach here, stairs lead down to sunbathing rocks.

**Manarola-Corniglia (45 min):** From the Manarola (#2) waterfront, it's easiest to take the high trail out of town. The broad and scenic low trail ends with steep stairs leading to the high road. The walk from #2 to #3 is a little longer, and a little more rugged, than from #1 to #2. If it's closed (as it has been for several years), you can climb around one fence, scamper across a washed-out section, and climb over the other fence. Any cat burglar can handle it. If you're concerned, ask other travelers about its current status.

**Corniglia-Vernazza (90 min):** The hike from Corniglia (#3) to Vernazza (#4)—the wildest and greenest of the coast—is most rewarding. From the Corniglia station and beach, zigzag up to the town. Ten minutes past Corniglia toward Vernazza, you'll see the well-hung Guvano beach far below. The trail leads past a bar and picnic tables, through lots of fragrant and flowery vegetation, and scenically into Vernazza.

**Vernazza-Monterosso (90 min):** The trail from Vernazza to Monterosso (#5) is a scenic, up-and-down-a-lot trek. Trails are rough but easy to follow. Camping at the picnic tables midway is frowned upon. The views just out of Vernazza are spectacular.

▲▲**Pesto**—This is the birthplace of pesto. Try it on spaghetti, *trofie*, or *trenette*. Basil, which loves the temperate Ligurian climate, is mixed with cheese (half *parmigiano* cow cheese and half *pecorino* sheep cheese), garlic, olive oil, and pine nuts, poured over pasta, and then into visitors. If you become addicted, small jars of it are sold in the local grocery stores.

▲▲**Wine**—The Vino delle Cinque Terre, famous throughout Italy, flows cheap and easy throughout the region. If you like sweet, sherry-like wine, the local *Sciachetra* (shock-ee-TRA) wine is worth the splurge (L5,000 per glass, often served with a cookie). While 10 kilos of grapes yield 7 liters of local wine, Sciachetra is made from near-raisins, and 10 kilos of grapes makes only 1½ liters of Sciachetra. If your room is up a lot of steps, be warned: Sciachetra is 18 percent alcohol, while regular wine is only 11 percent. In the cool, calm evening, sit on the Vernazza breakwater with a glass of wine and watch the phosphorous in the waves.

## Sights—Cinque Terre

▲▲**Riomaggiore–town #1:** The most substantial non-resort town of the group, Riomaggiore is a disappointment from the train station. But walk through the tunnel next to the train tracks (or take the high road, straight up and to the right), and you land in a fascinating tangle of pastel homes leaning on each other as if someone stole their crutches. There's homemade gelato at the Bar Central. With fewer locals making the wine and more tourists visiting, the local *trenino* (monorail wine train) now carries tourists to the Madonna di Montenero sanctuary high above the town.

▲**Manarola–town #2:** Like town #1, #2 is attached to its station by a 200-yard-long tunnel. Manarola is tiny and rugged, a tumble of buildings bunny-hopping down its ravine to the tiny harbor. This is a good place to buy your picnic (stores close from 13:00–17:00) before walking to the beaches of Corniglia.

▲▲**Corniglia–town #3:** A zigzag series of stairs that looks worse than it is leads up to the only town of the five not on the water. Originally settled by a Roman farmer who named it for his mother, Cornelia, its ancient residents produced a wine so famous that vases found at Pompei touted its virtues. Today its wine is still its lifeblood. Follow the pungent smell of ripe grapes into an alley cellar and get a local to let you dip a straw into her keg. Remote and less visited, Corniglia has a windy belvedere, a few restaurants, and more than enough private rooms for rent. At the town-end promontory, Maria Guelfi (tel. 812-178) and Sra. Silvana (tel. 513-830) offer rooms. Sra. Spora (tel. 812-293) offers rooms all over town. Villa Cecio rents cheap view rooms serves a tasty pasta and a mean house tiramisu (just above the town across the road, tel. 812-043).

Past the train station is the Corniglia beach and Albergo Europa, a bungalow village filled with Italians doing the Cinque Terre in 14 days.

▲▲▲**Vernazza—town #4:** With the closest thing to a natural harbor, overseen by a ruined castle and an old church, and only the occasional noisy slurping up of the train by the mountain to remind you these are the 1990s, Vernazza is my Cinque Terre home base.

The action is at the harbor, where you'll find a kids' beach, plenty of sunning rocks, outdoor restaurants, a bar hanging on the edge of the castle (great for evening drinks),

## Vernazza

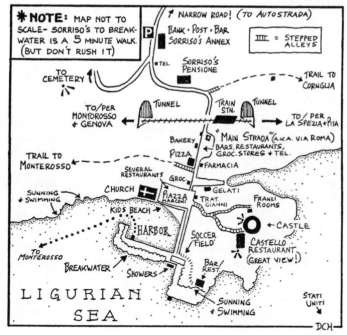

the tiny town soccer field, and a tailgate-party street market each Tuesday morning.

The town's thousand residents, proud of their Vernazzan heritage, brag that "Vernazza is locally owned. Portofino has sold out." Fearing the change it would bring, they stopped the construction of a major road into the town and region. Families are tight and go back centuries; several generations stay together. Leisure time is spent wandering lazily together up and down the main street. Sit on a bench and study Vernazza's passeggiata. Then explore the characteristic alleys called *carugi*. In October the cantinas are draped with drying grapes. In the winter the population shrinks, as many people move to more comfortable big-city apartments.

An hourly boat service connects Vernazza and Monterosso (L5,000 one way, L8,000 round-trip, calm summer days only). A 5-minute hike in either direction from Vernazza gives you a classic village photo op. Franco's Bar, with a panoramic terrace, is at the tower on the trail towards Corniglia.

**The Burned Out Sightseer's Visual Tour of Vernazza** (sit facing the town on the harbor breakwater):

**The Harbor**—In a moderate storm you'd be soaked as waves routinely crash over the *molo* (breakwater, built in 1972). Below the waterfall are the town's most popular sunning rocks. The train line (above) was built in 1930s. Plastered on the breakwater concrete is the schedule for the tiny shuttle-boat service from here to Monterosso. Vernazza's fishing fleet is down to three small fishing boats—the town's restaurants buy up everything they can catch. Vernazzans are more likely to own a boat than a car.

**The Castle**—On the far right, the castle still guards the town. The Belforte Bar (originally named "*bea forte*" or the "fort of warning screams," for the tower's function in pirating days) is a great perch. The lowest deck (follow the rope) is great for a glass of wine. (Inside the submarine-strength door, a photo of a major storm shows the entire tower under a wave.) The highest umbrellas mark the recommended Castello restaurant.

**The town**—From the lower castle, the houses were interconnected with an interior arcade—ideal for fleeing in times of attack. The pastel colors are regulated by a commissioner of good taste in the community government. The square before you is locally famous for some of the region's finest restaurants. The big red central house, the 12th century site where Genoan ships were built, used to be a guardhouse of sorts.

**Above the town**—The ivy-covered tower, another part of the city fortifications, reminds us of Vernazza's importance in the Middle Ages, when it was an important ally of Genoa (whose arch enemies were the other maritime republics of Pisa, Amalfi, and Venice). Franco's Bar, just behind the tower, welcomes hikers finishing (starting, or simply contemplating) the Corniglia-Vernazza hike with great town views. Vineyards fill the mountainside beyond the town. Wine production is down nowadays, as the younger residents choose less physical work. But locals still work their plots and proudly serve their family wine. A single steel train line (barely visible) winds up the gully behind the tower. This is a trenino line for the vintner's tiny service train.

**The church and city hall**—Vernazza's Ligurian Gothic church dates from 1318. The red house above and to the left of the spire is the city hall. Vernazza and Corniglia function as one community. In 1995, they elected their popular mayor, a Communist, to his second 5-year term. The party's banner (now the PDS or "people's democratic party of the left") decorates town walls. Also in the city hall is the elementary school. High school is in the "big city," La Spezia. Finally, on the top of the hill, with the best view of all, is the town cemetery where most locals already have a niche reserved (*tutto completo* . . . but a new wing is under construction).

▲▲**Monterosso al Mare–town #5:** This is a resort with cars, hotels, rentable beach umbrellas, and crowds. Walk east of the station through the tunnel for the Old World charm (and the about hourly boat to Vernazza). If you want a sandy beach, this is it. Adventurers may want to rent a rowboat or paddleboat and find their own private cove. There are several coves between #4 and #5, one with its own little waterfall (tourist office, 10:00–12:00, 17:00–20:00, closed Sunday afternoon, tel. 817-506).

## Sleeping and Eating in the Cinque Terre
### (L1,600 = about $1, zip code: 19018, tel. code: 0187)

While the Cinque Terre is too rugged for the mobs that ravage the Spanish and French coasts, it's popular with Italians. Room-finding can be tricky. Easter, August, and summer Fridays and Saturdays are tight. August weekends are miserable. If you're trying to avoid my readers, stay away from Vernazza and Mama Rosa's. Rich sun-worshipping softies like Monterosso. Winos and mountain goats prefer Corniglia. Students sleep cheap in Riomaggiore. Sophisticated Italians and Germans take Manarola. My home is Vernazza.

Real hotels, enjoying a demand that exceeds the local supply, are expensive, lazy, and require that you have dinner at the hotel in the summer. The budget alternative, a room in a private home, often gets you a more comfortable room for half the price. With any luck, you'll get a smashing view to boot. Any bar or restaurant has a line on local rooms for rent. Except for summer weekends and August, I'd arrive by midday without a reservation and ask on the street or in the local bars for *affitta camere* (rooms in private homes). If you're staying awhile, it's worth 30 minutes of shopping to get a place with a view balcony. Going direct cuts out a middleman and softens prices. Off season, empty rooms abound.

Sleep code: **S**=Single, **D**=Double/Twin, **T**=Triple, **Q**=Quad, **B**=Bath/Shower and Toilet, **CC**=Credit Card (Visa, MasterCard, Amex), **SE**=Speaks English (graded **A-F**); breakfast is included only in real hotels.

### Sleeping in Vernazza

Vernazza, the essence of the Cinque Terre, is my favorite town. (Have I mentioned that before?) There is just one real pension, but two restaurants have about a dozen simple rooms each, and a gaggle of locals rent extra rooms. Anywhere you stay here will require some climbing. Night noises can be a problem if you're near the station or the church bell tower. Address letters to 19018 Vernazza, Cinque Terre, La Spezia.

**Trattoria Gianni** (S-L55,000, D-L80,000, DB-L90,000, TB-L110,000, CC:VMA; Piazza Marconi 5, tel.

and fax 812-228, tel. 821-003, closed January–February, SE-D) rents 14 small, simple, comfortable doubles. Each is artfully decorated à la shipwreck, up lots of tight, winding, spiral stairs near the castle, where the views are Mediterranean blue and the only sounds you'll hear are the surf and the hourly ringing of the church bells (faintly through the night). The Franzi family splits the work: Gianni maintains the restaurant's good reputation, and perky Marisa (who doles out smiles like a rich gambler on a losing streak) runs the rooms. Pick up your keys at the restaurant/reception on the harbor square and hike up the stairs to #41 at the top. Alberto speaks English but communication can be difficult. No reply to your fax means they don't want to make a reservation. Ideally, telephone three days in advance and leave your first name and time of arrival.

**Pension Sorriso** knows it's the only real pension in town. Don't expect an exuberant welcome. Giovanni will hold a room for you without a deposit (D-L80,000, DB-L90,000, including breakfast, summertime dinner is required, and a room with dinner and breakfast costs L70,000 per person; CC:VM; 50 yards up the street from the train station, tel. 812224; while train sounds rumble through the front rooms of the main building, the annex up the street is quieter; closed January and February, SE-C). Call well in advance and reconfirm a few days before your arrival with another call. If you like sweet wine, you'll love his Sciachetra. Sciache-price (after much negotiation, with this book only), L3,000.

**Locanda Barbara** is run spittoon-style by Giacomo at the Taverna del Capitano (ten rooms with three public showers and WCs, S-L45,000, tiny loft D-L60,000, bigger D-L70,000; Piazza Marconi 21, tel. 812-201, closed December–January, Valerio speaks English and loves the girls). On the harbor square, many of his quiet, basic doubles (top floor of the big red vacant-looking building facing the harbor) have views. Their half-board deal gets you a discounted feast at their fine restaurant (good if you plan to really dine).

**Affitta Camere:** Vernazza is honeycombed with private rooms and apartments for rent. No English is spoken at these places. Most work with one of the eateries or shops on the main street. Ideally, get a local to call for you from your previous Italian stop. Each offers a handful of rooms and apartments (big, cheap for families, with kitchens) year-round. All are comfortable and inexpensive. Some are lavish, with killer views. **Affitta Camere da Nicolina** (three apartments and three rooms, L35,000 per person, great views; right over the harbor but close to the noisy church bell tower, ask at the harbor-side Vulnetia restaurant/pizzeria, tel. 821-193). **Affitta Camere da Filippo** (eight rooms, D-L60,000, DB-L70,000, T or Q-L80,000, no views, less noise; ask Francesca halfway down the main street at Trattoria Il Baretto, tel. 812-244). **Affitta Camere da Franco** (four quiet rooms, D-L60,000, DB with view-L70,000; going down the main street, turn left at the pharmacy, climb via Carattino to #64, tel. 821-082, German-speaking Franco runs the "Bar la Torre" at the top of the town. His wife, Anna Maria, speaks a little English. Franco's cigar-chomping cousin **Mike** (retired here after living in New York) has an apartment to rent next door (DB-L70,000, tel. 812-374). Mike can find you a place if he's full. The lady at the grocery store across from the gelateria has a line on rooms at **Affitta Camere da Giuseppina Villa** (three rooms including a gorgeous five-bed apartment with kitchen, D-L60,000, TB-L80,000, QB-L100,000, QuintB-L120,000; Via S. Giovanni Battista 5, tel. 812-026, SE-F) and **Antonia's** (DB overlooking main drag or a six-bed apartment, tel. 821-143). **Callo Giuseppe** (Piazza Marconi 26, tel. 715-744) has two fine rooms overlooking the harbor.

### Eating in Vernazza

If you're into Italian cuisine, Vernazza's restaurants are worth the splurge. The **Castello,** run by charming and English-speaking Monica and her family, serves good food just under the castle (12:00–22:00, closed Wednesday, tel. 812-296). **Trattoria Franzi** and **Trattoria del Capitano** (both harbor-front) are more atmospheric and famous. **Trattoria da Sandro** (often with an entertaining musical flair) is also popular. The more off-beat **Trattoria Piva** is less expensive, with good food and late-night guitar-strumming. The town's only gelateria is good, and most harborside bars will let you take your glass on a breakwater stroll. You can get good pizza by the L3,500 slice on the main street. Grocery store hours are 7:30–13:00, 17:00–19:30.

### Sleeping in Riomaggiore

**Youth Hostel Mama Rosa** is run with a splash of John
Belushi and a pinch of Mother Theresa by Rosa Ricci (an
almost-too-effervescent and friendly character who welcomes
backpackers at the train station), her husband, Carmine, and
their English-speaking son, Silvio. The only cheap dorm on
the Cinque Terre, this informal hostel is loved by the young,
rugged, and poor. It's a chaotic but manageable jumble with
the ambiance of a YMCA locker room filled with bunk beds
(L20,000 beds, price guaranteed through 1996, Piazza Unita
2, which is 20 yards in front of the station on the right past
the "sporting club" in an unmarked building; tel. 920-173 is
rarely answered, just show up without a reservation, no curfew). The ten coed rooms, with four to ten beds each, are
plain and basic with only roof vents. But a family atmosphere
rages with a popular self-serve kitchen, free laundry facilities,
trickle-down showers behind windblown curtains, and
Silvio's five unnamed cats (available as bed partners upon
request). This is one of those rare places where perfect
strangers become good friends with the slurp of spaghetti,
and wine supersedes the concept of ownership. You'll hardly
notice the cat-pee aroma. You can eat reasonably next door
at the **Vecchio Rio** restaurant (tel. 920-173, closed
Wednesday except in summer).

For affitta camere in Riomaggiore, try **Michielini Anna**
(five D-L70,000 with kitchens; Via Colombo 143, tel. 920-
411) and **Soggiorno Alle Cinque Terre** (near the castle at
the top of the town, Via de Gasperi 1, or Via Colombo 94,
tel. 920-587, Luciano Fazioli).

### Sleeping in Manarola

**Marina Piccola** has bright, modern rooms right on the
water, so they figure a warm welcome is unnecessary (nine
rooms, DB-L95,000, dinner never required, CC:VMA, tel.
920-103, fax 920-966).

Just up the hill, **Albergo ca' d'Andrean** (DB-L95,000;
Via A. Discovolo 25, tel. 920-040, fax 920-452, closed
November, Simone speaks English) is quiet, comfortable,
modern, and very hotelesque, with ten rooms and a cool garden complete with orange trees. One-night drop-ins are
okay, but not one-night reservations.

Farther up the street, **Casa Capellini** (D-L50,000, the *alta camera* on the top with a kitchen, private terrace, and knockout view-L70,000; take a hard right just off the church square, then two doors down the hill on your right, Via Antonio Discovolo 6, tel. 920-823, run by an older man and his daughter, who speak no English) is a private home renting four rooms.

### Eating in Manarola

**Il Porticciolo** (closed Wednesday) near the water on the main street, or **Trattoria da Billy** (closed Thursday), with the best view in town up in the residential area, are both reasonable for the overpriced area. At **Bar Aristade** (just after tunnel), Louis and his family party with guests at closing time.

### Sleeping in Monterosso
### (tel. code: 0187, post code: 19016)

Monterosso al Mare, the most beach-resorty of the five Cinque Terre towns, offers maximum comfort and ease. There are plenty of hotels, rentable beach umbrellas, shops, and cars. The TI (below the station, open 10:00–12:00 and 17:00–19:30, tel. 817-506) can find you a L40,000-per-person room in a private home.

**Hotel Villa Steno** (16 rooms, SB-L90,000, DB-L130,000, TB-L160,000, QB-L200,000, maximum prices in 1996 with this book, easy telephone reservations, with TV, telephones, and all the comforts; tel. 817-028, fax 817-056; 10-minute hike from the station at the top of the old town at Via Roma 109) features great view balconies, private gardens off some rooms, a tiny parking lot (free, but call to reserve spot), and the friendly help of English-speaking Matteo.

Near the station facing the beach is **Hotel Baia** (great beachfront balconies, modern and comfortable rooms, a real hotel, DB-L140,000 to L170,000, CC:VMA, tel. 817-363, fax 818-322), and the bare and basic **Pension Agavi** (eight rooms, DB-L100,000, including breakfast at beach bar, CC:VMA, tel. 817-171, fax 818-264). The tunnel then leads to the old town with **Albergo Marina** (D-L75,000, DB-L85,000, Via Buranco 40, tel. and fax 817-242 or 817-613, open March–October); the big, fancy, and a little more expensive **Albergo degli Amici** (next door at via Buranco 36, tel./fax 817-544 or 817-424); and **Restaurant/Pensione al Carugio** (rooms at top of town, D-L70,000, DB-L80,000, tel. 817-453) all require dinner mid-June through mid-September. Back in the new town, **Hotel Cinque Terre** (DB-L130,000, L170,000 in July and August, open April–October, CC:VMA, easy parking; Via IV November 21) is a slick new building with 51 similar rooms on the big road into town near the beach.

### Sleeping near the Cinque Terre

When all else fails, you can stay in a noisy bigger town like La Spezia. Each of these are within a block of the train station: **Hotel Terminus** (D-L50,000, DB-L60,000; Via Paleocapa 21, just down from the station, tel. 703-436) has filthy rooms with worn-out carpets, yellow walls, and old plumbing. **Albergo Parma** (D-L60,000, DB-L70,000, CC:VM; Via Fiume 143, 19100 La Spezia, tel. 743-010, fax 743-240), brighter and bleachy clean with TVs and folding metal furniture in the rooms, is located just below the station, down the stairs. The elegant old, newly restored **Hotel Firenze e Continentale** (DB-150,000 to 170,000, good group rates, CC:VMA, elevator, all the comforts but no parking; Via Paleocapa 7, 19122 La Spezia, tel. 739-757, fax 714-930, Maria Gabriella Liconti SE).

If you need the movie-star's Riviera, park your yacht at Portofino. Or you can settle down in nearby more personable **Santa Margherita Ligure** (20 min by bus from Portofino and an hour train-ride north of the Cinque Terre). While Portofino's velour allure is tarnished by snobby residents and a nonstop traffic jam in peak season, Santa Margherita tumbles easily downhill from its huggable train station. The town has a fun, resort character with a breezy promenade (TI: 0185/287-485). Buses go from the station and the harborfront to Portofino (3/hr, L2,000), but the boat does it with more class and without the traffic jams. Hikers count the SM-PF hike as one of the best on the Riviera. The friendly Sabini family offers 12 no-smoking rooms in the stately old **Hotel Nuova Riviera** (S-L50,000, SB-L55,000, D-L80,000, DB-L90,000, TB-L120,000 with a big breakfast, CC:V; easy parking, 10-minute walk from the station; walking or driving, follow signs to hospital, on Piazza Mazzini see hotel signs, Via Belvedere 10-2, 16038 S. Margherita Ligure, tel. 0185/287-403). Mama Sabini cooks a great dinner (L30,000) and Papa makes sure you enjoy the family wine.

## Transportation Connections
The five towns of the Cinque Terre are on a milk-run train line described earlier in this chapter. (Hourly trains connect each town with the others, La Spezia, and Genova.) While a few of the milk-run trains go to more distant points (Milan or Pisa), it's faster to change in La Spezia to a bigger train. **From La Spezia trains go to: Rome** (10/day, 4 hrs), **Pisa** (hrly, 60 min), **Florence** (hrly, 2½ hrs, change at Viareggio), **Milan** (hrly, 3 hrs, change in Genova).

Killing time in La Spezia's station? The station bar is OK, but a block down the street, **C'est Bon Casa del Cioccolato** serves crepes, gelati, and designer chocolates in turn-of-the-century splendor (10:00–13:00, 15:00–20:00, closed Tuesday, Piazza Saint Bon 1).

## Driving in the Cinque Terre
**Milan to the Cinque Terre (130 miles):** Drivers will speed south by autostrada from Milan, skirt Genoa, and drive along some of Italy's most scenic and impressive freeway toward the port of La Spezia. The road via Parma is faster but less scenic.

It's now possible to snake your car down the treacherous little road into the Cinque Terre and park above the town. This is risky in August and on Saturday or Sunday, when Italian day-trippers clog and jam the region. Throughout the tourist season you're likely to have to park far above the town. Vernazza has several parking lots above, and Riomaggiore has just built a huge but expensive garage. To drive into the Cinque Terre, leave the autostrada at Uscita Brugnato just west of La Spezia.

You can also park your car near the train station in La Spezia. Any spot with white lines and no sign should be free and legal. Look for diagonal parking spots in front of the station or on the streets below. Be patient; spots do open up. Confirm that parking is okay and leave nothing inside to steal. The "Autorimessa Stationi" garage immediately below the station can store your car for about L20,000 per day.

# MILAN (MILANO)

They say that for every church in Rome, there's a bank in Milan. Italy's second city and the capital of Lombardy, Milan is a hard-working, fashion-conscious, time-is-money city of 2 million. Milan is a melting pot of people and history. Its industriousness may come from the Teutonic blood of its original inhabitants, the Lombards, or from the region's Austrian heritage. Milan is Italy's industrial, banking, TV, publishing, and convention capital. The economic success of modern Italy can be blamed on this city of publicists and pasta power-lunches.

As if to make up for its shaggy parks and a recently-bombed-out feeling (WWII), its people are works of art. Milan is an international fashion capital with a refined taste. Window displays are gorgeous. Even the cheese comes gift-wrapped.

Three hundred years before Christ, the Romans called this place Mediolanum or "the central place." By the fourth century A.D., it was the capital of the western half of the Roman Empire. It was from here that Emperor Constantine issued the Edict of Milan, legalizing Christianity. After some barbarian darkness, medieval Milan rose to regional prominence under the Visconti and Sforza families. By the time of the Renaissance, it was called "the New Athens" and was enough of a cultural center for Leonardo to call it home. Then came 400 years of foreign domination (Spain, Austria, France, more Austria). Milan was a center of the 1848 revolution against Austria and helped lead Italy to unification in 1870.

Mussolini left a heavy Fascist touch on the city's architecture (such as the central train station). His excesses also led to the WWII bombing of Milan. But Milan rose again. The 1959 Pirelli Tower (the skinny, sleek skyscraper in front of the station) was a trendsetter in its day. Today the city has a pedestrian-friendly center, a great transit system, banks everywhere, and enough police to assure that those not looking for trouble won't find it.

Many tourists come to Italy for the past. But Milan is today's Italy, and no Italian trip is complete without seeing it. While it's not big on the tourist circuit, Milan has plenty

Milan

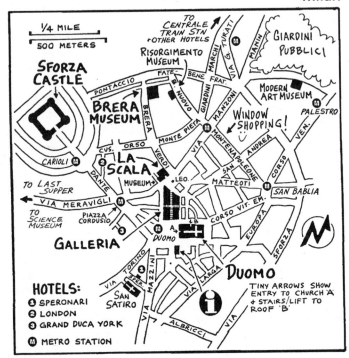

to see, it's no more expensive than other Italian cities, and it's well-organized and completely manageable. Our motto for Milan: don't worry, be clever.

## Planning Your Time

Okay, it's a big city. So you probably won't linger. But with two nights and a full day, you can gain an appreciation for the town and see the major sights. With 36 hours, I'd sleep in, and focus on, the center. Tour the Duomo and the La Scala museum, hit what art you like (Brera Gallery, Michelangelo's *Pietà*, Leonardo's *Last Supper*), browse through the elegant shopping area and the Gallery, and try to see an opera. Technology buffs could spend a day in the Science and Technology museum, while medieval art buffs could spend a day touring the city's very old churches. People-watchers and pigeon-feeders could spend an entire vacation never leaving sight of the Duomo.

Since Milan is a cold Italian plunge, and most flights to the U.S.A. leave Milan early in the morning, you may want to start your Italian trip softly by going directly from the Milan airport to Lake Como (Varenna) or the Cinque Terre (Vernazza) and seeing Milan at the end of your trip before flying home.

If you're just changing trains in Milan (as sooner or later you probably will) consider this 3-hour blitz: check your bag at the station, pick up a city map at the station TI, ride the subway to the Duomo, peruse the square, explore the cathedral's rooftop and interior, have a scenic coffee in the gallery, spin the Taurus, see the opera museum at La Scala, do the "Quadrilateral" high-fashion window-shopping stroll to Metro: Montenapoleone, and return by subway to the station. Art fans might make time for the Leonardo or the Michelangelo.

## Orientation (tel. code: 02)

### Tourist Information

There are two offices. The TI in the central train station (top level, with back to tracks, on the left next to a telephone center and the APT public transit info office) and on Piazza Duomo (to the right as you face the church, 8:30–20:00, Sunday 9:00–17:00, tel. 809-662 and 669-0532). Confirm your sightseeing plans and pick up the "Milan is Milan" map (with handy sketches of sights), the classy *Museums in Milan* booklet (with latest hours of top sights), the *Milano Mese* monthly (if you're interested in entertainment or special events), and the excellent *Youths in Milan* (listing shopping, restaurants, nightlife, and sports).

### Getting Around Milan

Use Milan's great subway system. The clean, spacious, fast, and easy three-line Metro zips you anywhere you may want to go. Transit tickets (L1,400 at newsstands, normally in the subway station) are good for one subway ride followed by 75 minutes of bus or tram travel. The L4,800 24-hour pass is a handy option (sold at major stations and some newsstands, 48 hours for L8,000). I've keyed all of the sightseeing to the subway system. While most sights are within a few blocks of each other, Milan is an exhausting city for walking, and the well-marked buses can be useful. Small groups go cheap and fast by

## Milan Metro

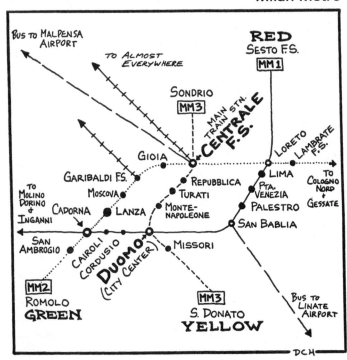

taxi (metered, drop charge L6,000 and L1,300 per km, often easiest to walk to a taxi stand rather than try to hail one).

Driving is bad enough in Milan to make the L35,000 a day you'll pay in a downtown garage a blessing. If you're driving, do Milan (and Lake Como) before or after you rent. If you have a car, use the huge, well-marked suburban Parcheggi, which offer affordable and safe parking at city-edge subway stations.

### Helpful Hints

**The Central Train Station:** This huge, sternly decorated, fascist-built station is a city and a sight in itself. Orient from the top level with your back to the tracks: train information (tel. 675-001) and baggage check on right; 24-hour drug store, TI, city transit information on left; airport shuttle-buses and Via Scarlatti (leading to recommended hotels) out the side exit on left; tickets and great supermarket/cafeteria (open 7:00–24:00) downstairs on right; metro station downstairs straight ahead.

You can buy tickets and arrange couchettes for the station price without the station lines near the Duomo at CIT (in Galleria Vittorio Emanuele, open until 19:00, tel. 669-0351), the Rinaldi Agency (on the Duomo Square), or American Express (up Via Verdi from La Scala, Via Brera 3, tel. 85571).

**Train Station to the Center:** For most quick visits, the giant city is one simple axis from the train station to Duomo. To get downtown from the station, go straight into the Metro, buy a L1,400 ticket (machines take paper and coins), follow signs for line 3 (yellow coded), direction S. Donato. To return to the station, take the yellow line 3, direction Sondrio. After one trip on the Metro, you'll dream up other excuses to use it.

**Theft Alert:** Be on guard. Milan's thieves target tourists. At the station and around the Duomo, thieves dressed as beggars roam, usually in gangs of three too-young-to-arrest children.

**Weather:** August is rudely hot and muggy. Locals who can, vacate, leaving the city just about dead. Those visiting in August find many shops closed and nightlife pretty quiet. I've listed which recommended hotels offer air conditioning.

## Sights—Milan

Compared to Rome and Florence, Milan's art is relatively mediocre, but the city does have unique and noteworthy sights. To maximize your time, use the Metro and note which places stay open through the siesta. I've listed sights in a logical geographical order.

There's much more to see in Milan than I've listed here. Its many thousand-year-old churches make it clear that Milan was an important beacon in the Dark Ages. Local guidebooks and the tourist information office can point you in the right direction if you have more time.

▲▲**Duomo**—Milan's cathedral, the city's centerpiece, is the third-largest church in Europe (after the Vatican's and Sevilla's). At 480 feet long and 280 feet wide, with 52 150-foot-tall sequoia pillars inside and more than 2,000 statues, the place seats 12,000 worshipers. If you do two laps, you've done your daily walk. Built from 1386 until 1810, this construction project originated the Italian phrase meaning

"never-ending": "like building a cathedral." It started Gothic
(notice the fine Gothic apse behind the altar) and was finished
under Napoleon. It's an example of the flamboyant, or "flame-
like," overripe final stage of Gothic, but architectural harmony
is not its forte. Note the giant stained-glass windows that try to
light the cavernous interior (open daily 7:00–19:00; enforced
dress code: no shorts or bare shoulders; Metro: Duomo).

The rooftop is a fancy forest of spires with great views of
the city, the square, and—on clear days—even the Swiss Alps.
Overlooking everything is the 13-foot-tall gilt Virgin Mary,
300 feet above the ground (climb the stairs for L5,000 or ride
the elevator for L7,000, 9:00–17:30, enter outside from the
north, clue: in Europe old churches face roughly east).

**Museo del Duomo**—The cathedral's museum is a scrap-
book of 600 years of cathedral history, offering a close look
at the stained glass, statues, and gargoyles (14 Piazza
Duomo, L7,000, open 9:30–12:30, 15:00–18:00, closed
Monday, Metro: Duomo).

▲**Piazza Duomo and nearby**—Piazza Duomo is a classic
European scene. Professionals scurry, label-conscious kids
loiter, young thieves peruse. For that creepy-crawly pigeons-
all-over-you experience, buy a bag of seed. Is the fountain the
Duomo facade in motion, or am I all wet? Behind the Duomo
is a pedestrian shopping zone. Within a block of the piazza
are a few interesting glimpses of old Milan. The center of
medieval Milan was Piazza Mercanti, a small square just
opposite the Duomo. It's a strangely peaceful place today.
The church of **Santa Maria presso San Satiro** (just off Via
Torino, a few yards past Via Speronari) was the scene of a
temper tantrum in 1242, when a losing gambler vented his
anger by hitting the baby Jesus in the Madonna-and-Child
altarpiece. Blood "miraculously" spurted out, and the beautiful little church has been on the pilgrimage trail ever since.
It's worth a visit to see the illusion of depth (*trompe l'oeil*),
designed by Bramante, behind the basically flat altar. The
**Duomo Center** is a modern mall with a mega music store,
book shop with maps and English travel guides, one-hour
photo service, decent pizzeria, and the recommended Ciao
cafeteria (with easy access WCs) upstairs.

▲▲**Galleria Vittorio Emanuele**—Milan is symbolized by
its great four-story-high, glass-domed arcade. This is the

place to turn an expensive cup of coffee into a good value with some of Europe's best people-watching. Stand under the central dome and enjoy the art above. For good luck, locals step on the testicles of the mosaic Taurus on the floor's zodiac design. Two local girls explained that it works better if you actually do a spin. (Metro: Duomo; under the dome is the CIT travel agency and an SIP cluster of public phone booths; the "Comune di Milan" office at the La Scala end has tourist information.)

▲▲**La Scala Opera House and Museum**—From the Galleria, you'll see a statue of Leonardo. He's looking at a plain but famous Neoclassical building, possibly the world's most prestigious opera house, Milan's Teatrale alla Scala. La Scala opened in 1778 with an opera by Antonio Salieri (of *Amadeus* fame). While tickets are as hard to get as they are expensive, anyone can have a peek into the grand theater from a box connected to the museum. Opera buffs will love the museum's extensive collection of things that would mean absolutely nothing to the MTV crowd: Verdi's top hat, Rossini's eyeglasses, Toscanini's baton, Fettucini's pesto, and original scores, busts, portraits, and death masks of great composers and musicians (L5,000, Monday–Saturday 9:00–12:00 and 14:00–18:00, and summer Sunday mornings; Metro: Duomo, tel. 805-3418).

The opera season is December–July; September–November is for ballet and classical concerts. La Scala is closed in August. Ask about the sky-high but affordable gallery seats that are often available two hours before the performance on the day of the show, or L10,000 standing room, which can be purchased in advance (tel. 720-03744, showtime usually 20:00).

▲**World Class Window-shopping**—The "Quadrilateral," the elegant, high-fashion shopping area around Via Montenapoleone, is worth a wander. In this land where cigarettes are still chic, the people-watching is as fun as the window-shopping. Via Montenapoleone and Via Spiga are the best streets. From La Scala, walk up Via Manzoni to the Metro stop: Montenapoleone, browse down Montenapoleone to Piazza San Babila and then down the pedestrians-only Corso Vittorio Emanuele II to the Duomo.

**Museums of Milan and of Contemporary History**—These museums (both at Via Sant'Andrea 6) are free and offer a quick walk through wall-sized pages of Milan's past, including the especially interesting 1914 to 1945 period (9:30–17:30, often with a lunch break, closed Monday; Metro: Montenapoleone).

▲**The Brera Art Gallery**—Milan's top collection of paintings (Italian, 14th to 20th centuries) is without a doubt world class, but it can't top Rome or Florence. Established in 1809 to house Napoleon's looted art, the gallery's highlights include works by the Bellini brothers, Caravaggio (*Supper at Emmaus*), Raphael (*Wedding of the Madonna*), and Mantegna's textbook example of feet-first foreshortening (*The Dead Christ*). Even if you don't go into the gallery, see Napoleon nude (by Canova) in the courtyard and wander through the art school on the ground floor (L8,000, open 9:00–17:30, Sunday 9:00–12:30, closed Monday; Metro: Lanza, tel. 722-631).

▲**Risorgimento Museum**—This tells the interesting story (if you speak Italian or luck out as I did with a bored and talkative English-speaking guard) of Italy's rocky road to unity: from Napoleon (1796) to the victory in Rome (1870). It's just around the corner from the Brera Gallery at Via Borgonuovo 23 (free, 9:30–17:30, closed Monday; Metro: Montenapoleone).

▲**Sforza Castle (Castello Sforzesco)**—This immense, much-bombed-and-rebuilt brick fortress is exhausting at first sight. It can only be described as heavy. But its courtyard has a great lawn for picnics and siestas, and its free museum is filled with interesting medieval armor, furniture, early Lombard art, an Egyptian collection, and, most important, Michelangelo's unfinished *Rondanini Pietà*. Michelangelo died while still working on this piece, which hints at the elongation of the mannerist style that would follow. This is a rare opportunity to enjoy a Michelangelo with no crowds (9:30–17:30, closed Monday, free; Metro: Cairoli).

▲**Leonardo da Vinci's** *Last Supper* (**Cenacolo**)—This Renaissance masterpiece is in the refectory of the church of Santa Maria delle Grazie. It captures the emotional moment when Jesus says to his disciples, "One of you will betray me," and 11 wonder nervously, "Lord, is it I?" Notice Judas with his 30 pieces of silver, looking pretty guilty. This ill-fated masterpiece suffers from Leonardo's experimental use of oil rather than the normal fresco technique. Deterioration began within six years of its completion. The church was bombed in WWII, but the *Last Supper* survived. Now undergoing extensive restoration, it's a faded mess with most of the original paint gone and much of the rest behind scaffolding (L12,000, 8:00–14:00, closed Monday; Metro: Cadorno).

▲**National Leonardo da Vinci Science and Technology Museum (Museo Nazionale della Scienza e Tecnica)**— The spirit of Leonardo lives here in Italy's top science and technology museum. Most tourists visit for the hall of Leonardo designs illustrated in wooden models, but Leonardo's mind is just as easy to appreciate by paging through a coffee-table edition of his notebooks in any bookstore. The rest of this immense collection of industrial cleverness is fascinating, with plenty of push-button action (no English descriptions): trains, radios, old musical instruments, computers, batteries, telephones, chunks of the first transatlantic cable, and on and on (L10,000, Via San Vittore 21, bus #50 or #58 from the Duomo, or Metro: San Ambrogio, 9:30–16:50, closed Monday).

**Nightlife**—For evening action, check out the arty, student-oriented Brera area in the old center and Milan's formerly Bohemian, now gentrified "Little Venice," the Navigli neighborhood. Specifics change so quickly that it's best to rely on the entertainment information in periodicals from the TI.

## Sleeping in Milan
### (L1,600 = about $1, tel. code: 02)
Milan has plenty of simple, central, and reasonable accommodations. Prices are the same throughout the year. None includes breakfast, which, if available, is a lousy value (eat down the street in a café). I have tried to minimize traffic noise problems in my listings. All are within a few minutes' walk of Milan's fine subway system. Anytime but summer, the city can be completely jammed by conventions; summer is usually wide open. Hotels cater more to business travelers than to tourists. I've limited recommendations to two areas: in the center near the Duomo and near the train station.

Sleep code: **S**=Single, **D**=Double/Twin, **T**=Triple, **Q**=Quad, **B**=Bath/Shower and Toilet, **CC**=Credit Card (Visa, MasterCard, Amex).

### Sleeping in the City Center (near the Duomo)

The Duomo (cathedral) area is thick with people-watching, reasonable eateries, and the major sightseeing attractions (just four stops on the Metro from the central train station).

**Hotel Speronari** is my home in Milan (S-L55,000, SB-L70,000, D-L75,000, DB-L80,000, DBWC-L115,000–L130,000, prices good in 1996 with this book, hallway showers-L5,000, CC:VM; ideally located on a pedestrian street off Via Torino, 1 block off the far left end of the Piazza Duomo with back to church, at Via Speronari 4, 20123 Milano, tel. 864-61125, fax 720-03178). It's perfectly located, safe and quiet, on a great pedestrian street full of fun delis and food shops, run by genteel and helpful Paolo Isoni, Maurizio, and family. It's bright and clean with no views or traffic noise. Consider breakfast at the Flut Bar across the intersection (from 7:00, closed Sunday).

**London Hotel** (30 rooms, SB-L100,000, D-L120,000, DB-L150,000, TB-L190,000, breakfast L12,000, CC:VM; elevator, TVs, telephones, air-conditioned; near Metro: Cairoli at Via Rovello 3, tel. 720-20166, fax 805-7037, SE-A) is a fine little hotel with all the comforts on a handy quiet street in the center.

**Hotel Grand Duca di York** (SB-L140,000, DB-L195,000, TB-L250,000, with breakfast, CC:VA; air-con; near Piazza Cordusio at Via Moneta 1, 20123 Milano, tel. 874-863, fax 869-0344, SE-A) is a real hotel with simple rooms and lavish public spaces stuck in the middle of banks and big-city starkness 3 blocks off the Duomo square.

Other one-star hotels in the center with rooms in the L70,000 range include: **Alba d'Oro** (5 Viale Piave, tel. 760-23880), **Hotel Kent** (Via F. Corridoni 2, tel. 551-87635), and **Hotel Roma** (4 Corso Lodi, tel. 583-09560). Nicer but farther out is **Hotel Del Sud** (at the Brenta Metro stop, Corso Lodi 74, tel. 569-3457).

### Sleeping near the Train Station

With Milan's fine Metro, you can get anywhere in town in a flash. For pure convenience and price, this is a handy, if dreary, area. The area between the station and Corso Buenos Aires has a seedy, frumpy, prostitutes-after-dark problem. Corso Buenos Aires is a bustling main shopping and people-watching drag. All listings below are within two subway stops or a 10-minute walk of the station. Via Scarlatti leads to the first five listings—leave the station's upper hall (with your back to the tracks) to the left. Across the parking lot, Hotel Bristol marks the start of Via Scarlatti. Business hotels employ sleazy hustlers in fake police uniforms to sell their push-list rooms. The deals are good, but honor (or at least cancel) any reservations you've made elsewhere. The self-service **Lavanderia Ondablu** (19 Via Scarlatti, 8:00–22:00 daily) washes and dries a 6½-kilo load in an hour for L12,000. The bar on the corner of Scarlatti and Settala is good for breakfast (cheap ham toasties and good seats).

**"The Best" Hotel** (SB-L70,000, DB-L90,000; at Via B. Marcello 83, 20124 Milano, tel. 294-04757, fax 201-966, elevator, phones in the room, free parking on square) actually is the best in its price range. It's run by friendly, English-speaking Luciana and Peter, with a homey lounge and rooms overlooking either a garden or an ugly car-filled square that becomes an open-air market on Tuesdays and Saturdays. Request a *tranquillo giardino* room. From the station, walk straight down Via Scarlatti, at Piazza Hanky Panky turn right, and you'll see it. (Don't miss it. On the next corner is a home for prostitutes having a hard time retiring.) In a sad battle of self-congratulatory names, the **Hotel Paradiso** next to "The Best" is sleepable, but fails to live up to its name (D-L70,000, DB-L90,000, hourglass-shaped elevator; Via B. Marcello 85, tel. 204-9448).

**Hotel Andreola** is a four-star business hotel that hires hustlers to bring in travelers during slow times when it has door-breaker prices. The rooms are little better than my other listings, but the location—a block from the station—is ideal, and the lounge-lizard public places will make you feel like you're in the U.S.A. While not worth its regular rates, from mid-June through August and during odd periods through the rest of the year, you can telephone and strike a deal. Call three days in advance (maximum low season prices: SB-L100,000, DB-L140,000, TB-L190,000 with breakfast, use breakfast as a bargaining chip, hustlers sell the rooms for even less, CC:VMA; air-con, elevator, request *tranquillo* back side; Via Scarlatti 24, tel. 670-9141, fax 667-13198, SE-A).

**Hotel Due Giardini** (S-L45,000, D-L65,000, T-L90,000, prices promised through 1996 with this book; walk

5 blocks down Via Scarlatti, right to Via Settala 46, 20124
Milano, tel. 295-21093, fax 295-16933, Salis family,
Giuseppe speaks English) is a plain, simple, and musty flop-
house with a peaceful garden.

**Hotel Serena** (DB-L130,000 with breakfast, CC:VMA;
a block off Corso Buenos Aires near the Lima Metro stop,
Via Boscovich 59, tel. 295-22152, fax 294-04958) is plain,
quiet, and handy with lot of stairs. Follow Scarlatti to the
huge Buenos Aires, turn right for a couple of blocks, then
right again on Boscovich.

**Hotel Virgilio** (S-L48,000, SB-L73,000, D-L75,000,
DB-L110,000, prices good through '96 with this book,
breakfast-L10,000, CC:VMA; elevator; air-con L10,000
extra; follow via Scarlatti, at Via Settala turn left until you
reach Via P.L. da Palestrina 30, 20124 Milano, tel. 669-
1337, fax 669-82587) is dark and designed for smoking busi-
nessmen, but a reasonable value for someone looking for a
real hotel near the station.

**Hotel Casa Mia**, reopening newly renovated in July
1996 (SB-L55,000 to L65,000, DB-L80,000 to L95,000 with
breakfast, CC:VM; a stone's throw from the Piazza della
Repubblica Metro stop, Viale Vittorio Veneto 30, tel. 657-
5249, fax 655-2228), is a simple, quiet, hardworking
Loguercio family affair, rare in downtown Milan.

## Eating in Milan

This is a fast-food city. But fast food in a fashion capital
isn't a burger and fries. The bars, delis, rosticcería, and
self-services cater to people with plenty of taste and more
money than time.

You'll find delightful eateries all over town. Notice the
fine (and free) munchies that appear late in the afternoon in
many bars. A L3,000 beer can (if you're either likable or
discreet) becomes a light meal.

### Eating near the Duomo and
### Recommended Hotel Speronari

For a low-stress affordable lunch facing the Duomo square,
eat at **Ciao**, a shiny, modern, second-floor self-serve cafeteria (daily 11:30–15:00, 18:00–23:00, view tables from top
"terrace" floor, easy public WC). For a more challenging

adventure in eating Milanese, and a classy hotel room dinner, hit the colorful shops on Via Speronari (off Via Torino, a block southwest of Piazza Duomo: rosticcería; classy cheese, bread, and produce shops). **Peck**, nearby on Via G. Cantu, off Via Dante, is an elegant rosticcería. The **Peck Snack Bar** (a block toward the Duomo, just off Via Orefici at Via Victor Hugo 4, 7:30–21:00, closed Sunday) is a classy cafeteria. Fast-food cheapskates eat facing the Duomo at Burghy or Amico.

For pizza, the **Pizzeria Dogana** at Via Dogana 3, serves up cheap, hearty, and tasty pizzas (indoor/outdoor, closed Monday). Worth the 2-blocks-farther walk, the local favorite, **Ristorante Pizzeria Calafuria Unione**, serves tasty L10,000 pizzas in a no-smoking room (where Via Falcone hits Via dell' Unione at Via dell' Unione 8, tel. 864-62091, closed Sunday).

**Ristorante Familiare della Cimbraccola** offers a dinner you'll never forget. Stefanini Arnaldo, with his imaginary mother in the kitchen, merrily stuffs his guests with a series of appetizers, pastas, and entrees, with endless wine, water, coffee, *grappa*, and three desserts—all for L30,000. Stefanini's found his niche, and you're at his mercy. The food is Tuscan and plain—the antipasti a bit old and dry—the walls are plastered with model ships, pipes, and dusty paper money; the clientele is local; and the ambience is one of disbelief (an olive toss off Via Dante, midway between the Duomo and the Fortress at Via S. Tomaso 8, tel. 869-2250, closed Sunday).

Floodlit Mary gazes down from the top of the Duomo on the **Odeon Gelateria** for good reason (next to Burghy on Duomo square, open nightly until 1:00).

### Eating near the Train Station and Recommended "Best" Hotel

**Ristorante Salernitano** (Via Vitruvio 8), **Trattoria Leo**, and several places on Via Tadino are reasonable, friendly, and relaxed. To eat classy in this area, try the bright, elegant, and full-of-fish **Ristorante Mediterranea Di Valerio e Maurizio** (Piazza Cincinnato 4, tel. 295-22076, closed Sunday).

Breakfast is a bad value in hotels and fun in bars. It's okay to quasi-picnic. Bring in a box of juice (*plastic bicchiere* = plastic cups) and some bananas (or whatever) and order a toasted

ham-and-cheese panino (*calda* = hot/toasted) or croissant with
your cappuccino.

## Transportation Connections
**Trains from Milan Central Station to: Venice** (hrly, 3
hrs), **Florence** (hrly, 3 hrs), **Genoa** (hrly, 2 hrs), **Rome**
(hrly, 5 hrs), **Brindisi** (4/day, 10–12 hrs), **Cinque Terre**
(hrly, 3–4 hrs to La Spezia, sometimes changing in Genoa,
trains from La Spezia to the villages go hourly), **Varenna** on
Lago di Como (the small line to Lecco/Sondrio/Tirano
leaves from Milan's Central Station every 2 hours for the
1-hour trip to Varenna—maybe 9:15, 12:15, 14:15, 16:15,
18:15), **Como** (maybe :25 after each hour, 30 min, ferries go
from Como to Varenna).

   **International destinations: Amsterdam** (4/day, 14 hrs),
**Barcelona** (2 changes, 17 hrs—before paying extra for the
Pablo Casals express, consider flying), **Bern** (7/day, 4 hrs),
**Frankfurt** (5/day, 9 hrs), **London** (2/day, 18 hrs), **Munich**
(5/day, 8 hrs), **Nice** (5 day, 7–10 hrs), **Paris** (4/day, 8 hrs),
**Vienna** (4/day, 14 hrs). Milan train info: tel. 67500.

### Milan's Airports
Most international flights land at Milan's surprisingly cozy
**Malpensa** airport, 30 miles northwest of the city. Customs
guards fan you through, and even the sniffing dog seems
friendly. The airport bank has fine rates (Banco di Milano,
8:00–20:00). Visit the bus/train information and ticket
office (convenient chance to buy train tickets and check
departure times for train trips from Milan, buy a L10,000
telephone card, and confirm your hotel). A shuttle bus connects Malpensa and the Central train station (2/hr, 45-min
ride, L12,000, tel. 400-99280). Taxis into Milan cost $80.

   Milan's second airport is **Linate** (5 miles to the east,
linked by regular shuttle-buses with Piazza Luigi di Savoia at
the central train station, 3/hr, 5:40–21:00, L4,000 tickets
from driver, tel. 669-84509).

   For flight information for either airport, call 02/748-
52200. (British Air, tel. 738-2028; American Airlines, tel.
290-04919; Alitalia, tel. 26852.)

# LAKE COMO (LAGO DI COMO)

Commune with nature where Italy is welded to the Alps, in the lovely Italian Lakes District. The million-lire question is: Which lake? For the best mix of accessibility, scenery, offbeatness, and a complete dose of Italian-lakes wonder and aristocratic-old-days romance, Lake Como is my choice. And the sleepy town of Varenna, at midlake, is my home base. Bustling Milan, just an hour away, doesn't even exist. Now it's your turn to be *chiuso per ferie* (closed for vacation).

Lake Como, lined with elegant 19th-century villas, crowned by snowcapped mountains, and buzzing with ferries, hydrofoils, and little passenger ships, is a good place to take a break from the intensity and obligatory turnstile culture of central Italy. It seems half the travelers you'll meet have tossed their itineraries into the lake and are actually relaxing.

Today the hazy lazy lake's only serious industry is tourism. Thousands of lakeside residents travel daily to nearby Lugano, in Switzerland, to find work. The area's isolation and flat economy have left it pretty much the way the 19th-century Romantic poets described it.

## Planning Your Time

If relaxation's not on your agenda, Lake Como shouldn't be either. Even though there are no essential activities, plan for at least two nights, so you'll have an uninterrupted day to see how slow you can get your pulse. The scenic approach is by train from Milan to Como (50-minute rides usually leaving at :25 past each hour) where you'll catch the 2-hour boat ride up the lake to Varenna. Knowing how great Varenna is, I zip there directly by train (1 hour from Milan), get set up, and limit my activities to midlake (Varenna, Bellagio, and Menaggio).

## Orientation

### Getting Around Lake Como

With the parking problems, constant traffic jams, and expensive car ferries, this is no place to drive if you don't need to.

Lake Como

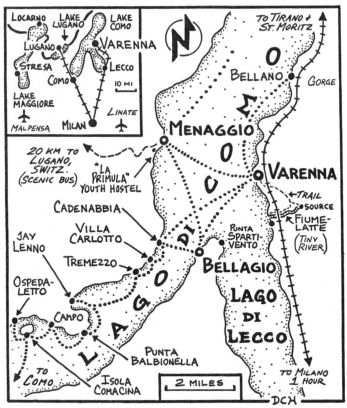

Lake Como is Milan's quick getaway. And, regardless of your destination at midlake, Varenna—with its handy Milan train connection—is the gateway. From Milan's Central Station, catch a train heading for Sondrio (but be certain it stops in Varenna). Trains leave about every two hours. Sit on left for great lake views. Get off at Varenna-Esino.

Lago di Como is well served by boats and hydrofoils. The lake service is divided into three parts: north-south from Como to Colico; midlake between Varenna, Bellagio, Menaggio, and Cadenabbia (Villa Carlotta); and the southeastern arm to Lecco. Unless you're going through Como, you'll probably limit your cruising to the midlake service (info: tel. 031/579-211). Boats go about hourly between Varenna, Menaggio, and Bellagio (15 min, L4,500 per hop).

Passengers pay the same for car or passenger ferries, but 50 percent more for the enclosed, stuffy, less scenic but very quick hydrofoil. The free schedule (at tourist office, hotel, or boat dock) lists times and prices. Stopovers aren't allowed, and there's no break for round-trips, so buy a ticket for each ride. The one-day L10,000 Midlake pass saves you money if you make three rides. (Boat-schedule literacy tips: *Feriale* = workdays, Monday–Saturday. *Festivo* = Sunday and holidays. *Partenze da* = departing from.)

While you can easily drive around the lake, the road is narrow, congested, and lined by privacy-seeking walls, hedges, and tall fences. It costs L12,000 to take your car onto a ferry. And parking is rarely easy where you need it, especially in Bellagio. Park in Varenna (free by the ferry dock or on the main road south of town) and cruise.

Don't try to go to Switzerland from Lake Como. As WWII was winding up, Mussolini tried. Locals caught him at the north end of the lake, shot both him and his mistress (April 28, 1945), and hung his body publicly in Milan. Dead meat.

## Sights—Lake Como

▲▲▲**Varenna**—This town (of 800 people) is the best of all lake worlds. Easily accessible by train, on the less-driven side of the lake, Varenna has a romantic promenade, a tiny harbor, narrow lanes, and its own villa. It's the right place to savor a lakeside cappuccino or *aperitivo*. The town is quiet at night. The *passerella* (lakeside walk) is adorned with caryatid lovers pressing silently against each other in the shadows.

There's wonderfully little to do in Varenna. A tiny public beach is just past the ferry dock, and a tiny private one (L2,000 entry, showers, rentable chairs and cabins, bar, open only in summer) is just beyond that. The ladies in the harborfront dress shop overcharge for their rental boats. The cooper welcomes gawkers in his grappa-keg-making shop. Varenna's TI is on the main square (Pro Local, open only 10:00–12:30, tel. 0341/830-367).

The best cheap meals in Varenna are at the **pizzeria** (19:00–24:00, closed Monday, good pizzas and spaghetti, #1, Piazza San Giorgio, below Hotel Royal Victoria, across from the church). **Ristorante del Sole** serves tasty Naples-style

### Varenna

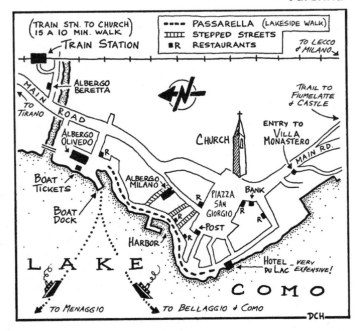

pizzas at Piazza San Giorgio 17 (tel. 830-206). The royal
**Hotel du Lac** serves an elegant-yet-affordable lunch with
lakeside splendor. For a splurge, consider the **Vecchia
Varenna** restaurant, with its romantic loggia on the old harborfront (L50,000 meals, tel. 830-793, closed Monday) or
the **Albergo Olivedo** (equal food, less ambiance, L40,000
meals). For the same great view but much cheaper eating,
the harborfront **Nilus Bar** serves dinner crepes, salads, and
hot sandwiches with a smile. For cold, sweet, and fruity
treats, check out the harborfront **Frulleria/frapperia**. The
**grocery stores** near the main square have all you need for a
classy balcony or breakwater picnic dinner. (For accommodations, see Sleeping, below.)

A steep trail leads to Varenna's ruined castle capping
the hill above. It's as intriguing as a locked-up castle can be.
While you can't get in, there's a fine view and a peaceful,
traffic-free, one-chapel, no-coffee town behind it. A kilometer south of Varenna, the town of Fiumelatte is named for its
milky river. It's the shortest in Italy (800 feet) and runs only

during the tourist season. Local brochures lay out a walk
from Varenna to the Fiumelatte to the castle and back.
▲**Bellagio**—The self-proclaimed "Pearl of the Lake" is a
classy combination of tidiness and Old World elegance. If
you don't mind that "tramp in a palace" feeling, it's a fine
place to surround yourself with the more adventurous of the
posh travelers and shop for umbrellas and ties. The heavy
curtains between the arcades keep the visitors and their poo-
dles from sweating. Steep-stepped lanes rise from the harborfront, and the shady promenade leads to the Lido
(beach). While Johnny Walker and jewelry sell best at lake
level, the locals shop up the hill. The town has a tourist
office (Piazza Chiesa next to the church, tel. 031/950-204,
loosely open 9:00–12:00, 15:00–18:00, closed Sunday and
Tuesday), a worth-a-look church, and some surprisingly
affordable funky old hotels (listed below). For something off-
beat to do in Bellagio, clink glasses with **Tony, the Wine
King**. He runs a wild little cantina behind the camera shop
near the ferry dock (11:00–13:00, 14:00 or 15:00–19:30,
Salita Genazzini 3, tel. 950-935). Tony, who speaks English,
greets you with an empty glass and ten or 15 open bottles of
wine and booze to taste. The tasting's free. His prices are
great. After 50 years in his cantina, he looks darn good.

Bellagio, the administrative capital of the midlake
region, is located where the two southern legs of the lake split
off. For an easy break in a park with a great view, wander
right on out to the crotch. Meander past the rich and famous
Hotel Villa Serbelloni, past the little Ortofrutta market (get
fruit and juice for the viewpoint, 8:00–12:30, 14:30–18:30,
closed Monday), and walk 5 minutes to the Punta
Spartivento, literally "the point that divides the wind." You'll
find a Renoir atmosphere complete with a bar, a tiny harbor,
and a chance to sit on a bench and gaze north past Menaggio
and Varenna and the end of the lake to the Swiss Alps.
▲**Menaggio**—Just 8 miles from Lugano in Switzerland,
Menaggio has more urban bulk than its neighbors. Since
the lake is getting a bit dirty for swimming, consider its
fine public pool. This is the starting point for a few hikes.
Only 25 years ago, these trails were used by cigarette
smugglers. As many as 180 people a night would sneak
through the darkness from Switzerland back into Italy with

tax-free cigarettes. The hostel (see Sleeping, below) has information about catching the bus to trailheads on nearby Mount Grona. The hostel also rents bikes for a 40-kilometer, 4-hour bike trip: pedal 15 level kilometers from the hostel to Argegno, catch the lift to 2,500-foot-high Pigra (L5,000 with bike), and coast scenically back to Lake Lugano and then 10 km along the traffic-filled road home to Menaggio. This is physically demanding and can be scary because of traffic.

**Villa Carlotta**—This is the best of Lake Como's famed villas. I see the lakes as a break from Italy's art, but if you're in need of a place that charges admission (L10,000, 9:00–18:00 daily in season), Villa Carlotta offers an elegant Neoclassical interior, a famous Canova statue, and a garden (its highlight, best in spring). If you're touring one villa on the lake, this is probably the best. Nearby Tremezzo and Cadenabbia are pleasant lake-side resorts an easy walk away. Boats serve all three places.

**Como**—On the southwest tip of the lake, Como has a good, traffic-free old town; an interesting Gothic/Renaissance cathedral; and a pleasant lakefront with a promenade (TI tel. 031/274-064). It's an easy walk from the boat dock to the train station (from Milan in 30 minutes, usually leaving at :25 past each hour). Boats leave Como about hourly for midlake (ferries take 2 hours and cost L9,500; hydrofoils do the trip in an hour for L14,300; tel. 031/304-060).

## Sleeping on Lake Como
### (L1,600 = about $1)

The area is tight in August, snug in July, and wide open most of the rest of the year. Many places close in winter. All places listed are family-run, have lake-view rooms, and some English is spoken. (Request "*con vista.*") View rooms are given (usually for no extra cost) to those who telephone reservations and request "*camera con vista.*" If ever I were to kill, it would be here . . . for the view. Prices go soft in the off-season. Shop around by phone to confirm the view and price. If you fail, ask to get a view balcony for your second night.

Sleep code: **S**=Single, **D**=Double/Twin, **T**=Triple, **Q**=Quad, **B**=Bath/Shower and Toilet, **CC**=Credit Card (**V**isa, **M**asterCard, **A**mex), **SE**=Speaks English (graded **A-F**).

## Sleeping in Varenna ($1 = about 1,600 lire, tel. code: 0341, postal code: 22050)

**Albergo Olivedo**, facing the ferry dock, is a neat and tidy old hotel (prices vary with season and views: S-L50,000 to L75,000, D-L70,000 to L100,000, DB-L95,000 to L120,000, including breakfast; plenty of sit-down tubs with "telephone showers" and toilets across the hall, tel. 830-115, Laura SE and runs a good restaurant). To reserve by telephone, leave a credit-card number for security (but you'll need to pay with cash). Each room has squeaky hardwood floors, World War II furniture, and Art Nouveau mattresses. Rooms without baths have glorious little lake-view balconies. Rooms with baths lack views. It's a fine place to hang out and watch the children, boats, and sun come and go.

**Albergo Milano** (DB-L120,000, a little more in July and August, discounted for three nights in off-season or with a side view; optional breakfast on the terrace with cheese, a trolley of sweets, and Amelia's charm is worth the L12,000, CC:VM; Via XX Settembre 29, 22050 Varenna/Como, tel. and fax 830-298, ideally reserve with a fax and credit-card number), located right in the old town, is your best splurge. Friendly but non-English-speaking Amelia obviously loves serving people. Her son, Giovanni, speaks English. Each of the eight rooms is comfortable and comes with great plumbing. Lakeside rooms 1 and 2 are smaller with royal balconies. Lakeside rooms 5 and 6 are bigger with small balconies. This place screams *luna di miele* (honeymoon).

**Albergo Beretta** (D-L70,000, DB-L90,000, D rooms 5 and 9 have view balconies, no breakfast, tel. 830-132), off the water on the main road below the station, has good beds but minimal character. **Albergo del Sol** (D-L45,000; Piazza San Giorgio 17, tel. 830-206) is a six-room, one-tub place on the main square offering decent cheap beds.

### Sleeping in Bellagio

**Hotel du Lac** (DB-L180,000 with breakfast, less off season, CC:VM; L12,000 garage; Leoni family, 22021 Bellagio/Como, tel. 031/950-320, fax 951-624) is your best splurge. Right on the harbor with a roof garden, it's completely remodeled (air conditioning, TVs, mini-bars) and gives you the old flavor with absolutely no loss of comfort. The cozier

**Hotel Florence** (DB-L175,000 with breakfast, June–October, less in April and May, closed off-season, CC:VMA; elevator, hand-held showers only; tel. 950-342, fax 951-722) is hardwood, pastel and family-run, with a rich touch of Old World elegance. **Hotel Suisse** (DB-L75,000, optional L10,000 breakfast; Piazza Mazzini 8, 22021 Bellagio, tel. 031/950-335, fax 951-755, CC:VM) somehow landed right on the harbor next to the stuffy places. It's frumpy with simple rooms, hardwood floors, fine bathrooms, terrible beds, and some great views and balconies (L5,000 extra). The similar one-star **Hotel Roma** (D-L55,000, DB-L70,000, L6,000 breakfast, CC:VMA; elevator, simple inexpensive restaurant, tel. 031/950-424, fax 951-966) cranes its well-worn neck behind and above Hotel Suisse. The fifth floor has the cheapest rooms (shower down the hall) with great view balconies. **Hotel Giardinetto** (D-L55,000, DB-L68,000, L9,000 breakfast; Via Roncati 12, tel. 031/950-168, SE-A), near the tourist office and about 100 steps above the waterfront, offers squeaky-clean, cool, and quiet rooms—some with a view balcony, above a breezy and peaceful garden. It's warmly run by the Ticozzi family. For a good back-street L25,000 dinner, try **Trattoria S. Giacomo** (Salita Servelloni 45, tel. 950-329).

### Sleeping in Menaggio
**La Primula Youth Hostel** is a rare hostel. Family-run for ten years by Ty and Paola (and their Australian sidekick, Paul), it caters to a quiet, savor-the-lakes crowd and offers the only cheap beds in the area. Located just south of the Menaggio dock (you'll see the sign from the boat), it has a view terrace, lots of games, a members' kitchen, a washing machine, bike rentals (L15,000 a day, L30,000 for non-hostelers), discount tickets to Villa Carlotta, discount boat passes, easy parking, and a creative and hardworking staff. (Closed 10:00–17:00 daily and from mid-November to mid-March, L14,000 per night in a four- to six-bed room with sheets and breakfast, L15,000 with private plumbing, hearty dinners with a local flair and wine are only L13,000; reserve dinner by 18:00). Ty and Paola print a newsletter to advertise their activities programs (inexpensive 14-day Italian language, 3- to 7-day hikes, bike trips, cooking

classes). The bike ride described under Sights—Menaggio is a favorite with hostelers. Show your copy of this book and receive a free La Primula recipe book. (Ostello La Primula, Via 4 Novembre 86, 22017 Menaggio, tel. and fax 0344/32356.) There are also hostels at the south and north ends of the lake (Como's Villa Olmo, tel. 031/573-800 and in Domaso, tel. 0344/96094).

## Transportation Connections

From anywhere covered in this book you'll get to Lake Como via Milan. The quickest Milan connection to any point at midlake (Bellagio, Menaggio, or Varenna) is via the train to Varenna. Trains run between Milan Centrale and Varenna (last year at 9:15, 12:15, 14:15, 16:15, and 18:15, 60 min, L6,000). Milan train schedules list Sondrio and Lecco, but often not Varenna; Varenna is a small stop. Some cars on long trains don't even get a platform. Ask for help so you don't miss the stop. You may have to open the door yourself. (Look for the button.) Trains leave Varenna for Milan at 5:30, 6:19, 7:27, 8:27, 10:27, and every two hours until 22:27. This makes a comfy last stop before catching the shuttle from Milan's station to the airport.

# THE DOLOMITES

Italy's dramatic limestone rooftop, the Dolomites, offers some of the best and most unique mountain thrills in Europe. Bolzano is the gateway to the Dolomites, and Castelrotto is a good home base for your exploration of Alpe di Siusi, Europe's largest alpine meadow.

## Planning Your Time

Train travelers should side-trip in from Bolzano (90 minutes north of Verona). To get a feel for the Alpine culture here, spend a night in Castelrotto. With two nights in Castelrotto, you can actually get out and hike. Tenderfeet ride the bus, catch a chairlift, and stroll. For mountain thrills, do a 6-hour hike. And for a mountain thrill that won't soon fade away, avid hikers will want to spend a night in a mountain hut. This means two nights in Castelrotto straddling a knight in a hut.

Car-hikers with a day can drive the 3-hour loop from Bolzano or Castelrotto (Val Gardena-Sella Pass-Val di Fassa) and ride one of the lifts to the top for a ridge walk. Connecting Bolzano and Venice by the Great Dolomite Road takes two hours longer than the autostrada (via Verona) but is more scenic (see below).

Hiking season is mid-June through mid-October. The region is packed and booming from mid-July through mid-September. Spring is dead, with no lifts running, the most exciting trails still under snow, and the huts closed. Ski season is busiest of all.

## Orientation

The sunny Dolomites are well developed, and the region's famous valleys and towns suffer from après-ski fever. The cost for the comfort of reliably good weather is a drained-reservoir feeling. Lovers of the Alps may miss the lushness that comes with the unpredictable weather farther north. But the bold limestone pillars, flecked with snow over green meadows under a blue sky, offer a worthwhile mountain experience.

A hard-fought history has left the region bicultural, with an emphasis on the German. Locals speak German first, and

## Northeast Italy

some wish they were still part of Austria. In the Middle Ages, the region faced north, part of the Holy Roman Empire. Later they were firmly in the Austrian Hapsburg realm. By losing WWI, Austria's South Tirol became Italy's Alto Adige. Mussolini did what he could to Italianize the region, including giving each town an Italian name. Even in the last decade, secessionist groups have agitated violently for more autonomy.

The government has wooed locals with economic breaks that make it one of Italy's richest areas (as local prices attest), and today all signs and literature in the autonomous province of Alto Adige/Süd Tirol are in both languages. Many include a third language, Ladin, the ancient Latin-type language still spoken in a few traditional areas. (I have listed both the Italian and German so the confusion caused by this guidebook will match that caused by your travels.)

In spite of all the glamorous ski resorts and busy construction cranes, the local color survives in a warm, blue-aproned, ruddy-faced, long-white-bearded way. There's yogurt and yodeling for breakfast. Culturally as much as geographically, the area reminds me of Austria. The Austrian Tirol is named for a village that is now part of Italy.

## Sleeping in the Dolomites

Most towns have no alternative to hotels, which charge at least L35,000 per person, or private homes, which offer beds for as low as L25,000 but are often a long walk from the town centers. Beds nearly always come with a hearty breakfast. Those traveling in peak season or staying for only one night are often penalized. Local TIs can always find budget travelers a bed in a private home (_Zimmer_). Drivers on a tight budget should pick remote Zimmers. Most mountain huts offer reasonable doubles, cheap dorm (_Lager_) beds, and inexpensive meals. Telephone any hut to secure a spot before hiking there. Most huts are open mid-June through September only.

In local restaurants there is no cover charge, and tipping is not expected. If you're low on both money and scruples, Süd Tirolian breakfasts are the only ones in Italy big enough to steal lunch from. A _Jausenstation_ is a place that serves cheap, hearty, and traditional mountain-style food to hikers.

## BOLZANO (BOZEN)

_Willkommen_ to the Italian Tirol! If it weren't so sunny, you could be in Innsbruck. This enjoyable old town of 100,000 is the most convenient gateway to the Dolomites, especially if you're relying on public transportation. It's just the place to gather Dolomite information and take a Tirolean stroll.

## Orientation

Bolzano is easy. Everything mentioned in Bolzano is within 3 blocks of Piazza Walther. Leaving the train station, veer left up the tree-lined Viale Stazione (Bahnhofsallee) and walk past the bus station (on your left) 2 blocks to Piazza Walther, where you'll find the city TI on your right (8:30–18:00, closed Saturday afternoon and Sunday, tel. 0471/993-808). The excellent—as if your safety depended on it—Dolomites information center (Monday–Friday 9:00–12:00, 15:00–17:00, Parrocchia 11, tel. 0471/993-809) is a block past the big church down Via Posta (Postgasse). The medieval heart of town is just beyond Piazza Walther. Choose your favorite Italian and bunny-hop down the arcaded Via dei Portici to the Piazza Erbe, with its ancient and still thriving open-air produce market.

**Mediocre Side Trip:** Many are tempted to wimp out on the Dolomites and see them from a distance by making the popular quick trip into the hills above Bolzano (cable car from near the Bolzano station to the cute but touristy village of Oberbozen, where you'll take a long, pastoral walk to the Pemmern chairlift; ride to Schwarzseespitze and walk 45 more minutes to the Rittner Horn). You'll be atop a 7,000-foot peak with distant but often hazy Dolomite views. It's not worth the trouble.

## Sleeping in Bolzano (about L1,600 = $1, zip code: 39100, tel. code: 0471)

While the cool, scenic, and nearby Dolomites make sleeping in hot and humid Bolzano a last resort, the town does have substantial charm.

Sleep code: **S**=Single, **D**=Double/Twin, **T**=Triple, **Q**=Quad, **B**=Bath/Shower and Toilet, **CC**=Credit Card (Visa, MasterCard, Amex), **SE**=Speaks English (graded A-F).

**Gasthof Weisses Kreuz** (ten rooms, D-L55,000, DB-L72,000, without breakfast; 1 block off Piazza Walther in the old town at Kornplatz 3, tel. 977-552, fax 972-273, SE-F) is your best value, but it's usually booked up. It couldn't be better located or more German—or at least anti-English. (Hotel signs and cards are quadrilingual, and English didn't make it.) The quirky **Hotel Figl** (D-L65,000, DB-L95,000 without breakfast, CC:VMA;

elevator; Kornplatz 9, tel. and fax 978-412) has more character than value.

The modern, clean, church-run **Kolpinghaus Bozen** (SB-L55,000, DB-L90,000, TB-L135,000 with breakfast; in the center, 2 blocks beyond the Dolomites information center at Spitalgasse 3, confusing elevator, tel. 971-170, fax 973-917, SE-B) has plenty of rooms with twin beds, all the comforts, and makes one feel thankful. Its institutional cafeteria (L12,000 dinners, 18:30–19:30 Monday–Friday) is open to all.

### Transportation Connections
**Trains from Bolzano to: Milan** (2/day, 4 hrs), **Verona** (hrly, 1½ hrs), **Trento** (hrly, 40 min), **Innsbruck** (hrly, 2½ hrs), **Merano** (hrly, 40 min), and **Venice** and **Florence** (via Verona, 3–4 hrs). Train info: tel. 974292.

**Buses from Bolzano into the Dolomites to: Castelrotto** (hrly, 40 min), continuing through the alpine meadow of Alpe di Siusi to **Saltria** (4–8/day, toll free info: tel. 167-846047). **Val di Fassa, Vigo di Fassa**, and **Canazei** (2/day, 4/day in summer, 2 hrs). **Val Gardena, Ortisei/St. Ulrich, St. Cristina** (4/day, 1 hr).

**Shuttle Buses To and Through the Alpe di Siusi:** Alpe di Siusi, a natural preserve, is closed to cars past Compatsch. June through mid-October "Buxi" shuttle-buses go about twice an hour (8:00–17:00, L2,000, discounted return tickets) from Castelrotto through the Alpe di Siusi to Saltria. Off season there's one "sad" 9:10 bus from Castelrotto and a 15:50 bus coming back.

### CASTELROTTO (KASTELRUTH)
Castelrotto (population 5,000, altitude 1,060 m), the ideal home base for exploring the Alpe di Siusi, has more village character than any town I saw in the region. Friday morning is the farmers' market, and a crafts market fills the town square on Tuesday mornings. It's touristy but not a full-blown resort—it's full of real people. Pop into the church to hear the choir practice or be on the town square at 15:00 as the bells peal and the moms bring home their kindergartners. The TI is on the main square (9:00–12:30, 15:00–18:00, closed Sunday afternoon, tel. 0471/706-333).

## The Western Dolomites

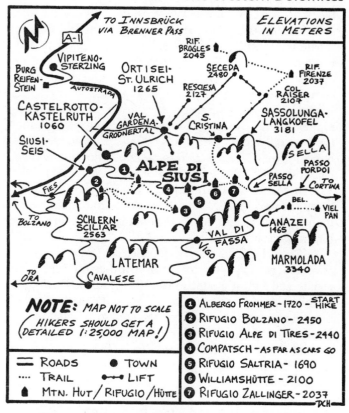

Map labels:
TO INNSBRÜCK VIA BRENNER PASS — A-1 — *ELEVATIONS IN METERS* — RIF. BROGLES 2045 — VIPITENO·STERZING — BURG REIFEN-STEIN — AUTOSTRADA — ORTISEI·St. ULRICH 1265 — SECEDA 2480 — RIF. FIRENZE 2037 — RESCIESA 2127 — COL RAISER 2107 — CASTELROTTO·KASTELRUTH 1060 — VAL GARDENA·GRÖDNERTAL — S. CRISTINA — SASSOLUNGA·LANGKOFEL 3181 — SIUSI·SEIS — ❶ ALPE DI SIUSI — SELLA — PASSO PORDOI — PASSO SELLA — TO CORTINA — FIES — ❷ — ❹ — ❼ — BEL. — VIEL PAN — ❺ ❻ — TO BOLZANO — SCHLERN·SCILIAR 2563 — ❸ — CANAZEI 1465 — VAL DI FASSA — Vigo — MARMOLADA 3340 — LATEMAR — TO ORA — CAVALESE

**NOTE:** MAP NOT TO SCALE
(HIKERS SHOULD GET A DETAILED 1:25,000 MAP!)

═ ROADS   ● TOWN
···· TRAIL   ●—● LIFT
🔺 MTN. HUT / RIFUGIO / HÜTTE

❶ ALBERGO FROMMER - 1720 - START HIKE
❷ RIFUGIO BOLZANO - 2450
❸ RIFUGIO ALPE DI TIRES - 2440
❹ COMPATSCH - AS FAR AS CARS GO
❺ RIFUGIO SALTRIA - 1690
❻ WILLIAMSHÜTTE - 2100
❼ RIFUGIO ZALLINGER - 2037

## Sleeping in Castelrotto
### (about L1,600 = $1, zip code: 39040, tel. code: 0471)

**Gasthof Zum Turm** is simple, clean, and traditional with great beds and modern bathrooms (DB-L100,000, TB-L135,000 with breakfast, L5,000 extra for one-night stays; behind the TI at Kofelgasse 8, tel. 706-349, fax 707-268, Herr and Frau Duregger speak no English). If you're driving, go right through the traffic-free town center (very likely with a police escort). Under the bell tower, go through the white arch to the right of the TI and park (free for guests) in the lot on your left.

**Gasthof Zum Wolf** is newly remodeled Tirolean mod with all the comforts (L80,000–L100,000 per person for bed, breakfast, and dinner, depending on the season; a block below the square at Wolkenstein strasse 5, tel. 706-332, fax 707-030, Arno speaks English). The L15,000 rebate is a lousy reason to skip dinner. Ask for a corner room or at least a balcony (worth the extra L10,000). **Hotel Cavallino D'Oro**, next door, has an even more complicated pricing scheme, which includes a mean-spirited 25 percent surcharge for stays of less than three nights. If you're loaded and love antiques by candlelight (or have only credit cards) this 600-year-old hotel is the best in town (DB-L140,000 to L250,000 depending on everything, CC:VMA; no elevator, tel. 706-337, fax 707-172, SE-A). In the town center, **Haus Harderer** rents out three rooms (DB-80,000 with breakfast, minimum two nights; Plattenstr 20, tel. 71702) but is more interested in long-term stays.

**Tirler Hof**, the storybook Jaider family farm, has 35 cows, one friendly *hund*, four Old World-comfy guest rooms, and a great mountain view (D-L55,000, T-L75,000 with breakfast; practical only for drivers, it's the first farm outside of town on the right on the road to St. Michael, Paniderstrasse 44, tel. 706017, the daughter SE). The ground-floor double has a private bath. The top-floor rooms share a bathroom and a great balcony. You'll take a stroll before breakfast.

## ALPE DI SIUSI (SEISER ALM)

Europe's largest high alpine meadow, Alpe di Siusi, (5 km by 12 km, 1,800 to 2,000 meters altitude), separates two of the most famous Dolomite ski-resort valleys. It's dotted by farm huts and wildflowers, surrounded by dramatic (if distant) Dolomite peaks and cliffs, and much appreciated by hordes of walkers. The Sasso Lungo (Langkofel) mountains at the head of the meadow provide a storybook Dolomite backdrop, while the spooky Schlern stands boldly looking into the haze of the Italian peninsula.

Not surprisingly, the Schlern, standing like a devilish winged victory, gave ancient peoples enough willies to spawn legends of supernatural forces. The Schlern witch, today's tourist brochure mascot, was the cause of many a broom-riding medieval townswoman's fiery death.

The Alpe di Siusi is my recommended one-stop look at the Dolomites because of Castelrotto's charm as a home base, because it's equally accessible to those with and without cars, because of its variety of walks and hikes, and because of its quintessentially Dolomite mountain views.

The meadow is a virtually car-free natural preserve. The Buxi park bus service shuttles hikers to and from key points along the tiny road all the way to Saltria at the foot of the postcard-dramatic Sasso peaks (Sasso Lungo, 3,180 meters). Meadow walks, for flower lovers and strollers, are pretty—or maybe pretty boring. Chairlifts provide springboards for more dramatic and demanding hikes. A few tiny service roads are technically closed, but people with reservations in distant chalets and huts drive them. Off season you may get away with some "car hiking."

Trails are well marked, and the brightly painted numbers are keyed into local maps. The Kompass Bolzano map #54 (1:50,000, L8,000) covers everything in this chapter. The Gardena/Alpe di Siusi 1:25,000 "Tobacco" map (L8,000) offers more detail on the Alpe di Siusi.

Compatsch, a kilometer into the park and as far as you're allowed to drive, is the park tourist village (1,870 m, grocery store, mountain bike rentals, tour bus corral, L5,000-per-day car-park, hotels, restaurants, shops, lifts, and so on).

**Sleeping in the Alpe di Siusi: Gasthof/Albergo Frommer** (DB-L90,000, tel. 727-917, SE-F) offers handy, comfortable, budget beds at the edge of the Alpe di Siusi. Arthur would heartily recommend this place. A rustic but classy old inn 100 meters from the Spitzbühl chairlift, with good meals, free parking, the Schlern peak out its window, and the Bolzano/Castelrotto/Buxi bus stop at its door, this is good for serious hikers who don't want to sleep in a mountain hut. Easy to find, it's a landmark place at the entry of the park about a kilometer before Compatsch.

## Hikes in the Alpe di Siusi (Seiser Alm)

Easy meadow walks abound, giving tenderfeet classic Dolomite views from baby-carriage trails. Experienced hikers should consider a tougher and more exciting trek from the Alpe di Siusi. Before attempting a hike, confirm your understanding of the time and skills required through the local tourist office.

**Summit hike of Sciliar (Schlern)**—For a challenging 12-mile, 7-hour hike with a possible overnight in a traditional mountain refuge, consider hiking to the summit of Sciliar (Schlern) and spending a night in Rifugio Bolzano (Schlernhaus). Start at the Spitzbühl lift and Albergo Frommer (1,725 m, free car-park, first bus stop in the park). The Spitzbühl chairlift drops you at Spitzbichl (1,935 m). Trail #5 takes you through a high meadow, down to the Saltner Schwaige dairy farm (1,830 m), across a stream, and steeply up the Schlern mountain. You'll meet trail #1 and walk across the rocky tabletop plateau of Schlern to the mountain hotel (Rifugio Bolzano/Schlernhaus, D-L52,000, L15,000 dorm beds, tel. 612-024, call for a reservation, 2,450 m, 3 hrs into hike). From this dramatic setting you get a great view of the Rosengarten range. Hike 20 more minutes up the nearby peak (Mt. Pez, 2,560 m) for a 360-degree Alpine panorama. From the Schlernhaus you can hike back the way you came or walk farther along the Schlern (12 km, 2 hrs, past the Tierser-Alpi-hutte, tel. 727-958, D or dorm beds, 2,440 m) and descend back into the Alpe di Siusi and the road where the Buxi bus will return you to your starting point or hotel.

**Loop around Sasso Lungo**—Another dramatic but not difficult hike is the 6-hour walk around Sasso Lungo (Langkofel). You can ride the bus to Saltria (end of the line), ride the chairlift to Williamshütte, walk past the Zallingerhütte (overnight possible), and circle the Sasso group.

**Easy Walks**—(1) From Compatsch, consider a 2-hour loop north to Arnikahütte and back via Puflatsch (elevation gain about 200 m). (2) From Compatsch, ride the lift to Panorama, hike 90 minutes to Molignonhütte (2,050 m) and back down to Compatsch; or continue 2½ hours (fairly level) to Zallingerhütte (2,060 m) and another 90 minutes to Saltria and the Buxi bus stop. (3) Bus to Saltria, 2½-hour loop to Zallingerhütte (2,040 m, 200-m altitude gain).

## MORE SIGHTS AND HIKES IN THE DOLOMITES

▲**Great Dolomite Road** (Belluno/Cortina/Pordoi Pass/Sella Pass/Val di Fassa/Bolzano) is the definitive

Dolomite drive. Connecting Venice with Bolzano this way
(the Belluno-Venice autostrada is slick) takes two hours
longer than the Bolzano-Verona-Venice autostrada. No public transit does this trip. While Cortina is the most famous
resort in the region, it has more diamonds than charm.

▲▲**The Abbreviated Dolomite Loop Drive**
(Bolzano/Castelrotto/Val Gardena/Sella Pass/Val di
Fassa/Bolzano) gives you the biggies in half the miles (allow
3 hours). **Val Gardena** (Grodner Tal)—famous for its
woodcarvers (ANRI is from the Val Gardena town of St.
Cristina), its traditional Ladin culture, and its skiing and
hiking resorts—is a bit overrated. Even if its culture has
been suffocated by the big bucks of hedonistic European
fun-seekers, it remains a good jumping-off point for trips
into the mountains. Within an hour you'll reach the **Sella
Pass** (2,240 m) viewpoint. After a series of tight hairpin
turns a mile or so over the pass, you'll see some benches
and cars. Pull over and watch the rockclimbers. **Val di
Fassa** is Alberto Tomba country. The town of Canazei, at
the head of the valley and the end of the bus line, has the
most ambience and altitude (4,600 feet). From there a lift
takes you to Col dei Rossi Belvedere, where you can hike
the Bindelweg past the Rifugio Belvedere along an easy but
breathtaking ridge to the Rifugio Viel del Pan. This is a 3-
hour round-trip hike with views of the highest mountain in
the Dolomites, the Marmolada, and the Dolo-mighty Sella
group along the way. In spring and early summer, passes
labeled "closed" are often bare, dry, and, as far as local drivers are concerned, wide open.

▲▲**Reifenstein Castle**—For one of Europe's most intimate
looks at medieval castle life, let the lady of Reifenstein (Frau
Blanc) show you around her wonderfully preserved castle.
She leads tours on the hour, in Italian and German. She's
friendly and will squeeze in what English she can.

Just before the Austrian border, leave the autostrada at
Vipiteno (Sterzing); follow signs toward Bolzano, then over
the freeway to the base of the castle's rock. It's the castle on
the west. While this is easy by car, it's probably not worth
the trouble by train (from Bolzano, 6/day, 70 min). The
pleasant mini-park beside the drawbridge is a good spot for a
picnic. (Pack out your litter.) Tours normally Easter–

November at 9:30, 10:30, 14:00, and 15:00, closed Friday
(L4,000, tel. 0472/765-879).

▲**Glurns**—Drivers deciding to connect the Dolomites and
Lake Como by the high road via Meran and Bormio or the
southwest of Switzerland should spend the night in the
amazing little fortified town of Glurns (45 minutes west of
touristy Meran between Schluderns and Taufers). Glurns
still lives within its square wall on the Adige River, with a
church bell tower that has a thing about ringing, and real
farms, rather than boutiques, filling the town courtyards.
This is a refreshing break after so many cute and wealthy
tourist towns. There are several small hotels in the town, but
I'd stay in a private home 100 yards from the town square,
near the church, just outside the wall on the river (Family
Hofer, six rooms, DB-L60,000 with breakfast, less for two
nights, tel. 0473/831-597, well marked).

# NAPLES, THE AMALFI COAST, AND POMPEII

If you like Italy as far south as Rome, go farther south. It gets better. If Italy is getting on your nerves, think twice about going farther. Italy intensifies as you plunge deeper. Naples is a barrel of cultural monkeys, Italy in the extreme—its best (birthplace of pizza and Sophia Loren) and its worst (home of the Camorra, Naples' "family" of organized crime). Serene Sorrento, just an hour to the south and without a hint of Naples, makes a great home base. It's the gateway to the much-loved Amalfi Coast. From the jet-setting island of Capri to the stunning scenery of the Amalfi Coast, from ancient Pompeii to even more ancient Paestum, this is Italy's Coast with the Most.

## Planning Your Time

On a quick trip, give the area three days. With Sorrento as your sunny springboard, spend a day in Naples, a day on the Amalfi coast, and a day split between Pompeii and the town of Sorrento. While Paestum, the crater of Vesuvius, Herculaneum, and the island of Capri are decent options, these are worthwhile only if you give the area more time. Consider a night train in or out of the area.

For a blitz tour, you could have breakfast on the early Rome-Naples express (7:10 to 9:10), do Naples and Pompeii in a day, and be back in Rome in time for Letterman. That's exhausting but more interesting than a third day in Rome. Remember that in the afternoon, Naples' street life slows and many sights close as the temperature soars.

For a small-town vacation from your vacation, spend a few more days on the Amalfi coast, sleeping in Positano, Atrani, or Marina del Cantone.

Driving south of Rome is not only stressful, it's impractical for most. Take advantage of the wonderful public transportation: the slick two-hour Rome-Naples express trains, the handy Circumvesuviana lacing together Naples, Pompeii, and Sorrento, and the regular bus service from Sorrento into the Amalfi region (where parking and car access are severely limited).

## NAPLES (NAPOLI)

Italy's third-largest city (more than 2 million people) has almost no open spaces or parks, which makes its position as Europe's most densely populated city plenty evident. Watching the police try to enforce traffic sanity is almost comical in Italy's grittiest, most polluted and crime-ridden city. But Naples surprises the observant traveler with an impressive knack for living, eating, and raising children in the streets with good humor and decency. Overcome your fear of being run down or ripped off enough to talk with people—enjoy a few smiles and jokes with the man running the cobblestone tripe shop or the lady taking her day-care class on a walk through the traffic.

Twenty-five hundred years ago, Neapolis ("new city") was a thriving Greek commercial center. It remains southern Italy's leading city, offering a fascinating collection of museums, churches, eclectic architecture, and volunteers needing blood for dying babies. The pulse of Italy throbs in Naples. Like Cairo or Bombay, it's appalling and captivating at the same time, the closest thing to "reality travel" you'll find in Europe. But this tangled mess still somehow manages to breathe, laugh, and sing—with a captivating Italian accent.

### Orientation (tel. code: 081)

For a quick visit, start with the museum, do the walk from there, and celebrate your survival with pizza. Of course, Naples is huge. But with limited time, if you stick to the described route and grab a cab when you're lost or tired, it's fun. Treat yourself well in Naples; this city is cheap by Italian standards.

#### Tourist Information

At the TI in the central train station (opposite track 16), pick up a map and the *Qui Napoli* booklet (if they say they're "finished" ask for an old one), 9:00–20:00, Sunday 9:00–13:00, tel. 268-779. (Ignore the toupee-topped con man.)

#### Trains

There are several Naples stations. Naples Centrale is the main one (facing Piazza Garibaldi, baggage check, Circumvesuviana stop for commuter trains to Sorrento and Pompeii, TI). Since Centrale is a dead-end station, through trains often stop at Piazza Garibaldi (actually a subway station just downstairs from Centrale) or Napoli Mergellina (equipped with a TI, across town, a direct 10-minute subway ride to Centrale, train tickets to Napoli Centrale and train passes cover you for the connecting ride to Centrale, subway trains depart about every 10 minutes). As you're coming in, ask someone which stations your train stops at. Get off at Mergellina only if it doesn't stop at Centrale or Garibaldi.

### Getting Around Naples
Naples' simple one-line subway, the Servizio Metropolitano, runs from the Mergellina station to the Centrale station through the center of town, stopping at Montesanto (top of Spanish Quarter and Spaccanapoli) and Piazza Cavour (Archaeology Museum). L1,200 tickets are good for 90 minutes. If you can afford a taxi, don't mess with the buses. Taxis are easy to hail, and a short ride costs L4,000–L6,000 (insist on the meter).

## Helpful Hints
**Traffic and Crime:** In Naples red lights are discretionary, and mopeds can mow you down from any place at any time. Don't venture into neighborhoods that make you uncomfortable; walk with confidence, as if you know where you're going and what you're doing. Assume able-bodied beggars are thieves. Give your money belt an extra half-hitch and keep it completely hidden. Stick to busy streets and beware of gangs of young street hoodlums. Remember, a third of the city is unemployed, and the local government sets an example the Mafia would be proud of. Assume con artists are more clever than you. Any jostle or commotion is probably a thief team smoke screen. Lately Naples has been occupied by an army of police which has made it feel safer. Still err on the side of caution.
**Baggage Check:** If you're doing Naples as a day trip, check your bags at the central train station (Deposito Bagagli in front of track #24, L1,500).

## Sights—Naples
▲▲▲**Museo Archeologico**—For lovers of antiquity, this museum alone makes Naples a worthwhile stop; it offers the

**Naples**

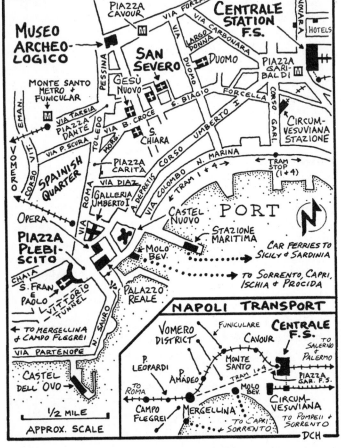

only peek possible into the artistic jewelry boxes of Pompeii and Herculaneum. The actual sights are impressive but barren. Somehow their best art ended up here.

**Paintings and artifacts:** Climb the grand stairs to the top floor and, from the grand ballroom, go left into a Pompeiian art gallery lined with paintings, bronze statues, artifacts, and an impressive model of the town of Pompeii (room LXXXIII), all of which make the relative darkness of medieval Europe obvious and clearly show the source of inspiration for the Renaissance greats.

**Mosaics:** From the same staircase, one floor (several flights) down, on the opposite side, you'll find a smaller but exquisite collection of Pompeiian mosaics (especially the fourth-century B.C. Battle of Alexander showing the Macedonians defeating the Persians).

**Farnese Collection:** The ground floor (on the distant left as you leave the stairs) has enough Greek, Roman, and Etruscan art to put any museum on the map, but its highlight is the Farnese Collection—a giant hall of huge, bright, and wonderfully restored statues excavated from Rome's Baths of Caracalla. You can almost hear the *Toro Farnese* snorting. This largest intact statue from antiquity (a third-century copy of a Hellenistic original) was carved out of one piece of marble and restored by Michelangelo. Read the worthwhile descriptions on the walls. (L12,000, 9:00–14:00, until 19:00 July–September, Sundays until 13:00, tel. 081/440-166, call to confirm times if visiting in the afternoon).

From the Centrale train station, follow signs to Metropolitano (tickets from window on left, ask which track—*Che binario?*—to Piazza Cavour, and ride the train one stop). As you exit, turn right and head gradually uphill. At the end of cluttered Piazza Cavour, you'll see the museum, a huge pink-brick building. The WC below and behind the main stairway is uncharacteristically pleasant.

▲▲▲**The Slice-of-Neapolitan-Life Walk**—Walk from the museum through the heart of town and back to the station (allow at least 2 hours plus lunch and sightseeing stops). Sights are listed in the order you'll see them on this walk.

Naples, a living medieval city, is its own best sight. Couples artfully make love on Vespas surrounded by more fights and smiles per cobble here than anywhere else in Italy. Rather than seeing Naples as a list of sights, see the one great museum, then capture its essence by taking this walk through the core of the city. Should you become overwhelmed or lost, step into a store and ask for help (for example, *"Dové il stazione centrale?"*) or point in this book to the next sight.

**Via Toledo and the Spanish Quarter (city walk, first half):** Leaving the Archaeological Museum at the top of Piazza Cavour (Metro: Piazza Cavour), cross the street, veer right, and dip into the ornate galleria on your way to Via Pessina. The first part of this walk is a straight one-mile ramble down the boulevard to Galleria Umberto I near the Royal Palace. Coffee will be waiting.

Busy Via Pessina leads downhill to Piazza Dante. After 2 blocks, a tiny pedestrian street (Via Micco Spadaro) leads to the Academy of Fine Arts (Belle Arti). Sneak a peek inside. Isn't that Michelangelo's *David*?! (The bar/pizzeria in front serves a decent quick lunch with pleasant outdoor seating.)

At Piazza Dante, notice poor old Dante in the center, looking out over the chaos with a hopeless gesture. Past the square, Via Pessina becomes Via Toledo, Naples's principal shopping street. About 5 blocks below Piazza Dante, at Via Maddaloni, you cross the long straight *Spaccanapoli* (literally, "split Naples"). Look left and right. Since ancient times, this thin street (which changes names several times) has bisected the city. (We'll be coming back to this point later. To abbreviate this walk, turn left here and skip down to the Spaccanapoli section.)

Via Toledo runs through Piazza Carita. You may meet a fascist here eager to point out the Mussolini photo in his wallet and the fascist architecture (from 1938) overlooking the square. Wander down Via Toledo a few blocks past the fascist architecture of two banks (both on the left). Try robbing the second one (Banco di Napoli, 178 Via Toledo).

Up the hill to your right is the Spanish Quarter, Naples at its rawest, poorest, and most historic. Thrill-seekers (or someone in need of a $20 prostitute) will take a stroll up one of these streets and loop back to Via Toledo. The only thing predictable about this Neapolitan tidepool is the ancient grid plan of its streets, the friendliness of its shopkeepers, and the boldness of its mopeds. Concerned locals will tug on their lower eyelid, warning you to be wary. Pop into a grocery shop and ask the man to make you his best ham and mozzarella sandwich. Trust him for the price—it shouldn't be more than L4,000.

Continue down Via Toledo to the Piazza Plebiscito. From here you'll see the church of **San Francesco di Paola** with its Pantheon-inspired dome and broad arcing colonnades. Opposite is the **Royal Palace**, which has housed Spanish, French, and even Italian royalty. The lavish interior is open for tours (L6,000, 9:00–14:00, Sunday until 13:00, closed Monday). Next door, peek inside the Neoclassical

**Teatro San Carlo**, Italy's second most respected opera house (after Milan's La Scala). The huge castle on the harborfront just beyond the palace houses government bureaucrats and is closed to tourists.

Enjoy a coffee break under the Victorian iron and glass of the 100-year-old Galleria Umberto I; go through the tall yellow arch at the end of Via Toledo or across from the opera house. Gawk up.

**Spaccanapoli to the Birth of Pizza and back to the station (city walk, second half):** To continue your walk, double back up Via Toledo past Piazza Carita to Via Maddaloni. (Consider going via the back streets.) Look east and west to survey the straight-as-a-Roman-arrow Spaccanapoli. Formerly the main thoroughfare of the Greek city of Neapolis, it starts up the hill near the Montesanto funicular (a colorful and safer Spanish Quarter neighborhood from where you can see how strictly Spaccanapoli splits Naples' historic center).

Turn right off Via Toledo and walk down Via Maddaloni to two bulky old churches (and a TI) on Piazza Gesu Nuovo. Check out the austere, fortresslike church of **Gesu Nuovo** with its peaceful but brilliant Baroque interior. Across the street, the simpler Gothic church of **Santa Chiara** offers a stark contrast (churches usually close 13:00–16:30).

The rest of this walk is basically a straight line (all of which locals call Spaccanapoli). Continue down traffic-free Via B. Croce to the next square, Piazza S. Domenico Maggiore. The classy Scaturcho café is filled with local ambiance and a unique Neapolitan pastry called *sfoigliatella* (sweet ricotta cheese with nuggets of candied fruit in a pastry). Walk behind the castlelike **San Domenico Maggiore** church (to the right as you face the church, take the first right after that), following yellow signs to the **Capella di Sansevero** (Via de Sanctis 19). This small chapel is a Baroque explosion mourning the body of Christ laying on a soft pillow under an incredibly realistic veil—all carved out of marble. It's like no statue I've seen (by Giuseppe "howdeedoodat" Sammartino, 1750). Lovely statues, carved from a single piece of marble, adorn the altar. *Despair* struggles with a marble rope net (on the right, opposite *Chastity*). Then, for the ghoul in all of us, walk down the stairway to the right for a creepy look at two 200-year-old studies in varicose veins (L6,000, 10:00–17:00, Sunday and Tuesday 10:00–13:00). Was one decapitated? Was one pregnant?

Back on Via B. Croce, turn left and continue the Spaccanapoli cultural scavenger hunt. As Via B. Croce becomes Via S. Biagio dei Librai, notice the gold and silver shops. And notice the Doll Hospital at #81.

Cross busy Via Duomo, and the street scenes along Via Vicaria intensify. Paint a picture with these thoughts: Naples has the most intact street plan of any ancient Roman city. Imagine life here as in a Roman city (retain these images as you visit Pompeii) with street-side shop-fronts that close up to form private homes after dark. Today is just one more page in a 2,000-year-old story of city activity: all kinds of meetings, beatings, and cheatings; kisses, near misses, and little-boy pisses. You name it, it occurs right on the streets today, as it has since Roman times. For a peek behind the scenes in the shade of wet laundry, venture down a few side streets. Buy two carrots as a gift for the lady on the fifth floor if she'll lower her bucket down to pick them up. At the tiny triangular park, veer right onto Via Forcella, and turn right on busy Via Pietro Colletta, which leads to Napoli's two most competitive pizzerias.

For a tasty and typically Neapolitan finale, drop by one of the two most traditional pizzerias in the birthplace of pizza. Naples, baking just the right combination of fresh dough, mozzarella, and tomatoes in traditional wood-burning ovens, is famous for its pizzas. **Antica Pizzeria da Michele** is for purists (cheap, filled with locals, 50 yards off Corso Umberto on Via Cesare Sersale, look for the vertical red Antica Pizzeria sign, 8:00–22:00, closed Sunday). It serves only two kinds: Margherita (tomato sauce and mozzarella) or Marinara (tomato sauce, oregano, and garlic with no cheese). A pizza with beer costs L8,000. Many locals prefer **Pizzeria Trianon** (10:00–13:30, 18:30–23:00, closed Sunday, across the street at Via Pietro Colletta 42, tel. 553-9426). Da Michele's arch-rival offers more choices and a cozier atmosphere.

To finish the walk, turn left on the grand-boulevardian Corso Umberto, and walk through all kinds of riffraff to the vast and ugly Piazza Garibaldi. On the far side is the Central Station. Run for it!

Naples has many more museums, churches, and sights that some consider important. For a rundown on these, refer to the TI's free *Qui Napoli* publication.

## Sleeping in Naples
### (L1,600 = about $1, tel. code: 081)

With Sorrento just an hour away, I can't imagine why you'd sleep in Naples. But if needed, here are two safe, clean places 200 yards from the station and a hostel. For the hotels, turn right out of the station and walk under an elevated road 1 block up Corso Novara. It's a thoroughly ugly but reasonably safe area. Be careful after dark.

Sleep code: **S**=Single, **D**=Double/Twin, **T**=Triple, **Q**=Quad, **B**=Bath/Shower and WC, **CC**=Credit Card (**V**isa, **M**asterCard, **A**mex), **SE**=Speaks English (graded **A-F**). Breakfast is normally included only in the expensive places (as noted).

**Hotel Ginerva** (S-L30,000, D-L50,000, DB-L60,000, special '96 price with this book, CC:VMA; right off Corso Novara down Via Genova to #116, tel. 283-210) is quiet, bright, and cheery. Little English spoken, but Bruno and Anna try hard. New beds, floral wallpaper, and a L5,000-per-load washing machine.

**Hotel Eden** (DB-L72,000, TB-L88,000, prices good through '96 with this book, CC:VMA; Corso Novara 9, tel. 285-344, fax 202-070) is a fine establishment run with panache by English-speaking Nicola (Danny DeVito) and his brother, Vincentzo. Clean, good beds, brown and gray tones, and all the comforts in sterile surroundings, which is exactly what you're after in Naples. Ask to see the hall lighting ambience.

**Ostello Mergellina** (L18,000 beds with sheets and breakfast, D-L40,000, small rooms with two to six beds; Metro: Mergellina, at Salita della Grotta a Piedigrotta 23, tel. 761-2346, closed 9:00–16:00 and at 24:00, cheap meals) is well run, cheap, and pleasant.

## Transportation Connections

Trains run from **Naples to Rome** (hrly, 2–3 hrs), **Brindisi** (ferries to Greece, 2/day, 7 hrs, overnight possible), **Milan**

(4/day, 7–9 hrs, overnight possible, more with a change in Rome), **Nice** (4/day, 13 hrs), **Paris** (3/day, 18 hrs), and **Venice** (4/day, 8–10 hrs).

The Circumvesuviana: **Naples, Herculaneum, Pompeii,** and **Sorrento** are all on the handy commuter train, the Ferrovia Circumvesuviana, from the basement of Naples' central station (clearly signposted). The Circumvesuviana also has its own terminal, one stop or a 10-minute walk beyond the central station. Take your pick. Two trains per hour marked "Sorrento" get you to Herculaneum (Ercolano) in 15 minutes, Pompeii in 40 minutes, and Sorrento, the end of the line, in 70 minutes (L4,200 one-way, no train passes). When returning to Naples Centrale station on the Circumvesuviana, don't go to the end of the line. Get off at the Collegamento FS or Garibaldi stop (Centrale station is just up the escalator). Naples train information: tel. 081/554-3188 or 680-635.

## SORRENTO

Wedged on a ledge under the mountains and over the Mediterranean, surrounded by lemon and olive groves, Sorrento is an attractive resort of 20,000 residents and—in the summer—as many tourists. It's as well-located for regional sightseeing as it is a pleasant place to stay and stroll. And there's not a hint of Naples. The Sorrentines have gone out of their way to create a pleasant, completely safe, and relaxed place for tourists to come and spend money. Everyone seems to speak fluent English and work for the Chamber of Commerce. This gateway to the Amalfi coast has a pleasant and unspoiled old quarter, a lively main shopping street, and a spectacular cliffside set-ting. Skip the port and its poor excuse for a beach unless you're taking a ferry.

### Orientation (tel. code: 081)

Sorrento is long and narrow. The main drag, Corso Italia (50 meters in front of its Circumvesuviana train station), runs parallel to the sea from the station through the town center and out to the cape, where it's renamed Via Capo. Everything mentioned (except the Via Capo hotels) is within a 5-minute walk of the station.

Sorrento

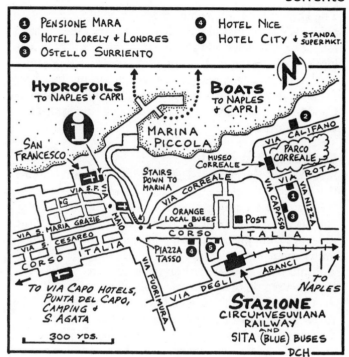

**①** PENSIONE MARA
**②** HOTEL LORELY & LONDRES
**③** OSTELLO SURRIENTO
**④** HOTEL NICE
**⑤** HOTEL CITY & STANDA SUPERMKT.

HYDROFOILS TO NAPLES & CAPRI

BOATS TO NAPLES & CAPRI

SAN FRANCESCO

MARINA PICCOLA

VIA CALIFANO

PARCO CORREALE

MUSEO CORREALE

VIA S.F.S.

STAIRS DOWN TO MARINA

VIA CORREALE

VIA ROTA

VIA NIZZA

VIA CAPASSO

VIA S. MARIA GRAZIE

VIA S. CESAREO

ORANGE LOCAL BUSES

POST

CORSO ITALIA

CORSO ITALIA

PIAZZA TASSO

VIA FUORIMURA

VIA DEGLI

ARANCI

TO NAPLES

TO VIA CAPO HOTELS, PUNTA DEL CAPO, CAMPING & S. AGATA

STAZIONE CIRCUMVESUVIANA RAILWAY AND SITA (BLUE) BUSES

300 YDS.

—DCH—

### Tourist Information

*Soggiorno e Turismo:* From the station, go left on Corso Italia, walk 5 minutes to Piazza Tasso; turn right at end of square down Via L. de Maio through Piazza Sant Antonino to the Foreigners' Club mansion at #35; 8:30–14:00, 17:00–20:00, tel. 807-4033. Get a free *Sorrentum* magazine with great map, and boat, bus, and events schedules. You'll pass many fake "tourist offices" on the way (travel agencies selling bus and boat tours) which can be helpful.

### Getting Around Sorrento

Orange city buses run from the station to the Punta del Capo, and down to the port (L1,000 tickets within the center, sold at *tabacchi* shops). Rental mopeds (L35,000) and Vespas (L50,000, tel. 878-1386) are at Corso Italia 210. In summer, forget renting a car unless you enjoy traffic jams in the Italian sun.

## Helpful Hints
The Foreigners' Club (behind the TI, city discount cards, public WC) provides reasonably priced snacks and drinks, relaxation and views, and a handy place for visitors to meet locals. It's lively, with music, on summer evenings. If you need immediate tanning, you can rent a chair on the pier by the port, though the best nearby sandy beach is at Punta del Capo (see below). There's a handy coin-op laundromat at Corso Italia 30.

## Sights—Sorrento
▲▲**Central Sorrento**—Take time to stroll and explore the surprisingly pleasant old city between Corso Italia and the sea. The evening passeggiata (along the Corso Italia and via San Cesareo) peaks around 22:00. Check out the old-boys' club playing cards, oblivious to the tourism, under their portico at Via San Cesareo and Via Tasso.
▲**Punta del Capo**—For clean water and a free pebbly beach on the tip of a peninsula, walk 40 minutes to Punta del Capo (or take the 10-minute bus ride from Piazza Tasso, two departures/hr, L1,000). It's a rocky but accessible, traffic-free swimming area with a stunning view of Sorrento and Naples. The very ruined Roman Villa di Pollio marks this discovered but beautiful cape. Leave the road at the American Bar, turn right, and amble down the covered walkway to the beach.

## Sleeping in Sorrento
**(L1,600 = about $1; tel. code: 081, zip code: 80067)**
Unlike many resorts, Sorrento offers the whole range of rooms. If you decide to splurge, get a balcony and view. (Ask, *"con balcon, con vista sul mare."*) *"Tranquillo"* is taken as a request for a room off the street. Hotels listed here are either near the station and city center or out toward the Punta del Capo, a 40-minute walk from the station. While many hotels close for the winter, you'll have no trouble finding a room during the off-season. Note: The spindly and more exotic Amalfi Coast town of Positano (see Amalfi Coast, below) is also a good place to spend the night.

## Sleeping near the Train Station and in the Town Center

From the station, turn right onto the Corso Italia, then left down Via Capasso for the first two listings. The next two are between the station and the town center on Corso Italia.

**Pension Mara** provides simple, clean rooms in a dull building with a good location (D-L50,000, DB-L65,000, T-L70,000, TB-L90,000, cheap quads, optional breakfast-L5,000; friendly Adelle, the English-speaking owner, can be talked out of her "quasi-obligatory" L60,000 per person half-board policy in August, ask for a balcony; from Via Capasso, turn right onto the unmarked Via Rota just past the police station, Via Rota 5, tel. 878-3665).

**Hotel Lorely** is a reasonable exception in an expensive neighborhood (DB-L100,000 with breakfast and sea-view balcony, less on the noisy street side; in July, August, and September, full-pension at L95,000 per person is required, but the food is delicious; follow Via Capasso to the water and turn right to see the big rose-colored hotel at Via Califano 2, tel. 807-3187, CC:VM; easy free parking on the street). The setting is drunk with character but the management is absentee and apathetic. This rambling, spacious, colorful old Sorrentine villa is ideal for those wishing to sit on the bluff and stare at the sea. Avoid the noisy street-side rooms. Don't avoid the elevator down to the hotel's private beach.

**Hotel City** (SB-L50,000, DB-L65,000, TB-L90,000, breakfast-L5,000, CC:VM; handy location near Piazza Tasso at Corso Italia 221, tel. and fax 877-2210) is small and bright. The manager, Gianni, caters to budget English-speaking travelers and runs a newsstand and travel agency in his lobby.

**Hotel Nice** (SB-L54,000, DB-L80,000 with breakfast, third and fourth roommates-L28,000 each; Corso Italia 257, tel. 878-1650) is a good, basic value very near the station on the busy main drag. Ask for a room off the street.

**Hotel Del Corso** (D-L60,000, DB-L80,000, breakfast-L10,000; half-pension at L75,000 per person required in July and August; CC:A; in town center, Corso Italia 134, tel. 807-1016), a well-worn Old World hotel, is clean and comfortable, with spacious rooms and urban noise. I'm not sure if the manager is wry or unfriendly.

### Sleeping with a View on Via Capo

These hotels are outside of town near the cape (straight out the Corso Italia, which turns into Via Capo; 30 minutes on foot from the center, L15,000 by taxi, or a L1,000 bus-ride away). It's an easy walk to the Punta del Capo from here. If you're in Sorrento to stay put and luxuriate, these are best (although, I'd rather luxuriate on the Amalfi Coast).

**Pension La Tonnarella** (DB-L110,000–L150,000 with view and breakfast; obligatory L100,000 per person half-pension with dinner in the summer; many rooms with view balconies; CC:VMA; Via Capo 31, tel. 878-1153, fax 878-2169) is a Sorrentine villa with several terraces, stylish tiles, and sea views.

**Hotel Desiree** (DB-110,000 with breakfast, shares La Tonnarella's driveway and beach; at Via Capo 31, tel./fax 878-1563), run by helpful English-speaking Ingeborg Garguilio, is a simpler affair with humbler views but all the comforts and no half-board requirements.

**Hotel Minerva** (SB-L100,000, DB-L160,000, TB-L190,000 with breakfast and no summer half-pension require-ment, CC:VMA; at Via Capo 30, tel. 878-1011, fax 878-1949). The friendly, English-speaking owners have lovingly restored this dream palace. Getting off the elevator on the fifth floor, you'll step into a spectacular terrace with outrageous Mediterranean views and a cliff-hanging swimming pool com-plementing large tiled rooms with balconies. Peasants sneak in a picnic dinner and enjoy just hanging out here.

**Pension Elios** (D-L64,000, DB-L70,000, including breakfast, special '96 prices with this book; Via Capo 33, tel. 878-1812), run by Luigi and Maria, offers simple but spacious rooms, many with balconies and views, and a fine roof terrace.

### Eating in Sorrento

Dining out can be reasonable here. If you fancy a picnic dinner on your balcony, on the hotel terrace, or in the public garden, you'll find many markets and take-out pizzerias in the old town. The supermarket at 223 Corso Italia has it all (8:30–13:00, 16:30–20:30, closed Sunday and Thursday afternoons).

In the city center, **Sant Antonino's** offers friendly ser-vice, red-checkered tablecloths, an outdoor patio, decent prices, and good pasta (just off the P. Sant Antonino on Santa Marie delle Grazie 6). The nearby and smaller **Pizzeria Da Gigino** (first road to the right of Sant Antonino) is also good. **Pizzeria Giardiniello** (Via Accademia 7) is a family show offering good food at good prices. The **Osteria Gatto Nero**, a hole-in-the-wall at Via Santa Maria della Pieta 36 (tel. 878-1582, closed Monday), is a mom-and-pop place that respects its budget eaters. The restaurant on the terrace of **Hotel Lorely** serves the best reasonably priced great-view meals in town. **La Favorita-O'Parrucchiano** (Corso Italia 71) is venerable, expensive, and a decent splurge for fine regional cooking.

For cheap eats, skip the center and the views and walk a couple of blocks past the station on Corso Italia to **Master Hosts** (cheap good pizza and pasta) or **Pizza A' Kilo** (behind the station).

## Transportation Connections

**From Sorrento to Positano and Capri by boat:** Sorrento's busy port launches ferries to Capri, Ischia, Positano, and Naples (schedules available at TI, walk or shuttle-bus to port from Piazza Tasso). To **Positano** (L7,000, July and August only). To **Capri** (about hourly, L5,000). Several lines compete, using boats and hydrofoils. Buy only one-way tickets (there's no round-trip discount) for schedule flexibility, so you can take any company's boat back. Prices are the same. Fifteen-minute hydrofoil and "jet-boat" crossings to Capri cost L7,500. Check times for the last return crossing upon arrival.

**From Sorrento to the Amalfi Coast by bus:** Blue SITA buses depart from Sorrento's train station nearly hourly and stop at all Amalfi Coast towns (Positano in 45 minutes for L2,000 Amalfi in 90 minutes, L3,400), ending up in Salerno at the far end of the coast in just under 3 hours. Buy tickets at the tobacco shop nearest any bus stop before board-ing. (There's a tabacchi at the Sorrento station.) You may have to change in Amalfi to get to Salerno. Leaving Sorrento, arrive early to grab a seat on the right for the best views. There are often two or three buses leaving at the same time.

**From Sorrento to Pompeii, Herculaneum, and Naples by Circumvesuviana train:** This handy commuter

train runs at least hourly between Naples and Sorrento.
From Sorrento, it's 30 minutes to Pompeii, 45 minutes to
Herculaneum, and 70 minutes to Naples (L4,200 one-way).
See the Naples chapter for tips on arriving there smartly.

## THE AMALFI COAST

### Sights—The Amalfi Coast
▲▲▲**Bus ride along Amalfi Coast**—One of the world's
great bus rides, this trip from Sorrento along the Amalfi
Coast will leave your mouth open and your film exposed.
You'll gain respect for the Italian engineers who built the
road—and even more respect for the bus drivers who drive
it. The hyperventilation caused by winding around so
many breathtaking cliffs makes the Mediterranean, 500
feet below, really twinkle.

Cantilevered garages, hotels, and villas cling to the vertical terrain, and beautiful sandy coves tease from far below and
out of reach. Gasp from the right side of the bus as you go and

## The Amalfi Coast

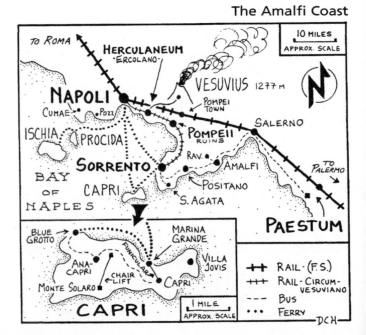

the left on the way back (if you return by bus). Those on the wrong side really miss out. Traffic is so heavy that in the summer, local cars are allowed to drive only every other day—even-numbered license plates one day, odd the next. (Buses and tourists foolish enough to drive are exempt from this system.)

The Amalfi Coast towns are pretty to look at but generally touristic, congested, overpriced, and a long hike above tiny beaches. The real thrill here is the scenic drive. Catch a blue SITA bus from the Sorrento train station (see above for details).

▲▲**Positano**—Specializing in scenery and sand, Positano sprawls halfway between Sorrento and Amalfi on the most spectacular stretch of the coast. The village, a three-star sight from a distance, is a pleasant (if expensive) gathering of women's clothing stores and cafés, with a superb beach. There's little to do here but enjoy the beach and views and window-shop. Consider a day trip from Sorrento; take the bus out and the afternoon ferry home.

To minimize your descent, use the last Positano bus stop (on the Amalfi town side, ask for "Sponda"). It's a 15-minute stroll/shop/munch from here to the beach. To catch the bus back to Sorrento, remember it may leave from Sponda 10 to 15 minutes before the main Positano departure, which is at the other end of town. You can also take the orange bus up to the highway and catch the SITA bus from the small town square (2/hr, tickets from the adjacent café). Boats to Sorrento, Amalfi, and Capri depart from Positano. For accommodations in Positano, see Sleeping, below. Positano TI: tel. 875067.

**Amalfi**—The waterfront of this most famous of the Amalfi Coast villages is dominated by a bus station, a parking lot, and two gas stations. The main street through the village—hard for pedestrians to avoid—is packed with cars and bully mopeds. Neighboring Atrani, a 15-minute walk away, and Minori, a bit further on, are more pleasant.

▲**Bus ride to Sant Agata and Sorrento's Peninsula**—The trip from Sorrento to Sant Agata is a beautiful cliff-hanger punctuated by lemon groves, olive orchards, and wildflowers. Catch the sunset here for the single best view over both sides of the peninsula. From the end of the line, Sant Agata, walk toward Sant Agata's church. Follow signs to the monastery,

Il Deserto. Go through the gate and climb into and on top of the monastery for the views surveying both the Golfo di Napoli and the Golfo di Salerno (ask for *Colle di Fontanelle.*) The village of Sant Agata is nothing special, but you'll find it refreshingly unspoiled. It's a decent place for dinner or a *granita caffè con panna* at the old wooden bar about 100 meters from the bus stop (departures—2 per hour, 20-minute ride—on blue SITA buses from the Sorrento station, buy two one-way L1,800 tickets in the station café).

This is the gateway to the scenic but ignored Sorrento peninsula that stretches 20 kilometers from Sorrento to the Campanella point. From Sant Agata, the bus continues to Marina del Contone and Termini. From Termini a 7-kilometer walk takes you to the point under a ruined Norman Tower where you can almost reach out and touch Capri (bring water, get local directions, not good for swimming).

**Marina del Contone**, a tiny fishing village near Nerano on a Sorrento Peninsula dead end, is the place to establish a sleepy, fun-in-the-sun residency (1 hour by bus from Sorrento, 5/day). Sleep at Pensione La Certosa (80068 Massa Lubrense, tel. 081/808-1209) which runs a beachfront restaurant, organizes boat excursions, and can direct you to a number of peaceful little beaches.

## Sleeping on the Amalfi Coast
### (L1,600 = about $1, zip code: 84017)

### *Sleeping in Positano*
These hotels, arranged by altitude from nearest the bus stop to nearest the beach, are on Via Colombo, which leads from the Sponda SITA bus stop down into the village. **Albergo California** (DB-L110,000, CC:A; Via Colombo 141, tel. 089/875-382, Maria SE) has great views, spacious rooms, and a comfortable terrace. **Residence La Tavolozza** (DB-L100,000, also a royal family apartment; Via Colombo 10, tel. 089/875-040) is a tiny, unassuming hotel warmly run by Celeste. Flawlessly restored, each room comes with view, balcony, fine tile, and silence. **Hotel Bougainville** (DB-L100,000 with view balcony, L80,000 without view, breakfast included only with this

book; CC:VMA; Via Colombo 25, tel. 089/875-047, fax 811-150, Carlo SE), is a fine, spotless place with eager-to-please owners and comfortable rooms. The pizzerias on the beach are a bit overpriced but pleasant. Consider a balcony, terrace, or beach picnic dinner.

### Sleeping in Amalfi and Atrani

If marooned in Amalfi, stay at the **Hotel Amalfi** (DB-L80,000–L100,000 including breakfast, cheaper for more than one night; Via dei Pastai 3, tel. 089/872-440) or hike 15 minutes (or ride the bus) to the tiny beach town of Atrani, and stay in **A' Scalinatella** (L20,000 per bed with spaghetti in Filippo's restaurant, D-L30,000, DB-L60,000, tel. 089/871-492; 84010 Atrani). This informal hostel with dorm beds, private rooms, family apartments, and a guest washer and dryer (L7,000/load) is ideal for a small town Amalfi hideaway without the glitz and climbing of Positano. Owner Filippo speaks English and is eager to please (near main square, tel. 871492). There's a youth hostel in Agerola on Piazza G. Avitabile (tel. 081/802-5048).

## CAPRI

Made famous as the vacation hideaway of Roman emperors Augustus and Tiberius, these days Capri is a world-class tourist trap packed with gawky tourists in search of the rich and famous and finding only their prices. The 4-mile-by-2-mile "Island of Dreams" is a zoo in July and August. Other times of year it provides a relaxing and scenic break from the cultural gauntlet of Italy. While Capri has some Roman ruins and an interesting 14th-century Carthusian monastery, its chief attraction is its famous Blue Grotto, and its best activity is a scenic hike.

At the ferry dock, confirm your plans at the tourist information office (tel. 081/837-0424, 837-5308, or 837-0686; room-finding service, baggage deposit service nearby).

## Sights—Capri

**Capri and Anacapri**—From the ferry dock at Marina Grande, a funicular lifts you 500 feet to the cute but most-touristy town of Capri. From there buses go regularly along a cliff-hanging road to the still cute but more bearable town of Anacapri.
**Blue Grotto**—To most, a visit to the Blue Grotto is an overrated "must." While the standard tour is by ferry from

Marina Grande, you can save money by catching the bus from Anacapri and hiking for an hour. Admission, by rowboat with a guide, is L12,000. (Those who hike, dive in for free.) Touristy and commercial as this all is, the grotto, with its eerily beautiful blue sunlight reflecting through the water, is an impressive sight (daily 9:00 until an hour before sunset, except in stormy weather).

**Hike down Monte Solaro**—From Anacapri, ride the chairlift to the 1,900-foot summit of Monte Solaro for a commanding view of the Bay of Naples and a pleasant downhill hike through lush vegetation and ever-changing views, past the 14th-century Chapel of Santa Maria Cetrella, and back into Anacapri.

**Villa Jovis**—Emperor Tiberius' now-ruined Villa Jovis is a scenic 1-hour hike from Capri town. Supposedly Tiberius ruled Rome from here for a decade (in about A.D. 30).

While you can take a boat between Naples and Capri, the ferry from Sorrento is quicker and cheaper (L5,000, nearly hourly). There is also a Positano-Capri boat. For an untouristy alternative to Capri, consider the nearby island of Ischia (easy boat connections from Naples and Sorrento).

## POMPEII, HERCULANEUM, AND VESUVIUS

Pompeii (▲▲▲), stopped in its tracks by the eruption of Mount Vesuvius in A.D. 79, offers the best look anywhere at what life in Rome must have been like 2,000 years ago. An entire city of well-preserved ruins is yours to explore. Once a thriving commercial port of 20,000, Pompeii grew from Greek and Etruscan roots to become an important Roman city. Then it was buried under 30 feet of hot mud and volcanic ash. For archaeologists this was a shake 'n' bake windfall, teaching them about ancient Roman culture. It was rediscovered in the 1600s, and the first excavations began in 1748 (L12,000, daily 9:00 to an hour before sunset, 20:00 in summer, ticket office closes an hour before that).

### Orientation

Pompeii is halfway between Naples and Sorrento, about a half-hour from either by direct Circumvesuviana train (runs

### Pompeii

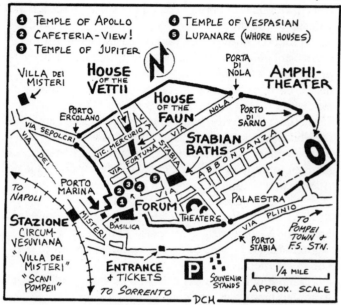

**1** Temple of Apollo
**2** Cafeteria-View!
**3** Temple of Jupiter
**4** Temple of Vespasian
**5** Lupanare (Whore Houses)

at least hourly). Get off at the "Villa dei Misteri, Pompei Scavi" stop. (The modern town is Pompei, the ancient sight is Pompeii.) Check your bag at the train station for L1,500 or at the site for free. From the station, turn right and walk down the road to the circus-like entrance. The TI (look for the "i" across the street above the locked door) may have a Pompeii layout. The *Pompeii and Herculaneum* "past and present" book has a helpful text and allows you to re-create the ruins with plastic overlays—with the "present" actually being 1964; L20,000 price but pay no more than L15,000. To understand what you're seeing, a guidebook is essential.

## Touring Pompeii

Allow 3 hours. Entering through the Porta Marina, you'll walk past the Antiquarium (first building on right, artifacts and eerie casts of well-preserved victims) to the Forum.

The Forum (Foro), Pompeii's commercial, religious, and political center, is the most ruined part of Pompeii. It's nonetheless impressive, with several temples; the "basilica" (Pompeii's largest building, used for legal and commercial business); and some interesting casts of volcano victims displayed with piles of pottery behind the fence on the left as you enter the Forum.

From the Forum, walk toward the volcano—past the convenient 20th-century cafeteria (decent value, gelati, overpriced cards and books, WCs with rooftop views)—down Via del Foro, which becomes Via di Mercurio, into Pompeii's oldest quarter for the most interesting houses. The House of Vettii (Casa dei Vettii), home of two wealthy merchant brothers who enjoyed erotic wallpaper (notice as you enter), is best. After a wander through the nearby House of the Faun (Casa del Fauno), go back to the Forum and walk left down Via dell' Abbondanza to explore Pompeii's more recent excavations.

The Stabian Baths (Terme Stabiane, public baths, on the left), are the best preserved baths in the city. Behind the baths, the Vico del Lupanare leads to Lupanare, a simple whorehouse with stone beds, stone pillows, and art to get you in the mood.

Continuing down Via dell' Abbondanza, you'll pass a variety of businesses. Ask guards to let you into various houses and buildings, many of which are locked, or tag along with a tour if you can. Inside homes, you'll find frescoes, paintings, and mosaics that give you a feel for (at least the rich man's) workaday Roman life. The flat stones that cross the streets like crosswalks allowed pedestrians keep their sandals dry during rainstorms.

At the far end is the huge, rebuilt Amphitheater (Anfiteatro). It's a long walk, but you'll get a look at the oldest (80 B.C.) and best-preserved Roman amphitheater in Italy. From the top, look into the giant rectangular Palestra, where athletes used to train. (Pompeii's best art is in the Naples museum, described above.)

▲▲Herculaneum (Ercolano)—Smaller, less ruined, and less crowded than its more famous big sister, Herculaneum offers in some ways a closer peek into ancient Roman life. Caked and baked by the same eruption in A.D. 79, Herculaneum is a small community of intact buildings with plenty of surviving detail (15 minutes from Naples and 45 minutes from Sorrento on the same train that goes to Pompeii, turn right and follow the yellow signs, 5 minutes downhill from the Ercolano station, L12,000, open 9:00 until one hour before sunset).

▲**Vesuvius**—The 4,000-foot summit of Vesuvius, mainland Europe's only active volcano (sleeping restlessly since 1944), is accessible by car or by the blue Vesuvio bus (from the Herculaneum station, 45-minute ride, irregular, often 5/day, often only taxis). The trip, with a 2-hour wait on the mountain, costs about L12,000 (including the L3,000 admission). From the bus and car-park, you'll hike 30 minutes to the top for a sweeping Bay of Naples view, desolate lunar-like surroundings, and hot rocks. On the top, walk the entire crater lip for the most interesting views. The far end overlooks Pompei. Be still and alone to hear the wind and tumbling rocks in the crater. Any steam? Closed when erupting.

## PAESTUM

Paestum is one of the best collections of Greek temples anywhere—and certainly the most accessible to western Europe. Serenely situated, it's surrounded by fields and wildflowers and has only a modest commercial strip.

Founded as Poseidonia in the sixth century B.C., a key stop on an important trade route, its name was changed to Paestum by occupying Romans in the third century B.C. The final conquerors of Paestum, malaria-carrying mosquitoes, kept the site wonderfully desolate for nearly a thousand years. Rediscovered in the 18th century, Paestum today offers the only well-preserved Greek ruins north of Sicily (L12,000 tickets include the museum, daily 9:00 until one hour before sunset, ticket sales end 2 hours before sunset, tel. 0828/811-023, TI tel. 811-016).

### Orientation

Buses from Salerno (see Connections, below) stop at the "secondary entrance" that leads to the lonely Temple of Ceres, across from a good bar/café with sandwiches and cappuccino. Get a feel for the manageable scale of this three-temple set of ruins by looking through the fence, then visit the museum opposite the entrance.

**The Museum:** Orient yourself at the site plan (upstairs on the right). If you're not buying a guidebook, establish your sightseeing plan here. The large carvings overhead adorned various temples from the nearby city of Hera. Most are scenes from the life of Hercules. Don't miss the Greek sculptures in the ground-floor back room. Find the plans for the Temple of Neptune, the largest and most impressive of Paestum's temples, and notice the placement of the decorative carvings and the gargoyle-like heads behind you.

## Touring Paestum

Allow 2 hours with the museum. Enter the ruins at the Ionic Temple of Ceres, the northern end of ancient Paestum, and do a loop through the ruins, exiting where you entered. The key ruins are the impossible-to-miss Temples of Ceres and Neptune and the Basilica, but the scattered village ruins are also interesting. Faint remains of swimming pools, baths, houses, a small amphitheater, and lone columns will stretch your imagination's ability to re-create this ancient city.

The misnamed Temple of Neptune, a textbook example of the Doric style, constructed in 450 B.C. and dedicated to Hera, is simply overwhelming. Better preserved than the Parthenon in Athens, this huge structure is a tribute to Greek engineering and aesthetics. Walk right in, sit right down, and contemplate the word "renaissance"—the rebirth of this grand Greek style of architecture. Notice how the columns angle out and how the base bows up (scan the short ends of the temple). This was a trick ancient architects used to create the illusion of a perfectly straight building. All important Greek buildings were built using this technique. Now imagine it richly and colorfully decorated with marble and statues.

Adjacent is the almost-delicate Basilica (also dedicated to the Goddess Hera, 550 B.C.). Beyond these temples, you'll find traces of the old wall that protected Paestum. If you have time, walk out toward the train station to see the wall's eastern limit.

Should you get stuck in Paestum, the **Albergo della Rosse** (DB-L70,000, tel. 0828/811-070), which has a respectable restaurant, is just across from the main entry.

## Transportation Connections

**Salerno to Paestum:** Salerno, the big city just north of Paestum, is your transfer point. From Naples or Sorrento you'll change buses or trains in Salerno for Paestum. Several companies offer a Salerno-Paestum bus service from the same stop (2/hr, 60 min, buy L4,200 ticket on

### Salerno Connections

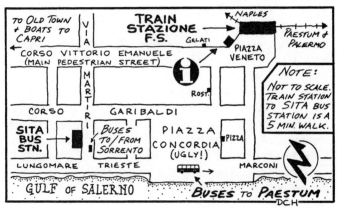

board, schedules are more difficult on Sunday). The Salerno-Paestum train (6/day, 40 min) is usually less efficient, but check schedules at the Salerno station. Northbound buses leave Paestum from the far side of the street bordering the ruins. Flag down any bus, ask "Salerno?" and buy the ticket on board. Most buses stop in front of the Salerno train station.

**Naples to Salerno by train:** Hrly, 1-hr trip

**Sorrento to Salerno by bus:** The scenic 3-hour Amalfi Coast drive (blue SITA bus, 12/day) drops you in Salerno, 75 yards from the Paestum bus stop (head toward waterfront) and 150 yards from the train station. Ask the driver to direct you to the station and/or Paestum bus stop.

**Sorrento to Paestum by train:** Ride the Circumvesuviana for an hour to Naples and catch the Salerno train at the central station (hrly, 1 hr).

**Drivers:** While the Amalfi Coast is a thrill to drive, summer traffic is miserable. From Sorrento, Paestum is 3 hours via the coast and a much smoother 2 hours by autostrada. Driving toward Naples, catch the autostrada (direction: Salerno), skirt Salerno staying on the autostrada (direction: Reggio), exit at Eboli, drive straight through the modern town of Paestum, and you'll hit the ruins about when you're worried that you missed a turnoff. Along the way, you'll see signs for *mozzarella di bufalo*, the soft cheese made from the milk of water buffalo that graze here.

# APPENDIX

## Telephone Information

Smart travelers use the telephone every day—especially in Italy. Hotel reservations by phone on the morning of the day you plan to arrive are a snap. If there's a language problem, ask someone at your hotel to talk to your next hotel for you.

The key to dialing long distance is understanding area codes and having a local phone card. Hotel-room phones are reasonable for calls within Italy (the faint beeps stand for L200 phone units), but a terrible rip-off for calls to the U.S.A. Never call home from your hotel room unless your hotel allows toll-free access to your AT&T or MCI operator (many don't).

To call from Italy to other countries, dial the international access code (00 in Italy), followed by the country code of the country you're calling, followed by the area code without its zero, and finally the local number. When dialing long distance within Italy, start with the area code (including its zero), then the local number. Orange SIP public telephones are everywhere and take coins or cards.

Italy's phone cards aren't credit cards, just handy cards you insert in the phone instead of coins. The L5,000 or L10,000 phone cards (buy at post offices, tobacco shops, and machines near phone booths; many phone booths indicate where the nearest phone card sales outlet is located; rip off the corner to "activate" the card) are much easier to use than coins for long-distance calls. Buy one on your first day to force you to find smart reasons to use the local phones.

Dial slowly and deliberately, as if the phone doesn't understand numbers very well. Repeat as needed.

### Telephone Directory

Directory Assistance (for L1,000 an Italian-speaking
robot gives the number twice, very clearly) .......12

English language telephone help ..............170
(usually offering free directory assistance)

To call Italy from the U.S.A: ..............011-39-
area code without the zero-local number

To call U.S.A. from Italy ...................00-1-
area code-local number

## *Italian Area Codes*

| | |
|---|---|
| Assisi 075 | Milan 02 |
| Bagnoregio (Città) 0761 | Naples 081 |
| Bolzano (Dolomites) 0471 | Rome 06 |
| Cinque Terre 0187 | Siena 0577 |
| Florence 055 | Sorrento 081 |
| Lake Como 0341 | Venice 041 |

## *Country Codes*

After you've dialed the international access code, then dial
the code of the country you're calling.

| | | |
|---|---|---|
| Austria: 43 | France: 33 | Netherlands: 31 |
| Belgium: 32 | Germany: 49 | Norway: 47 |
| Britain: 44 | Greece: 30 | Portugal: 351 |
| Canada: 1 | Hungary: 36 | Russia: 7 |
| Czech Rep.: 42 | Ireland: 353 | Spain: 34 |
| Denmark: 45 | Italy: 39 | Sweden: 46 |
| Estonia: 372 | Latvia: 371 | Switzerland: 41 |
| Finland: 358 | Lithuania: 370 | Turkey: 90 |
| | | U.S.A. 1 |

## Climate Chart—Rome

*1st line, avg. daily low; 2nd line, avg. daily high; 3rd line, days of no rain*

| J | F | M | A | M | J | J | A | S | O | N | D |
|---|---|---|---|---|---|---|---|---|---|---|---|
| 39° | 39° | 42° | 46° | 55° | 60° | 64° | 64° | 61° | 53° | 46° | 41° |
| 54° | 56° | 62° | 68° | 74° | 82° | 88° | 88° | 83° | 73° | 63° | 56° |
| 23 | 17 | 26 | 24 | 25 | 28° | 29 | 28 | 24 | 22 | 22 | 22 |

## Train Connections

| from . . . to | duration of trip | frequency | cost 2nd class |
|---|---|---|---|
| Milan-La Spezia | 3-4 hours | 6/day | L20,000-L25,000 |
| La Spezia-Pisa | 1 hour | hourly | L6,000 |
| Pisa-Florence | 60-90 minutes | hourly | L7,000-L9,000 |
| Florence-Siena | 80-120 minutes | hourly | L7,200 |
| Siena-Orvieto | 2-3 hours, 1 change | 7/day | L10,000 |
| Siena-Assisi | 3½ hours, 2 changes | 4/day | L16,000 |
| Assisi-Rome | 2-3 hours, 1 change | 8/day | L14,000-L20,000 |
| Siena-Rome | 3 hours, 1 change | 6/day | L20,000-L25,000 |
| Orvieto-Rome | 75-90 minutes | 10/day | L11,000 |
| Orte-Rome | 40-80 minutes | 20/day | L7,000 |
| Rome-Naples | 2-3 hours | hourly | L16,000 |
| Salerno-Naples | 40 minutes | 2/hour | L4,500 |
| Rome-Venice | 5-7 hours | 2/day | L50,000 |
| Venice-Bolzano | 3½-4 hours, 1 change | 8/day | L20,000-L28,000 |
| Bolzano-Milan | 3½ hours, 1 change | 8/day | L20,000 |

## Italy's Public Transportation

**KEY:** — RAIL ─── BUS ···· SHIP
*NOT TO SCALE* ● OVERNIGHT STOPS (ON 22 DAYS ROUTE)

—DCH—

## Basic Italian Survival Phrases

| Hello. / Goodbye. | Ciao. | chow |
|---|---|---|
| Do you speak English? | Parla inglese? | PAR-lah eeñ-GLAY-zay |
| Yes. / No. | Sì. / No. | see / noh |
| I don't understand. | Non capisco. | nohn kah-PEE-skoh |
| I'm sorry. | Mi displace. | mee dee-speeAH-chay |
| Please. | Per favore. | pehr fah-VOH-ray |
| Thank you. | Grazie. | GRAH-tseeay |
| Where is...? | Dov'è...? | doh-VEH |
| ...a hotel | ...un hotel | oon oh-TEHL |
| ...a youth hostel | ...un ostello della gioventù | oon oh-STEHL-loh DAY-lah joh-vehn-TOO |
| ...a restaurant | ...un ristorante | oon ree-stoh-RAHN-tay |
| ...a grocery store | ...un negozio di alimentari | oon nay-GOH-tsoh dee ah-lee-mayn-TAH-ree |
| ...the train station | ...la stazione | lah stah-tseeOH-nay |
| ...tourist information | ...informazioni per turisti | een-for-mah-tseeOH-nee pehr too-REE-stee |
| ...the toilet | ...il gabinetto | eel gah-bee-NAYT-toh |
| men | uomini, signori | WAW-mee-nee, seen-YOH-ree |
| women | donne, signore | DON-nay, seen-YOH-ray |
| How much? | Quanto costa? | KWAHN-toh KOS-tah |
| Cheaper. | Più economico. | peeOO ay-koh-NOH-mee-koh |
| Included? | È incluso? | eh een-KLOO-zoh |
| I would like... | Vorrei.... | vor-REHee |
| Just a little. / More. | Un pochino. / Di più. | oon poh-KEE-noh / dee peeOO |
| A ticket. | Un biglietto. | oon beel-YAYT-toh |
| A room. | Una camera. | OO-nah KAH-may-rah |
| The bill. | Il conto. | eel KOHN-toh |
| one | uno | OO-noh |
| two | due | DOO-ay |
| three | tre | tray |
| four | quattro | KWAHT-troh |
| five | cinque | CHEENG-kway |
| six | sei | SEHee |
| seven | sette | SEHT-tay |
| eight | otto | OT-toh |
| nine | nove | NOV-ay |
| ten | dieci | deeEH-chee |
| hundred | cento | CHEHN-toh |
| thousand | mille | MEEL-lay |

## Faxing Your Hotel Reservation

Most hotel managers know basic "hotel English." Faxing is the pre-ferred method for reserving a room. It's more accurate and cheaper than telephoning and much faster than writing a letter. Use this handy form for your fax. Photocopy and fax away.

## One-Page Fax

To: _____ @ _____
                  *hotel*                               *fax*

From: _____ @ _____
                  *name*                               *fax*

Today's date: ____ / ____ / ____
             *day*  *month*  *year*

Dear Hotel _____ ,
Please make this reservation for me:

Name: _____

Total # of people: ____    # of rooms: ____    # of nights: ____

Arriving: ____ / ____ / ____  My time of arrival (24-hr clock): ____
       *day*  *month*  *year*  (I will telephone if I will be late)
Departing: ____ / ____ / ____
        *day*  *month*  *year*

Room(s):  Single___  Double___  Twin___  Triple___  Quad___
With:  Toilet___  Shower___  Bath___  Sink only___
Special needs:  View___  Quiet___  Cheapest Room___

Credit card:  Visa___  MasterCard___  American Express___
Card #: _____
Name on card: _____
Expiration Date:_____

You may charge me for the first night as a deposit. Please fax or mail me confirmation of my reservation, along with the type of room reserved, the price, and whether the price includes breakfast. Thank you.

_____
*Signature*

_____
*Name*

_____
*Address*

_____
*City*                *State*        *Zip Code*    *Country*

# INDEX

# Rick Steves' Phrase Books

Unlike other phrase books on the market, my well-tested phrases and key words cover every situation you are likely to encounter in your travels. With these books you'll laugh with your cabby, disarm street thieves with insults, and charm new European friends.

*Each book in the series is 4" x 5½", paperback, with maps.*

**RICK STEVES' FRENCH PHRASE BOOK**
U.S. $4.95/Canada $6.95

**RICK STEVES' GERMAN PHRASE BOOK**
U.S. $4.95/Canada $6.95

**RICK STEVES' ITALIAN PHRASE BOOK**
U.S. $4.95/Canada $6.95

**RICK STEVES' SPANISH & PORTUGUESE PHRASE BOOK**
U.S. $5.95/Canada $8.50

**RICK STEVES' FRENCH, ITALIAN & GERMAN PHRASE BOOK**
U.S. $6.95/Canada $ 9.95

# Other Books from John Muir Publications